No other book that I know describes so succinctly the forces that in less than forty years turned Australia from a vassal of the United Kingdom ('Britain is at war, therefore Australia is at war', said Prime Minister Menzies on September 3, 1939) into an independent power which, if it owes any allegiance, owes it politically to the United States and economically to Japan.

Times Literary Supplement

The author has done well. This is an entertaining record, dealing with a period of outstanding interest and importance in Australian political history.

History

Provocative, lively and insightful. Particularly good is the treatment of Robert Menzies and the way in which he shifted Australia out of the British and into the American orbit.

Library Journal

His book shows considerable talent for compressing great events into short space without distorting them too much in the process. Griffiths' book is a refreshing change from the timid or pedantic approach of many other academics.

Age

Unlike many textbooks it is easy to read, somewhat provocative, pithy and rather racy in style.

Economic Record

We are given a readable account of the Australian political scene, very much as a well-informed and very impartial Australian might have seen it. There is ample detail; but of what use is the broad-sweep style of history without the detail it reviews? To understand modern Australia, study this.

Times Educational Supplement

Beautiful Lies

Tony Griffiths has taught Australian
and Scandinavian history in Australia,
Japan and Europe. He lives in Adelaide,
but revised this book while a Visiting
Fellow at the Robert Schuman Centre
for Advanced Studies at the European
University Institute in San Domenico
di Fiesole.

Contemporary Australia
Scandinavia
The Irish Board of Works

Beautiful Lies
Australia from Menzies to Howard

Tony Griffiths

**Wakefield
Press**

Wakefield Press
Box 2266
Kent Town
South Australia 5071
www.wakefieldpress.com.au

First published as *Contemporary Australia* 1977
This fully revised and updated edition published 2005

Edited by Gina Inverarity
Indexed by Helen Stafford
Bibliography compiled by Gerritt Stafford
Designed by designBITE
Printed by Hyde Park Press

National Library of Australia
Cataloguing-in-publication entry

Griffiths, A. R. G. (Anthony Royston Grant), 1940– .
Beautiful lies: Australia from Menzies to Howard.
Rev. ed.
Bibliography.
Includes index.
ISBN 1 86254 590 1.
1. Australia – History – 20th century. 2. Australia – Politics and
government – 20th century. I. Title.

994.04

CONTENTS

Philip Knightley, reviewing the first edition of this book almost thirty years ago in the *Times Literary Supplement*, wrote:

> No other book that I know describes so succinctly the forces that in less than forty years turned Australia from a vassal of the United Kingdom into an independent power, which, if it owes any allegiance, owes it politically to the United States and economically to Japan.

While the relationship between social change and political power has remained constant in Australia since the second world war, the author believes that all the *TLS* would have to do in the third millennium is change the word 'Japan' for 'China'.

Mark Twain observed more than a century ago that Australian history is 'always picturesque; indeed, it is so curious and strange, that it is itself the chiefest novelty the country has to offer and so pushes the other novelties into second and third place. It does not read like history, but like the most beautiful lies; and all of a fresh new sort, no mouldy old stale ones. It is full of surprises and adventures, and inconguities, and contradictions, and incredibilities; but they are all true, they all happened.'

This is still the case, most recently demonstrated when Prime Minister John Howard won his record fourth election despite a damaging row in the Liberal Party over whether or not a senior government senator had described the prime minister as a lying rodent.

Tony Griffiths,
Florence, 2005

During the last fifty years, as Australia has turned slowly from a largely Anglo-Saxon-Celtic constitutional monarchy in the direction of a multicultural republic, strange revelations have been more often the rule than the exception. In the last sixteen years, one former prime minister, Harold Holt, has been identified as a Chinese spy. Another, Malcolm Fraser, has been found wandering without his trousers in an American motel. John Brown, a Minister for Sport, Tourism and Recreation, celebrated a Labor Party victory by making love on a ministerial desk top. Prime Minister Paul Keating chose Danpork, the leader of the Danish pig industry, to manage his family enterprise.

What did these developments mean? Was Holt a double agent since his student days? Was Fraser the victim of a South African secret service plot? Did the minister's wife, Jan Murray, leave her underpants in the ashtray to show the government's contempt for the Public Service, as she claimed? Should Keating be remembered not as the Placido Domingo of Australian politics, but as the Pavarotti of the pig industry?

The book does not answer all these diverting questions, but it does set out the important events and trends of the half century since the fall of Singapore and the bombing of Pearl Harbour.

Lest the reader smile too much, it should be remembered that

Australian history has not changed in some respects since the nineteenth century. As Mark Twain observed almost a century ago, Australian history 'is almost always picturesque; indeed, it is so curious and strange, that it is itself the chiefest novelty the country has to offer and so it pushes the other novelties into second and third place. It does not read like history, but like the most beautiful lies; and all of a fresh new sort, no mouldy old stale ones. It is full of surprises and adventures, and incongruities, and contradictions, and incredibilities; but they are all true, they all happened.'

Tony Griffiths,
Adelaide, 1993

The selection of facts which have significance is one of the most difficult tasks for an historian. If some are selected others must be left out, and their subsequent rise to importance may nag like a decayed tooth. In the flux of contemporary Australia facts which at first sight appear trivial may turn out not to be so. Prime Minister McMahon ate neither butter nor margarine, but would not be led on his liking for dripping when questioned in Parliament. Prime Minister Hold exposed the lack of *haute cuisine* on the VIP aircraft in scathing terms, revealing that he and Dame Zara were forced to eat pies and pasties on more than one occasion. A Minister's wife advertised Sheridan printed bedsheets in the *Australian Women's Weekly*. Prime Minister Gorton had matchboxes marked with his title of office. Did these facts indicate a fatal case of megalomania, the commercialisation of the Crown, an offensive abuse of power, or the death of the dairy industry? Did other events signal the points better, and in any event did the second-level generalisations reveal anything significant about the uniqueness of Australian society? As Voltaire observed, a man who ventures to write contemporary history must expect to be attacked both for everything he has said, and for everything he has not said.

The scope and purpose of this book is to outline the making of contemporary Australia since 1939. The concluding date of

1975 was chosen because that was the end of the Labor Party's period of office: the Labor Prime Minister was then dismissed by the Governor-General, an action overwhelmingly confirmed by the electorate, and the Liberal National Country Party again took power in new economic circumstances. The Cabinet records of the war period are only now being released in the search room of the Australian Archives, Canberra, so the book is based on the evidence provided by the special studies and general works listed in the bibliography. The absence of the deepest level of primary evidence (minutes, submissions, agendas, bundles of folders from government departments) constitutes the chief defect of all contemporary histories. The accounts by participants in high-level diplomacy and politics given in memoirs and apologies published during their lifetimes are notoriously suspect. Parliamentary debates are orchestrated by the government of power. Questions are pre-arranged, inconvenient business never allowed to escape the gag. Newspaper editorial opinion reflects the preoccupation of the proprietors. Scholarly accounts of current affairs in the *Keesing's Contemporary Archives* tradition are often written in Australia by political scientists and historians with little idea of where events are heading and no long-term perspective or sensitive intuition. The law of libel inhibits the free expression of some important facts, leaving most contemporary histories of Australia vapid and emasculated, which is scarcely surprising when one considers that such history is usually written more by the seat of the pants than by other deeper faculties.

Tony Griffiths,
Cambridge, 1977

CHAPTER 1

Coming Through with Dug-Out Doug

The federal parliament was sitting in Canberra on 3 September 1939 when Britain declared war on Germany. But the conservative Australian Prime Minister, R. G. Menzies, without consulting the House of Representatives or the Senate, immediately broadcast on national radio, 'Britain is at war, therefore Australia is at war.' To Menzies there was one king, one flag, one cause. And so the Australian people saw it.

Menzies lost office on 29 August 1941. Disaffection within the conservative ranks alienated the voters at a time when solid leadership was essential. The nation was fighting for survival. When the Japanese bombed Pearl Harbor, the anxieties of a century were fulfilled. Australia's security was threatened as never before. From the fall of France until the Japanese surprise attack, Great Britain conducted the war against Germany and Italy on its own. Three days after Pearl Harbor, the British Navy suffered an appalling loss when Japanese bombers sank, with ease, the battleships *Prince of Wales* and *Repulse*. In an engagement which lasted only a couple of hours, Admiral Tom Phillips and six hundred men were lost, and Britannia ceased to rule the waves of the Far East. For England, 10 December 1941 was the darkest hour of the war so far. For Australia, it exploded a cherished illusion: insularity was no longer any guarantee of safety. To inhabit an island continent was to live in fear.

It was starkly clear that the nation's own exertions would deter-mine its future. Australia still had to depend upon its most important allies but, to survive, its own civilian sweat and military blood had to be expended.

The Prime Minister of Australia in December 1941 was John Curtin. He had been in office for less than two months, and was leading the first Labor government for a decade. It was his task to bring the country through the greatest psychological shock it had ever faced. Before Christmas 1941, the Japanese had a superior set of aircraft carriers and their well-planned amphibious attacks on the Philippines and Northern Malaya showed that it was only a matter of time before they would be in the Dutch East Indies, and thence, perhaps, into Australia – although a clear understanding of Japan's intentions at that time was lacking.

On 16 December 1941, Curtin formally asked for approval of the government's actions in declaring war on Japan. Not only was this action of overriding significance in the history of Australia, said Curtin, but it created a condition 'the consequence of which will affect the life of this Commonwealth for hundreds of years to come'. The organisation of a non-military people for the purpose of complete war, he said, necessarily effected 'a revolution in the lives of the people', and the transformation would be so great that there would be confusion, problems, difficulties, dislocations, disturbances, fretfulness and criticism. But the complete conversion of a nation from the pursuits of peace to those of war would entail losses trivial beside those if the war were lost.

Curtin was prepared to act ruthlessly in planning the war effort: there were absolute requirements for home defence forces, including the defence of New Guinea. The maximum number of men needed varied according to the degree of the threat of invasion, which was mainly dependent on the deterrent effect of American and British naval strength in the Pacific Ocean, and Australia's own capacity to resist. With the *Prince of Wales* and

Repulse at the bottom of the sea, few were optimistic about Britain's ability to protect Australia, and those still with illusions lost them when Singapore fell in the new year.

There was never any doubt in Curtin's mind that an American crusade in the Pacific was his country's only hope. In the mounting climate of fear and terror that followed Pearl Harbor, Curtin had no time to think about the possible costs for Australia when confronted with the material riches of the American way of life.

Seeking inspiration and national leadership, the Melbourne *Herald* requested a new year message from the prime minister. Curtin responded, and the subsequent editorial, headed 'The Task Ahead', contained an appreciation that Australia had reached a watershed in its history: the year 1942 would see immense changes in Australian life. Curtin's statement caused an immediate sensation, as it was taken to mean that Australia would henceforward align itself with the United States rather than the British empire, a shift of loyalties regarded as a public sell-out. Although Curtin subsequently tried to play down the nexus, the Australian government was already working for a concerted plan in which the United States and Australia would co-operate. With no inhibitions of any kind, Curtin made it clear that Australia looked to America, free of any pangs about its traditional links or kinship with the United Kingdom. Australia knew the problems that the United Kingdom faced. It knew the constant threat of invasion. It knew the dangers of dispersal of strength. But it knew, too, that Australia could go and Britain could still hold on. Curtin was therefore determined that Australia should not go. He decided to exert all his energies towards the shaping of a plan, with the United States as its keystone, that would give the country some confidence of being able to hold out until the tide of battle swung against the enemy. Summed up, the Australian aim was a Pacific strategy with the United States as the leader consolidating

Australian, British, Chinese and Dutch forces.

The enemy was at the gate in the months of February and March 1942. On 15 February the Japanese captured Singapore, and it was clear that the Dutch East Indies, with their fuel, would be taken. Singapore held out for only two weeks before General Percival and 60,000 troops surrendered.

Curtin characterised the fall of Singapore as Australia's Dunkirk. Into Japanese prison camps went 13,000 Australians of the 8th Division, and the battle for Australia began with accusations of imperial betrayal. The government blamed Churchill for putting Singapore at the bottom of his list and not enquiring into its defences. The fall of Singapore ended the long-held delusion of Australian independence and revealed precisely how much Australia had been relying upon the protection of Great Britain for its overseas defence. Once Singapore had gone, Australia felt more isolated and vulnerable than ever before.

Four days after the fall of Singapore, Darwin was bombed. It was the first attack ever on the Australian mainland by a foreign power. The raid on Darwin began at 10 AM when high-level bombers dived in from the south-east and, at 14,000 feet, dropped their bombs in pattern over the town. Then dive-bombers, escorted by fighters, machine-gunned shipping in the harbour, the RAAF aerodrome and civil aerodrome, and the hospital at Berrima. The American Kittyhawk aircraft assigned to defend the town were nearly all shot down while making for height, and the anti-aircraft batteries were too small to be effective. Five merchant ships and three warships were sunk in the harbour, among them the American destroyer *Peary*, which went down with guns blazing.

After forty minutes the first raid was over. Most of the town was destroyed. The hospital ship *Manunda* was damaged by a direct hit, the civilian hospital almost wrecked by eight bombs in the grounds, the post office blown to bits. There were bodies in the bomb shelters, bodies in the mangrove roots.

The Administrator of the Northern Territory miraculously survived a direct hit on Government House. The town's operating theatres were busy, and the dead and wounded were being collected, when fifty-four land-based bombers began a second raid at 11.45 AM. It lasted twenty minutes and obliterated the RAAF aerodrome. In Darwin there were two hundred and fifty dead or dying from their injuries and about three hundred and fifty wounded who were to survive.

The psychological shock to the Australian community of the two day-time raids was tremendous. When the second raid was over, many Darwin townspeople grabbed their portable goods and rushed out of the town to the Adelaide River railway station and the train south; cars, trucks, carts and bicycles passed those just running. The deserted town was looted by merchant seamen and members of the forces, including an officer and an NCO in the military police. Canberra was in a state of jitters and morale was shakiest at the top. Curtin concealed the truth about Darwin because he had no faith in the people. The official announcement made to the Australian press was that there were seventeen killed and twenty-four wounded, several ships hit, and buildings, the harbour wharves, and several aircraft on the ground damaged. But rumour soon spread that the loss was greater, that Darwin had been caught napping, and that the military police had led the looting.

The public gloom and pessimism lifted after the appointment was announced of General Douglas MacArthur as Supreme Commander of the Allied Forces in the South-West Pacific. The Allied commands were then rationalised into three theatres: the Pacific, directed by the United States joint chiefs of staff; the Indian Ocean and the Middle East directed by the British chiefs of staff; and the European-Atlantic, a joint responsibility of the British and the Americans. As MacArthur travelled south from Darwin his train stopped for water at Terowie (a small railway junction in northern South Australia) and MacArthur explained to the press that the President of the United States had ordered him to break through the Japanese lines and go from Corregidor to Australia, for the purpose of organising an American offensive against the Japanese. 'I came through,' said MacArthur, 'and I shall return.' MacArthur was informed that the Australians were in a state of near panic, and planned to withdraw to a line drawn at Brisbane, leaving the northern ports open to the Japanese. When he heard this news, MacArthur was stunned. He turned deathly white, his knees buckled, his lips twitched, he whispered, 'God have mercy upon us,' and, unable to sleep on the 'Overland' between Adelaide and Melbourne, spent the night pacing the train's corridors. At Spencer Street railway station in Melbourne, where he was welcomed by a guard of honour, the leaders of the armed forces, and the public, MacArthur emerged in creased trousers, his shirt bare of medal ribbons, to make a terse speech which ended, 'My success or failure will depend primarily upon the resources which the respective governments place at my disposal. My faith in them is complete. In any event, I shall do my best. I shall keep the soldier faith.'

Because of his strength of personality, MacArthur was soon to restore Australian morale and to reassure and inspire Curtin. 'Mr Prime Minister,' directed MacArthur, 'we two, you and I, will see this thing through together . . . you take care of the rear and I will handle the front.' Curtin was looking for a saviour and clutched at MacArthur.

MacArthur's admirers, without self-consciousness, described him as a soldier-statesman whose genius rivalled that of Alexander the Great, Hannibal, Julius Caesar and Napoleon; his critics called him a dangerous militarist and a threat to democracy. Who was right? In March 1942, MacArthur was a glorious failure. He was partly responsible for defeat in the Philippines. During the crucial battle of Bataan, he was not as conspicuous as he had been in the front line in France during 1918. His troops sang:

> Dug-out Doug MacArthur lies a-shaking on the rock
> Safe from all the bombers and from any sudden shock

possibly a libel, but one which no such experienced and esteemed field commander ought to have exposed himself to. Together Curtin and MacArthur promoted a military strategy to General George C. Marshall, the US Army Chief of Staff, based on the incorrect assumption that the Japanese wished to invade Australia. In mid-March 1942, Japanese strategy was limited to two simple objectives: the conquest of Burma and the reduction of Bataan and Corregidor. Their objective was to secure their rear, and clear the way for the exploitation of the strategic tin, rubber and oil deposits in South-East Asia. The irony was that MacArthur and Curtin had relatively little to do with the final defeat of Japan, which was the result of the magnificence of the US Navy during the battles of the Coral Sea and at Midway, and the dropping of atomic bombs on Hiroshima and Nagasaki.

Within six months of Pearl Harbor there were 88,000 US infantry troops in Victoria, South Australia and Queensland. The ports of Perth and Sydney swarmed with ever-increasing numbers of US marines. Later, after the battle for Guadalcanal in 1943, the 1st Marine Division was rested near Melbourne, while the northern coastal towns of Rockhampton and Townsville were taken over by the Americans for naval bases and R and R. The American general headquarters was set up at Brisbane. To these places the Americans brought demands for material and administrative machinery, airports, offices, camps, hostels, hotels, telephones, cinemas, timber and meat. American soldiers were better paid and spent more. By the end of the war there were 862,000 Americans in the South-West Pacific area. Most of these spent some leave in Australia. The highest number of US Army troops actually in Australia was 120,000 at the end of September 1943, when the troop numbers were drastically reduced. At that time the population of Australia was 7,250,000. In June 1944 there were 55,000 troops in Australia and 5,600 a year later.

The Australian government was opposed to the landing of black GIs, but when the first white Americans arrived Curtin was gratified and heartened. Great Britain, Curtin pointed out, could not carry the burden of the Pacific war while engaged in a life and death struggle with Germany and Italy; thus the aid from the United States was a double blessing. Expressing his own and the national fear and insecurity, Curtin added, 'We will not be left quite alone.' On behalf of the people of Australia, Curtin welcomed the first Americans and assured them that they would continue to be made to feel at home and enjoy the warmth of their first honeymoon fortnight. Curtin welcomed them as 'visitors who speak like us, think like us, and fight like us'. Curtin maintained this delusion throughout the war, but in the community at large there were growing reservations that by the end of 1945 amounted to undisguised hostility. The Americans were not trained, nor did they fight, like the Australians. The Americans arrived unready for jungle warfare, and unable to meet the Japanese veterans on equal terms. The Australian soldier lived hard during training. In battle he was familiar with crises; problems and discomfort he had experienced before. The Americans, on the other hand, went into combat over-equipped and under-trained. It took very little personal contact to realise that the Americans also spoke and thought differently. They communicated in the English language, but they did not share the same ideas and values. By embarrassing mismanagement the first Americans landed without pay. But as soon as the dollars began to flow much of the popular appreciation changed to envy. Australian women preferred the Americans, feeling perhaps that a pair of nylon stockings in the hand was worth two in the bush. Americans in Sydney met the complaint that the Yanks were overpaid, oversexed and over here.

Curtin and the Advisory War Council first met MacArthur in Canberra on 26 March 1942. In the absence of significant numbers of British troops, the effect of MacArthur and the Americans was magnified. When Curtin accepted the Americans as crusaders, he tacitly agreed that their culture had something to commend it. Gratitude and admiration for the American presence led the prime minister to imitate some aspects of American life. In the wartime political atmosphere, Curtin adopted a more personal, almost presidential style of government, directing the conduct of domestic and external policy without relying on lengthy consultations with cabinet, caucus or parliament, and calling on outside experts who had no standing in parliament or the civil service. Curtin's presidential style of government was not always apparent to contemporary critics, who claimed that like other ALP leaders he was too much dominated by caucus. But the federal government was able to take over the direction of a whole range of matters that would have been ruled outside its province in time of peace, and the prime minister, as the chief executive, was allowed power unthinkable except in national crisis.

On 5 May 1942 the battle of the Coral Sea began and the sense of doom and impending disaster was at its height. Political divisions and constitutional practices were effaced by the sense of national danger. This reinforced the tendency for Australian politics to polarise around a leader rather than party platforms. In the charged and dramatic situation, Curtin stressed that he was the national leader. Since federation, the more successful prime ministers had looked at public opinion and tried to tune in to it. In response the community had merely contented itself with a sporting analogy: it picked the team with the most inspiring captain. The more heroic the personality, the greater the vote-catching ability. This personality cult response reached its peak in the 1930s and was personified by the almost magical appeal of J. T. Lang, the Premier of New South Wales. Without joking, Lang's supporters cried, 'Lang is mightier than Lenin!' Lang went down fighting, expelled from the Labor Party, sacked from his premiership by the governor of New South Wales, but he was a portent which showed national leaders what Australians responded to: in the absence of any established political tradition, liberal or conservative, Australians reacted to the captain's style.

During the war the captain was less of a sporting figure, more of a chieftain. His skill and determination were taken out of the sporting arena and became a matter of national survival. Curtin's importance to the nation was seen most clearly in his identification with the battles in New Guinea where the Japanese posed the most obvious threat. Although they were repulsed at the battles of the Coral Sea and at Midway, the Japanese still tried to take Port Moresby and New Guinea by amphibious attacks. In 1940 there were less than 2,000 Australians living in Papua: by 1945, almost 4,000 had died there. Australians had periodically thought of New Guinea as their bulwark against an invasion from the north, and during 1942 it was true. While the Americans carried out their crusade in the Pacific, making their way towards Japan, 50,000 Australian troops were fighting in New Guinea. From July 1942 the fighting was bitter on the Kokoda Track, as the Japanese pressed southwards. They landed in August at Milne Bay, on the eastern tip of New Guinea. But the Japanese offensive in January-February 1943 (from Salamaua to Wau on the tablelands of south-eastern New Guinea) was turned back, and thereafter Japanese outposts were put down one by one. In 1943, the 9th Australian Division, the last in the Middle East, returned home. As the division marched in triumph through the streets of Brisbane, it was clear that a turning-point in the war had been reached.

The Australian divisions had been released from the European war zone at Curtin's request. The 6th, 7th and 9th Divisions were then all in Australia, while the 8th was behind wire in Singapore. The battle honours of the 9th Division at El Alamein were important to the build-up of Curtin's image. These seasoned veterans were rightly eulogised by the press, MacArthur and Curtin, as they were the last lever needed to reconquer New Guinea. By mid-1944 the coast of New Guinea was recaptured. When Morotai was taken in September 1944 the Australians had advanced over 1,500 miles in little over a year, and cut off 200,000 Japanese troops. The mop-up operation culminated in the capture of Wewak in May 1945, and Australian troops were freed to take part in the invasion of Borneo in June-July. The seventh edition of Ernest Scott's *A Short History of Australia* was being drafted at the beginning of 1945 – just in time to note how General MacArthur had organised a series of brilliant actions against the Japanese, which gave him a chain of bases along the north coast of New Guinea, and enabled him to carry out a successful invasion of the Philippines.

Curtin's background as a union organiser and a political journalist gave him the appearance of being in touch with the aspirations of organised labour during the war, and a subsequent generation has idealised him, regarding 1941–49 as Labor's golden age. During the war, however, there was not one Labor programme but three. There were also three Labor leaders. Curtin, the prime minister, was intent only on securing Australia's physical safety, and worked with MacArthur in trying to convince Marshall and President Roosevelt that the South-West Pacific theatre had a strategic importance it did not, in reality, possess. J. B. Chifley, treasurer of the Labor government, (who in 1939 at the outbreak of the war had been adviser on labour to the Menzies government) was intent only on the question of economic development and social reconstruction. H. V. Evatt, the attorney-general, focused his energies on a constitutional reorganisation of the federal-state relationships.

What did the Labor Party do with its wartime power?

The first task of the government was to control the workforce and to restrict non-essential production. The economy was directed by the Department of War Organisation of Industry, which was set up within weeks of Pearl Harbor. W. C. Wurth, who had already established a powerful reputation as head of the New South Wales Public Service Board, was appointed Director-General of Manpower. By March 1942, all persons over sixteen years old were required to register with the directorate, civilians were issued with identity cards, and the unemployed were directed to jobs by John Johnstone Dedman, the minister responsible for carrying out economic policies.

The people accepted the encroachment of the state into their economic lives only in return for a *quid pro quo* – or at least, that is how Labor leaders saw it, and *quid* had more than one meaning in the 1940s. While the prime minister was able to reform taxation law, peg prices and ration food, he had in return to extend social services: widows were given pensions, a national welfare scheme was considered, unemployment benefits were increased and free medicine doled out to those who needed it. Most important of all, Evatt laid plans for post-war reconstruction, which he considered was a task for both the commonwealth and the states. The activities of the states had to be co-ordinated with the general commonwealth plan. Unfortunately, the commonwealth lacked the legislative power for the task: after the war the use of defence power could not be prolonged. Asked by the enthusiasts for state rights who was better able to deal with post-war depression than the states, Evatt replied that the commonwealth was one, and the states were many: in the depression of 1929–33 the problems were insoluble because they were Australia-wide problems, and no government had the power to deal with them on an Australia-wide basis. Evatt was prepared to change the constitution not only to restore industry, but also to control prices and profits and to encourage the growth and settlement of the population in less congested cities. He was prepared to unify the country on a master plan, and believed that he knew how to do it. All he required was effectual power.

The wartime Labor government's first attack on the problem of poverty was to focus on the plight of the widows. Almost every civilised country, explained E. J. Holloway, the Minister for Social Services, had recognised that the premature death of the breadwinner was one of the most important causes of poverty. In the late 1930s widows and children had been provided for by contributory schemes, but the government believed that it was unreasonable to expect the community at large to support every widow regardless of age and circumstances. Some women were left in relatively comfortable circumstances. Young widows without children usually found no difficulty in providing for themselves. The government therefore decided to concern itself mainly with those who had young children, those beyond middle age, and those in ill health. The need of these women justified government aid, and Holloway stressed that this was only the beginning. The further development of federal social services would continue until 'real social security' was provided for all the people. The act provided pensions for widows with destitute children, widows over fifty who were in ill health or in destitute circumstances after the death of their husbands, deserted wives and women whose husbands were in mental hospitals. As was the case in Great Britain during the 1914–18 war, the new legislation was a recognition of the importance of women to the war effort, in the munitions industry, for example, which employed large numbers of women. Overall, the number of women employed rose by 35 per cent between 1939 and 1944, from 644,000 to 855,000.

On 22 December 1942 Curtin appointed Ben Chifley as Minister for Post-War Reconstruction. Chifley continued to hold the Treasury portfolio. His first important action was to establish a Rural Reconstruction Commission, which investigated the problems of primary industry. On 15 January 1943 Chifley appointed Dr H. C. Coombs as Director-General of Post-War Reconstruction. Once Coombs had assembled his department – almost exclusively from outside the civil service – he and Chifley initiated the planning of post-war social policy, singling out full employment as the chief force in national prosperity.

In the 1920s and 1930s, as Chifley knew from personal experience, too many lives were dominated by the fear of unemployment, and too little effort was made by governments and administrators to banish it. During the war the fear of unemployment was absent. In winning the war, Chifley said, Australia was learning ways of controlling its affairs and of ending enforced idleness. Labor was determined to see that work was not only available to all but adequately rewarded and directed towards worthwhile ends. This meant, above all, placing permanently within the reach of everyone freedom from basic economic worries, the realisation of some personal ambitions, and the opportunity to bring up healthy, well-educated families. To this end, Curtin had far-reaching plans for medical, hospital, dental, child, maternal, unemployment and sickness benefits and welfare schemes. But at the time all the government could afford was a marginal increase in maternity allowances, and provision of subsidised funerals for old age and invalid pensioners. Under war conditions the strain on medical and nursing services was already heavy, and it was clearly beyond resources to bring all of the pie down from the sky at once. On 30 March 1944, for example, Holloway introduced a bill to give everyone in the commonwealth free medicine, as a new instalment of the plan promised by Chifley the year before. But general practitioners refused to co-operate, fearing a diminution of their income. Even more significant was the government's admission that there were insufficient administrative manpower and equipment available to put the legislation into effect.

It proved far easier for Labor to secure full employment under the war economy than social reforms. 'War economy means what it says,' said Curtin. 'We are at war, therefore all our economic resources – all the methods of buying and selling, of carrying on the business of feeding and housing and clothing and transportation and amusing ourselves – must be placed second after the requirements of national defence and offence. War comes first.'

Tea was rationed on 30 March, clothing on 9 May, and sugar on 31 August 1942. Curtin spoke from personal experience when he said that excessive beer-drinking impaired the national war effort, so beer and spirit production were reduced by one-third in March 1942. Butter was rationed in June 1943. Australians were allowed half a pound of butter a head per week (in Britain the amount was two ounces) and cotton materials were put on the coupon at the same time. Meat rationing, in January 1944, was an irritation rather than a health hazard, as a man could have as many sausages as he wanted, and housewives had to adopt more imaginative cooking methods with less expensive cuts of meat.

The linchpin of Curtin's plans was a system of price control established in February 1943. As prime minister, Bob Menzies had introduced price control at the beginning of the war, restricting price increases to those required by unavoidable increases in costs. Chifley's innovation was to put a ceiling on all goods and services, placing the burden of increases in production costs on the investor and entrepreneur. The aim was to dampen down the rate of inflation in the new boom conditions of war. Full employment, increased government expenditure and extra overtime put more money in the pay-packet, and Chifley intended to divert it into government bonds and savings banks by limiting the consumer's range of purchases and guaranteeing stable prices. Chifley invented 'the unspendable margin', which could find no outlets other than in war loans or idle bank deposits. Although flouted by a booming black market, on the whole the treasurer's scheme achieved its ends.

Chifley also managed to take over the lion's share of tax-gathering in Australia. When the states rejected his proposals on income tax reform, the treasurer countered with four federal tax bills which provided that, for the duration of the war, and during the financial year in which the war came to an end, the commonwealth would be the sole authority to tax incomes. The states were to be reimbursed from the central fund. Stripped of the power to finance their own policies, the premiers screamed in protest. But Chifley, convinced that the war effort demanded centralised control by the commonwealth, was ruthless. National rights had to take precedence over state rights.

Menzies later compared Chifley's methods with those of eighteenth-century highwaymen. They gave their victims a choice – their money or their life. Chifley proposed that the commonwealth should give financial assistance to those states that suspended their power to collect taxes in the interests of national defence. Opposition was obdurate in Victoria and South Australia. The Victorian premier proposed to test the commonwealth's action in the High Court, and the Adelaide *Advertiser* commented on 18 May 1942 that the federal system was about to be destroyed. If Chifley realised what he was doing to the future of commonwealth-state relations, he kept his thoughts private. The High Court began to hear the challenge on 22 June 1942 and by 23 July the verdict was known. Chifley's tax acts were upheld, and a huge change in the constitutional relationships and political structure of Australia was made, without any formal amendment to the constitution. Forgan Smith resigned as Labor Premier of Queensland, muttering, 'My breeding and training are such that I will not be a vassal to anyone,' but the other premiers sat tight and prepared for a life of log-rolling. The introduction of pay-as-you-earn taxation on 1 January 1941 had given the commonwealth reserves enormous potential, and the premiers greedily antici-pated their share.

During the war Labor was overwhelmingly popular. Australians voted on 21 August 1943 for both the House of Representatives and the Senate, and the Labor Party routed the conservative coalition, who were still clinging to the dis-credited platitudes of the 1930s. The Labor slogan 'Victory in war, victory for the peace' was not an empty catch-phrase, it was a battle cry, and it rang out as such. Curtin said, 'You cannot risk a government from the United Australia Party and the Country Party. They would make the same terrible mistakes they made before Japan came into the war. Who would be the boss among them all? Who would be the leader of leaders?' This was Curtin's theme: he recognised that he was the leader of leaders with such wartime charisma that the opposition could not match him.

When the votes were counted Menzies was literally speechless. 'You do not have much comment left in you,' he said, 'if you have been hit on the head by a sledge hammer or run over by a traction engine.' For the first time since 1916 Labor held majorities in both the lower and upper houses. Curtin was modest: the electorate had endorsed the chieftain's conduct of the war for survival. Evatt took a larger view (which was incorrect) that the voters not only approved of Curtin's conduct of the war, but also of Chifley's blueprint for post-war reconstruction. The people supported the Curtin government and not the Labor government. Curtin faced no concerted oppo-sition, and made skilful use of his best weapon – that he had successfully brought Australia through the biggest national crisis in the country's history. The people voted against the conser-vatives as well as for Curtin. The accepted Leader of the Opposition was Fadden, head of the Country Party, but he quarrelled angrily with Menzies, who, he said, stabbed him in the back during the campaign.

There was an entrenched hostility to the extension of federal power in any field other than that of winning the war, which not even social reform could mitigate. Evatt was the first to feel public opinion: as attorney-general he had to draft proposals for a referendum aimed at altering the constitution and putting more power in the hands of the commonwealth. On 19 August 1944, Australians had to decide whether or not the federal parliament should be given the exclusive right to legislate for five years after the war on fourteen matters which, up to that time, had been the responsibility of the state parliaments. The Adelaide *Advertiser* saw the referendum as a 'grave threat to the Australian federation', and was pleased at the overall majority of 'No' votes. If complete power over jobs, homes, primary production and social security had been given to the commonwealth on a permanent basis, as the amendments to the constitution proposed, the federal system would have been destroyed. It was clear (to the *Advertiser*) that the majority was not willing to let wartime power spill over into the years of peace. But even before it was clear that the 'Vote No' slogans were more prominent than the 'Vote Yes' ones, the representatives of non-Labor organisations, as Menzies styled them, had planned a new political party.

Following its election debacle, a special committee of the council of the New South Wales branch of the United Australia Party began to draft a new party platform in October 1943. Formed in 1931 to meet the national crisis of the depression, the UAP needed both a different title and a fresh outlook to weld conservative functions together and to counter the new cohesive Labor movement. The UAP's only hope lay in Labor's referendum defeat, which Menzies interpreted as showing that a great body of Australian opinion was liberal and progressive but nevertheless distrustful of, and opposed to, excessive government control and interference in commerce and industry. During a conference held in Canberra from 13 to 16 October

1944, Menzies was able to cajole, coerce and persuade delegates from eighteen separate conservative political organisations – but not the Country Party – to sink their differences and join a new firm. Curtin, Chifley, Evatt and Calwell had shown that socialism was their goal. Socialism became the conservatives' Russian Bear.

Searching for an economic policy, Menzies turned to the theories of the Institute of Public Affairs, a body founded in 1943 by a group of Melbourne investors and company directors. Their manifesto, *Looking Forward*, published in 1944, spelled out the free enterprise solution to industrial problems, detailing the ransom the rich would have to pay to the poor for the continued enjoyment of their privileges. From his new political platform, Menzies called for a true revival of liberal thought, which would work for social justice, security and national progress, and for the full development of the individual. In December 1944, a second and larger conference held at Albury adopted the title 'Liberal Party'. Menzies subsequently created an elaborate federal party structure: there was a federal council with seven members from each state (who controlled Liberal affairs) and an executive of eleven who ran the day-to-day activities of the secretariat. Menzies tried desperately to keep the Liberals independent from the tied contribution of large companies and professional organisations, but in this he failed, and the Liberal Party (like the UAP) derived its initial funds and its strength from the financiers of Melbourne.

Facing a revived conservative opposition, defeated on a leading issue by a referendum, with the prospects of the war ending and the saviour-image going with it, Labor was badly affected by Curtin's death on 5 July 1945. Nevertheless, despite the refusal of the people to accept an extension of federal power in the immediate post-war years, in 1946 the Labor Party basked in the sun of its greatest peacetime electoral victory. The Labor Party had clean hands when the war started. It was not a 'war party' like Churchill's conservatives. Its progressive liberal ideas were moderate enough to be acceptable to the middle class. Labor began its post-war administration in the hands of Ben Chifley, elected by caucus, who had the task of relating to the Australian community how the war against Japan had ended with the dropping of atomic bombs on Hiroshima and Nagasaki.

CHAPTER 2

Smart but not Extreme

✦

The crusade in the Pacific and the war in Europe ended with Labor firmly in the saddle. Because of the untimely death of Curtin, the Labor Party, which governed Australia, faced the problems of post-war reconstruction with a new leader, Ben Chifley. Chifley's chief tasks were to guide the Labor movement and solve the industrial issues of post-war economic recovery. But he was not able to devote attention to the needs of the bourgeoisie; his attack on the banks was seen as an attack on the middle class. The plans to nationalise the banks lost Labor the 1949 election, and forced the middle class into a conservative political position which was to last over twenty years, and had the effect of fossilising Australia's social and political life.

Chifley was happy in the wings between 1941 and 1945. Curtin was the leader and, arm in arm with MacArthur, he had galvanised the nation into the war effort. Chifley's role was that of unobtrusive lieutenant. He was a secondary and unpopular figure, the architect of increased taxation, wartime domestic restrictions and the plotter of future state intervention. Chifley's best year was 1945 when as national leader he announced the surrenders of Germany and Japan and initiated his post-war reconstruction programme. But it was in a tottering world economy that the state premiers agreed to co-operate with Chifley and expedite demobilisation. Within days of the

Japanese capitulation, the United States government had ended lend-lease and created a worldwide balance of payments crisis and an acute dollar shortage to which the Australian economy remained exposed.

Nevertheless Chifley's demobilisation plans were an early and brilliant success. At the end of the war there were half a million servicemen in uniform. A quarter of a million were demobbed before the end of 1945: ex-servicemen were given preferential employment, facilities for retraining and education, cheap soldier-settler smallholdings and subsidised housing loans. The co-ordinator of demobilisation and dispersal was Lieutenant-General Stan Savige, who had no difficulty convincing employers that they would serve both their own interests and the national task of re-establishment by offering soldiers opportunities to apply the enterprise and efficiency they had developed during the war.

Chifley himself was a prime minister on trial. He had been selected and installed in office by his caucus friends alone, so at the immediate post-war election Chifley decided to lie low. Chifley thought that elections were determined psychologically some time before the climax of the campaign, and that, although there might be a lot of people who did not make up their minds until the last few days, what caused them to make a final decision had already been planted in their minds. His 1945 policy speech was little more than a pedestrian report and routine prospectus of a well-established enterprise, while Menzies's growing brilliance as leader of the new Liberal Party underlined the prime minister's dullness. On the crucial question of industrial peace Menzies said that he would make strikes illegal and prosecute offenders. He also promised to cut taxation drastically, extend child endowment, and end wage pegging and other wartime controls. Chifley offered only to ease wage pegging and taxes as the general economic situation improved. A referendum to retain the commonwealth's wartime power to make defence regulations during the period of reconstruction was defeated, and Chifley was left with a mandate to introduce popular moderate reforms through his twin pillars, the creation of full employment and social welfare.

During the four years in which Chifley led the country, he made substantial contributions to the development and shaping of Australian society. In 1947 he initiated a government-financed immigration scheme which Arthur Calwell as Minister for Immigration administered. Calwell set himself an annual target of 70,000 migrants, but the economic condition of post-war Europe allowed an intake of 150,000 a year within five years.

Calwell believed in a White Australia Policy, saying no red-blooded Australian wanted to see 'chocolate-coloured Australia' and made the notorious pun, 'Two Wongs don't make a White'. The white newcomers brought skills that played a large part in breaking the bottleneck in steel production, housing and public works, as well as contributing to the obvious enrichment of Australian culture. Calwell's immigration achievement was one of the historic successes of Chifley's government; it lay behind industrial growth and the success of the ambitious development projects of the next decades. In 1950 Menzies praised the immigration policy of the Labor government: all his conservative colleagues agreed that the attack on the problem of immigration in Australia under Chifley and Calwell deserved the deep gratitude and praise of every Australian.

Chifley's contribution to Australian primary industry was greater than that made by all the previous Country Parties put together. Between 1945 and 1948 there was legislation to help the wool, dried fruits, sugar, meat, dairy, cotton, timber, egg, hide, leather and apple producers, but his main success was the far-sighted achievement of wheat price and production stabilisation. In 1946 Chifley had suggested that the wartime arrangements for the marketing of wheat be kept on. Both the haughty state governments and the recalcitrant wheat-growers objected, however, because Chifley intended to control production as well as marketing. But when Australian wheat reached a production record of 220 million bushels in the summer of 1948, the prudent acceptance of long-term stabilisation plans by most wheat-growers was inevitable. The federal and state governments then co-operated with wheat-growers to guarantee a good living for efficient farmers. Thus the fluctuations between prosperity and disastrous slump were ended, leaving only drought and seasonal ups and downs outside the control of the primary producers. When wheat-growing became less of a gamble, the whole community benefited.

Nor was the defence of Australia neglected. In 1947 a guided missile range was established at Woomera, about a hundred miles north of Port Augusta in South Australia. The rocket range extended over 1,200 miles of desert and there Australian scientists co-operated with the British to design and test guided missiles and aircraft. The Jindivik pilotless jet aircraft was one of the first projects off the drawing board. Woomera was the base camp for extensions of defence planning into the field of atomic weapon testing at Maralinga, 500 miles west of Woomera in Central Australia, on the edge of the Nullarbor Plain. There was little concern for the the welfare of the Aboriginal inhabitants of the area. Equally significant was the establishment by Chifley of an effective security service. The Australian Security Intelligence Organisation (ASIO) was to collect information and organise counter-espionage against subversive elements within Australia. Finally, Chifley began the most ambitious development project ever undertaken by any Australian government, the Snowy Mountains Hydro-Electric and Irrigation Scheme. But his achievements still left the prime minister exposed to danger: on Labor's vulnerable left flank lurked the cadres of the Australian Communist Party in the industrial trade unions.

Chifley's headaches with industrial unrest began in earnest

nine days after the 1946 election, when Melbourne suffered the first combined rail and tramway stoppage in Victoria's history. Chifley disregarded the storm signals and, after consulting his senior ministers, decided that wage pegging would have to be retained even after the expiry of the National Security Act on 31 December. Meanwhile, in the workshops of the Victorian railways and the state foundries, there were, in quick succession, an overtime ban that was unamenable to arbitration, a lock-out that turned into a strike, threats of deregistration, and finally the inevitable compromise. The Victorian metalworkers' strike lasted six months and was one of a succession of industrial disputes that had sprung up since the end of the war in the Pacific. During the war, the workers had accepted industrial conscription in return for full employment and abundant overtime. As was the case in the United Kingdom during 1914–18, skilled craft unions even allowed unskilled workers and women to do the work hitherto reserved for tradesmen, and in return the management allowed such concessions as lengthy tea-breaks during the long wartime working day. In post-war Australia, however, there were spontaneous grass-roots campaigns for better wages and working conditions. The workers took home less pay with the run-down in plant and equipment after six years of war. And there were bottle-necks caused by disputes in the New South Wales coal industry.

There were two important features about the coal industry disputes. First, the Chifley government learnt nothing from them, in so far as the prime minister decided that even tougher legislation would be needed to curb trade union demands. Accordingly, the Arbitration Court inserted a clause in the metal trades award forbidding overtime bans. When this was ruled illegal in 1951, Menzies amended the act to allow for penal sanctions. Secondly, the 1946 strikes brought the Communist Party into the limelight and sent diligent right-wingers hunting for reds under beds. Yet the influence of the Communist Party was not part of a giant communist conspiracy to weaken the economy and destroy Australian society. The stoppages were not directed by cold and calculating brains at CPA headquarters, as most union activists were not members of the Communist Party (only six out of the thirty-six members of the Melbourne District Committee were cardholders).

Were strikes the result of genuine worker demands for a better deal, or were they part of subversive class war conducted by guerilla shop stewards? Chifley did not know. He only knew that he could not win. If the strikes continued, he was showing his weakness; if they were stopped, he illustrated his callous disregard for the workers. In 1947 he had tried to draw the sting of the militants by amending the Conciliation and Arbitration Act and appointed fifteen conciliation commissioners. At the same time the court's functions were reduced to making determinations related to basic wage rates, hours of work, and annual leave. In September 1947, after almost two years' hearings, the court delivered a unanimous judgment in favour of the forty-hour week. Nearly a million workers were affected by the decision, which was based on the assumption that the Australian economy was booming and could absorb the added costs involved. Despite this concession, industrial unrest continued to grow, and daily life in the community was disrupted increasingly by strikes on the wharves and in the mines.

In mid-winter 1949 came the government's most critical test. On 27 June a coal strike broke out in New South Wales in support of the miners' claims for a three-dollar a week increase in wages, a thirty-five-hour working week, and three months' paid holiday once every seven years. In anticipation of the stoppage, drastic fuel rationing was announced in Sydney on 17 June, including immediate cuts of 50 per cent in coal supplies to rail, tram, gas, electricity services, of 75 per cent in supplies to general industry, and of over 90 per cent in the steel industry.

Hospitals, water-works, and food processing plants were exempt from rationing. On 20 June the New South Wales government was forced to prohibit the industrial use of electricity altogether, as well as electric lighting in shops, theatres and warehouses. Each household was permitted to burn only two electric light globes, electric cooking was prohibited until noon and electric water heaters were banned altogether. Chifley and the Labor Premier of New South Wales, James McGirr, then made a joint statement explaining to the miners that no threat or strike, however prolonged, would influence the commonwealth or state government's determination that the dispute be settled by the normal process of arbitration. Indeed, the issue of arbitration was at stake. The strike, called in defiance of a stay-at-work order of the coal industry tribunal (which had the miners' claims before it), amounted to a repudiation of the conciliation machinery set up at the miners' demand during the war.

Subsequent events illustrated how little there was to choose between socialist and conservative policies; Menzies and Fadden could scarcely have acted more resolutely. On 30 June 1949, Chifley's government launched a newspaper campaign that described the negotiations preceding the strike and denounced the stoppage as a communist-inspired, wholly unjustifiable repudiation of conciliation and arbitration at a time when they were functioning effectively. When the strike began, the miners' leaders immediately removed funds from the union's bank account to help miners in need and also so that they would then have money to pay fines levied by the Arbitration Court. The Miners' Federation, the Federated Ironworkers' Association, the Waterside Workers' Federation and the Amalgamated Engineering Union were all subsequently charged with removing $108,000 in defiance of the National Emergency Coal Strike Act, which parliament had passed to deal with the situation. Subsequently three workers' leaders were imprisoned, inevitably stirring up more industrial action. Commonwealth police, instructed by the security service, raided Marx House, the Communist Party's headquarters in Sydney. Prison sentences and injunctions continued. The Communist Party was prevented from using its funds to help the strikers. Three more miners were given twelve months' gaol. The Communist Party's bank account was frozen, and there were strikes at all Australian ports. Premier McGirr turned out to be a scab as he tried to import 100,000 tons of Transvaal coal to New South Wales. By 21 July, the army was ready to move on to the coalfields, and, at midnight on 2 August 1949, troops began working the open-cut mines.

At that stage in the life of the commonwealth, a blacker page in Labor history would be difficult to find. The cabinet had chosen, rather inappropriately, Arthur Calwell as its Minister of Information. In a calculated exercise of propaganda against the strikers, he addressed a Labor rally in Sydney on 31 July. The meeting was marked by the customary disruption and arrests, Calwell described the communists as a collection of pathological exhibits, said that the best place for them was a concentration camp, and added that they had made the names of miners stink in the nostrils of all decent people. It was, he said, an anti-Australian strike: the communists wanted to smash the arbitration system, but they would not be allowed to succeed, as the government would smash them first.

The strike ended on 11 August when the general council of the Australian Miners' Federation endorsed the decision of the acting executive council to return to work. The army, which had produced 100,000 tons of coal, was withdrawn on 14 August, and the resumption of work became general. A turning-point in Australian history, the strike illustrated how little there was to choose between the policies of the two major parties, making the question of administrative expertise all-important; it also cost the country 2,000,000 tons of coal and put 600,000 men out of work.

If the Communist Party of Australia received unmerited

publicity through the strike, it was largely Chifley's doing. And in making it a scapegoat, he was providing successive conservative governments with the myth of communist influence on the Labor movement, which helped them to retain office throughout the 1950s and 1960s. Chifley's view, at the end of August 1949, was that the strike had been planned by the communists. The prime minister could not believe that any citizen could so callously plan to hold up community life and impose such intolerable hardships as the strikers had done, but it happened. Chifley characterised it as a revolt against the whole community. The Communist Party replied that a great struggle had ended, in which the right-wing leaders of the Labor Party, headed by Chifley and Evatt, had demonstrated that their real concern was the defence of capitalism at all costs, and that as lackeys of monopoly capitalism these Labor traitors had shown they were prepared to go to any lengths to defeat the workers. Not since the strikes of the 1890s, from which the Australian Labor parties sprang, was the evidence of class conflict so clear, so blatant and so unconvincing. For the miners' strike in 1949 appeared to be waged not against capitalism but against the Labor government, and it was broken because Labor Party leaders, supported by many union officials, campaigned against the miners on the coalfields.

Chifley received scant co-operation from organised labour, but less still from organised capital. His decision to nationalise the banks was the most serious error of his career and, combined with the industrial unrest and Menzies's strong leadership of the revived Liberal Party, was the beginning of Labor's long years in the wilderness. When he became prime minister, Chifley retained the treasury portfolio. Only two hours after the Japanese surrendered he conferred with Treasury and taxation experts, believing that he held the vantage point from which to drive through his plans for full employment and social reform. Chifley's study of public accounting had convinced him of the possibility of an international economic recession that was likely to threaten his programme of social reform. Social reform could be saved only by the twin pillars of bank nationalisation and peacetime price control. He admitted that the United States was doing a great job with Marshall aid in Europe. Australia, however, faced both a crucial shipping shortage – which hampered export of primary produce – and a crisis in foreign exchange. While the country's London sterling funds were buoyant (they rose from 199 million in June 1947 to 452 million in June 1949), the North American dollar problem was acute. Australia had to get $164 million from the sterling area pool to balance its annual dollar accounts for the year 1947–48. This was the background to Chifley's fight for bank nationalisation.

The new left view, and indeed the old left view, is that Chifley's attempt at bank nationalisation was not part of an attack on capitalism. It was simply forced upon him by circumstances. If the free enterprise banks had worked harmoniously within the 1945 legislation, Chifley would not have tried to nationalise them. On the other hand, Chifley had seriously considered bank nationalisation for at least a decade. He had served in 1937 with the Banking Commission, disagreed with its bland findings, and issued a minority report in which he said that there was no possibility of any well-ordered progress in the community so long as there were privately owned trading banks that had been established for the purpose of making a profit. A banking policy should have one aim, Chifley said: service for the general good of the community. Private banking systems made the community the victim of every wave of optimism or pessimism that surged through the minds of the financial speculators. Later, as treasurer in March 1945, Chifley had steered through the House of Representatives legislation that provided a uniform legal framework for regulating the banking system. It co-ordinated banking policy under the direction of the Commonwealth Bank, controlled credit and bank interest rates, and was designed to mobilise and provide machinery for the control of the foreign exchange and gold resources.

Perhaps Chifley stumbled into bank nationalisation when his method of control was successfully challenged on 13 August 1947. The Melbourne City Council claimed in a test case that the Australian Labor Party's banking legislation was unlawful under the constitution. And the High Court upheld its case. On the other hand, it is equally likely that Chifley, having bank nationalisation in the back, and sometimes the front, of his mind since 1937, decided that if it were done, it were best done quickly. On 14 August 1947 Chifley called a meeting with the two senior members of the cabinet, Evatt and McKenna, the Governor of the Commonwealth Bank, the Bank's Secretary and Economic Adviser and two Treasury men. This group informally considered the implications of the Melbourne City Council decision, and Chifley asked the bankers whether it would be technically possible to nationalise the banks. He gave the question no special emphasis, and the bankers were left in the dark about the prime minister's plans. Evatt knew. He had given his opinion on the legal issues involved, and McKenna was told on 15 August, because his Department of Health and Social Security was the chief weapon in the social reform armoury.

The cabinet sat on 15 August to consider a variety of items including the Snowy Mountains Hydro-electric Scheme, and the British pound-dollar crisis and its implications for Australia. At the end of the meeting Chifley asked ministers to remain in Canberra until Saturday evening to polish off the business and discuss the Melbourne City Council case. The prime minister distributed no documents on the High Court decision, and only Evatt and McKenna knew what was up his sleeve. On Saturday morning, when the routine business was over, Chifley asked Evatt to outline the legal position of the commonwealth. He then put the alternatives: the government could either accept the decision and wait for the private banks to attack the entire

1945 Act, or they could remove the challenge by nationalising the banks. In the cabinet room there was stunned shock, followed by jubilation as every minister recommended nationalisation. There was complete unanimity.

Staggered by the decision, Menzies first assumed that it sprang from pique over the defeat of the banking case in the High Court. But as a masterly tactician he soon realised that Chifley had handed him an executioner's sword. The community was alarmed, and Menzies soon made political capital out of this widespread fear. Within a couple of days Menzies was claiming that Australians were called to a great battle to defend their freedom against dictatorship at home. Twenty years later, some bank officers could still vividly recall the shocking Saturday afternoon in August when they learnt of the government's decision. Coming home from the football they had seen the newspaper banners, or at home they had heard it on the radio while gardening, or read it in the evening news.

The morning newspapers spoke of serfs and totalitarianism. The Melbourne *Age* branded Chifley a 'revolutionary', the *Sydney Morning Herald* spoke of financial extremism that would lead to the economic enslavement of the Australian people. Of the weeklies *The Bulletin* was apoplectic, and the Sydney *Catholic Weekly* ominously suggested that conscientious Catholic ministers and members of the Labor Party rank and file would resign from the Labor Party if bank nationalisation heralded the introduction of socialism and the abolition of private property. Cardinal Gilroy declared that bank nationalisation was not the business of his church unless a moral issue was involved but then, as later, the damage was done. Fadden composed a doggerel rhyme:

> We thought the Kelly Gang was dead,
> But the spirit still lives on.
> In the place of brothers Dan and Ned
> We've Bert and stubborn Ben instead.

In reply, the Labor members quoted Bernard Shaw to the effect that a national or municipal bank would bring down the price of capital, just as nationalisation of the coal mines brought down the price of coal by eliminating the profiteer.

The Australian Labor Party's previous banking legislation in 1945 had been objectionable because it removed the central bank board and put the treasurer of the day in ultimate control of credit policy, while giving the central bank and, in effect, the treasurer, full power to determine the trading banks' class of advances and to regulate the volume of credit they might employ. It was argued that if the government succeeded in taking over the trading banks holus-bolus, they would be in a position to appoint their staffs, dismiss the incumbent boards and managers, and pry into the details of depositors' accounts. A group calling itself the Sane Democracy League took large and expensive advertisements in the daily press, pointing out that the proposed bank grab delighted the communists, whose party was loudest in applauding the Chifley government's bank nationalisation proposal. The communists said that the decision to nationalise the banks was one of the most important and best ever reached by a Labor government. Four days later, the federal congress of the Australian Council of Trade Unions (ACTU) passed a resolution moved by the communists, in almost identical terms. The Sane Democracy League urged Australians to remember that the ACTU was a body that directed Labor's policy. By their logic the Chifley government had become an instrument of communist policy, which threatened the freedom of every man, woman and child in Australia.

All of the people who had accounts in the trading banks were liable to be affected if the Chifley nationalisation plan was successful. If they could be mobilised and convinced, all bank depositors were potential Liberal voters. Menzies had little difficulty in the task. He began by pointing out that it was Chifley's job to argue the case for change. Why should private banks be outlawed and customers deprived of rights which they had enjoyed almost from the foundation of Australia? Menzies traced Chifley's plan to Karl Marx's thesis that since private banks were conducted primarily for profit, their business should be transferred to public ownership. This revolutionary doctrine, Menzies argued, could be transformed into complete socialism. If it had been adopted at the beginning of the nineteenth century, the whole industrial expansion of the English-speaking world, the increase in population and living standards would never have occurred. Nor would Australian land settlement, manufacturing industry or even the Australian trade union movement have existed. In all this Menzies used the techniques of debate – irony, ridicule, and the quotation of Labor statements against Labor arguments – that were so effective in future years.

The legal fate of the Bank Nationalisation Act was complicated. Following the act's swift passage, eight Australian and three British trading banks lodged writs on 28 November 1947 seeking an interim injunction by the Australian High Court to restrain the commonwealth from nationalising the banks under the act. The same action was taken by the states of South Australia, Victoria and Western Australia. Justice Sir Owen Dixon granted the injunction on 5 December, and a month later referred the case to the High Court. The High Court hearing was the longest in the history of the court, lasting thiry-five days, and ended with the court declaring so many sections of the act invalid that it became a dead letter. Garfield Barwick, leading counsel for the banks, successfully submitted that the act was not authorised under section 51 of the federal constitution, did not provide just terms, and was an infringement of the constitutional integrity of the states. Evatt was unable to convince the court that the act was within the commonwealth parliament's legislative powers.

Menzies was in London when the decision was handed down, and described it as not only a legal but also a political landmark. He was correct. The court had shown that there was a sharp limit to the power of the federal parliament to nationalise industry. People in Britain, Menzies added, would be interested to observe how much more difficult it was for the socialists to have their way in a federal country than it was in a unitary country like Britain. Menzies recalled how in all recent referenda the Australian electors had shown that they were not willing to extend the central powers of the federal parliament permanently. The decision of the full High Court, though based on purely legal considerations, was in line with the mood of the people. It was one of Menzies's greatest gifts that he could gauge the popular attitude on current political issues, and mould his policies accordingly. His successors were to prove far less sensitive.

Chifley then appealed to the Privy Council against the High Court's verdict. Not surprisingly, the appeal before the Privy Council was also the longest hearing in its history. Evatt and Barwick again appeared. Finally dismissing the appeal, the Privy Council put the issue in a nutshell. Section 46 of the Banking Act, in effect, provided for nationalisation of the business of banking in Australia, whereas, by section 92 of the constitution, trade, commerce and intercourse among the states had to be absolutely free. The business ended in May 1950 when the 1947 act was repealed. At the same time the conservatives established a small board of directors for the Central Commonwealth Bank. Fadden pointed out that it was in line with the policy of a number of commonwealth countries for a board of directors to control and manage the Central Bank. When the Bank of England was nationalised in 1946 the system of board management continued. In sum, both socialists and conservatives were prepared to use arguments and weapons, which on ideological grounds they might have been expected to eschew, Labor appealing for help to an extra-national court and the Liberals quoting aspects of British socialist administration to justify their own policy.

The bank grab fiasco finished Chifley. It showed that Fadden had hit the nail on the head by describing him as 'stubborn Ben', insensitive to the mood of the electorate and pig-headed in his determination to rout his opponents. The long legal battle also showed up the defects of his successor. Whenever legal proceedings were afoot, Evatt could not resist running into court. Appearing before the High Court in the vital banking case, Evatt antagonised the bench by asking two judges to disqualify themselves from hearing the case on the grounds that their families held shares in free enterprise banks. Such political insensitivity was the hallmark of his characteristically disastrous court appearances.

In 1945 *The Bulletin* assured its readers that they could vote Labor, reasonably supposing that it was the party of reform and not of socialisation. In 1949, Menzies pointed out that a vote for Labor was a socialist vote for the master state, the one employer, the one planner, the one controller. As in the monstrous totalitarian states, which had disfigured the twentieth century, all free choice would be gone. One could not have a controlled economy without controlling human beings, who were yet the greatest of all economic factors. One could not socialise all means of production without socialising men and women. Unless people did what they were told, worked where they were told to work, learned what they were drafted to learn – in all, fitted obediently into their appointed place – the socialist planned state would fall to pieces like the false and shoddy thing it was. The socialists of Great Britain, concluded Menzies, were already introducing industrial conscription. Faced with this onslaught, all Chifley could do was to stand on his achievements as champion of the people.

Chifley's achievements were the basis of much of Australia's prosperity and stability in the 1950s and the 1960s, but in 1949 they were too embryonic to count. Many of his development plans were so ambitious and far-sighted that their realisation seemed mere dreams. Other decisions with more obvious short-term effects reinforced conservative political criticism. In 1947, for example, Chifley acquired all the shares of Qantas Empire Airways, giving the federal government overall control of Australian international air transport. During 1947 the Australian government took part in tariff negotiations which formed the General Agreement on Tariffs and Trade. This reduced the possibility of tariff wars and helped stimulate trade in the era of world-wide shortages. Australia received an enormous compliment when Foreign Minister Evatt was elected, by 31 votes to 20, President of the third session of the United Nations Assembly. For Evatt his election was the last personal triumph in his life.

Public opinion polls suggested that after the slump in 1947, the ALP recovered majority support for much of 1948 and early 1949. The party's popularity faded only after the coal strike, Mao Tse-tung's triumph on the Chinese mainland, and a perceptible rise in domestic inflation. Even if he had abandoned petrol rationing and granted child endowment for the first child, Chifley would probably still have lost the 1949 election; the bank grab had weakened his standing irretrievably.

When the country went to the polls on 10 December 1949, Labor held an enviable majority of 43 seats in a house of 74 effective members. Although the House of Representatives had been increased by 48 seats for the 1949 election, Labor picked up hardly any. Four days before the polls J. T. Lang delivered a symbolic *coup de grace*. He produced a list of mortgages registered in the names of Mr and Mrs J. B. Chifley. The loans totalled only $30,000 and covered a period from 1930 to 1942, but they bore interest at rates ranging from 5 to 9 per cent. Because of the embargo on radio political broadcasting before an election, Chifley was unable to reply to the press. He went down as a hypocrite who, while attacking the banks for lending money at high rates of interest, had been doing the same thing himself.

The allegations about Chifley were technically true but in essence very unfair. Nor was Chifley's image helped by his description of J. T. Lang as a Labor rat whom he would not pursue into a sewer.

The election in December 1949 was a victory for the coalition. Menzies and Fadden combined to defeat the Labor Party, which had held office for eight years. Menzies led a new house, enlarged by over half. The electoral redistribution had been carried out under Chifley but without Labor noting that the redistribution would affect the party badly. The larger membership of parliament was necessary to keep pace with the growth in population since the establishment of the commonwealth – from 3,765,000 to 7,581,000; the number of registered electors from 1,893,000 to 4,780,000. The new house was to give the coalition a reservoir of talent. But the real dynamic of the conservative government was to come from the expansion of the civil service, which inevitably accompanied the growth in the House of Representatives.

Menzies's first priority as prime minister was to 'develop the maximum strength of Australia', a hope vague enough to serve any political leader. He was determined to maintain the closest ties and machinery for consultation with Britain and other Commonwealth countries, so that on important world issues they could speak with one voice. At the time of Suez this aim was to clash with his other objective, which he spelt out in rather more detail. Menzies said it was a cardinal point of government policy to develop real friendship with the US, not just because the United States was Australia's powerful friend in wartime, but because the British and American peoples really understood each other and were prepared to work and do business together. Menzies's phrase 'powerful friend' echoed by his successors for twenty-five years, eventually became a liability when the American dream soured both at home and in Vietnam. Like Evatt, Menzies saw himself as a world statesman, whose historic role was to be a special link in Anglo-American relations.

The conservative victory and the Labor defeat marked the end of an era. Looking back on his term as prime minister, Ben Chifley said that his job had been difficult and man-killing. He described himself (mixing his metaphors) as an evangelist crying in the wilderness – fortune's wheel had made him prominent, but the strength to turn plans into reality could only have come from the roots of the Labor movement, and they were choked and strangled.

The post-war period ended with Chifley's defeat at the 1949 elections; in the 1950s the Labor party was sociologically inappropriate to Australian society. Menzies's triumph lay in his capacity to grasp that social reform was right for the middle class but electoral suicide if extended to the workers. A prime minister might safely reflect changing attitudes and standards by increasing pensions and child endowment, but he could not so easily reduce the hours of work for miners, waterside workers and fitters. Thus, when the first mass-produced Australian motor car rolled off the line it was priced at $1,400 and was too expensive for the workers who made it. The Holden was General Motors' stake in the Australian economy.

The Holden was featured in the 1949 election campaign advertising. A proud Menzies stood behind a new Holden marked 'Free Enterprise' and helped a woman out of a broken-down 1929 model, left-hand drive, chauffeured by a glass-eyed Chifley. GMH knew who the market buyers were when they based their first sales campaign on the slogan that epitomised bourgeois values: the Holden was floated as 'smart without being extreme'. The same could have been said of the Liberal-Country Party.

CHAPTER 3

Facing the Nest of Traitors

The 1950s saw the re-establishment of liberal capitalism in Australia as in Western Europe and America. In developing new industrial and financial institutions, the middle class were the vanguard. Side by side with the growth of economic prosperity went a fear of communism. As the Cold War deepened, Menzies was able to exploit the middle-class neurosis about the 'reds' in the Australian unions, and the 'reds' in Europe and Asia. Communist candidates at the 1949 elections attracted only 87,958 voters, but Menzies characterised them as a traitorous minority with the power 'to destroy us' and argued that in the 1950s Australia was 'fighting for its life'. While Menzies's administration was at first founded upon public disillusion with the Labor Party, what kept the Liberals in office was the general level of insecurity in the community. For the conservatives to stay in power the people had to be convinced that Australia's prosperity was endangered by left-wing threats. Menzies soon developed the technique of whipping up fear and offering the bourgeoisie security.

The legislative campaign against communism began in March 1950. Menzies announced to the House of Representatives that because of a series of strikes among members of the Communist-led Waterside Workers' Federation in Brisbane, the governor-general, the establishment's traditional constitutional spearhead, had issued a proclamation under the Crimes Act declaring that the existence of a serious industrial disturbance prejudiced and threatened trade and commerce between the Australian states.

The Crimes Act provided that, while the proclamation remained effective, any person taking part in a strike in the transport industry, or in any essential service, or inciting, aiding or encouraging a strike, was liable to imprisonment for not more than one year, or, if not born in Australia, to deportation. The Waterside Workers' Federation had carried out a series of rolling strikes against a system whereby waterside workers were allotted work in particular ships in the order in which they were picked from a roster, this having the effect of splitting up teams or groups. The port of Brisbane was immobilised from December 1949 until March 1950, and cargoes of export meat, butter and wool lay in holds perishing while inward cargoes of steel could not be unloaded and sent to factories. Menzies fore-shadowed further action, saying that the government was leg-islating to deal with the communists but, in the meantime, it was not prepared to allow the position to drift and would carry the fight to the traitors. On 27 March the President of the Australian Council of Trade Unions, A. E. Monk, convened a special union congress for 16 May to consider the government's action in enforcing the Crimes Act for industrial disputes, and two days later the Waterside Workers' Federation advised dockers to return to work.

But victory over the watersiders was not followed by the general extermination campaign Menzies favoured. And his failure to manipulate the parliament, the courts and the elec-torate to drive the Communist Party underground was probably his greatest political miscalculation. Had he succeeded, the communist weapon in Australian politics would have been even blunter. Communist influence was on the wane by the early 1950s. There is ground for thinking that the peak came around 1945. But even so, the conservatives could not disregard the influence of communists in the industrial unions. In April 1950 Menzies introduced a bill to dissolve the Communist Party for 'the safety and defence of Australia'. He clearly hoped to be able to preclude known communists from government and key trade union posts.

The provisions of the bill were of the gravest importance since they involved a dramatic attack on civil liberties. The preamble declared that the Communist Party sought to assist or to accelerate the coming of a new revolutionary situation in which, acting as a revolutionary minority, it would be able to seize power and establish a 'dictatorship of the proletariat'. Communists were said to be prepared to attain political, economic and industrial ends by force, violence and fraud. The government believed that the Australian Communist Party was an integral part of the world communist movement, which was engaged in espionage, treason and sabotage, and that these activities were designed to dislocate, retard and disrupt production in industries vital to the security and defence of Australia (including coal-mining, iron, steel, engineering, building and transport).

It was a good story. Events were to prove the Australian Communist Party a paper tiger. During the period 1920–55, the communists (wrote an ex-card-carrier) were not able to give a serious alternative to a modification of capitalism, unless the strenuous advocacy of nationalisation of the larger monopolies is to be accepted as such. But Menzies was taking no chances. His bill declared the party unlawful and provided that party funds could be confiscated by the federal government without right of appeal. The governor-general was also given power to ban affiliated organisations. People declared communist were to be disqualified from employment in the Commonwealth Public Service. Trade unions could also be declared.

For the unions, A. E. Monk declared that the ACTU was

opposed to every section of the bill, which was adroitly worded to give unfettered power to the government to deal with those whom it wished to remove from political or industrial office. Chifley condemned the bill as a violation of freedom of expression and said that it was opening the road to totalitarianism. The parliamentary Labor Party then underwent a *volte-face* on a colossal scale. In what Menzies rightly described as the most abject surrender in the Labor Party's history, the federal executive of the Labor Party decided that the bill should be passed, and the bill went through, Menzies pressing the rout by pointing out that the executive were not even members of the parliamentary party – a point of such importance that it was to win a future election for the coalition. Chifley was distracted: he addressed members of the parliamentary party in ominous terms, saying that the Labor Party had to accept the executive's decision, and be humiliated, in order to go forward: recriminate, he said, and we shall split.

Although the Labor Party failed the Communist Party, the country did not. The Australian Communist Party and the trade unions (including the Waterside Workers' Federation, the Australian Railways Union, the Amalgamated Engineering Union, the Seamen's Union, the Ironworkers' Association, the Miners' Union, the Sheet-metal Workers' Union, the Ship Painters and Dockers' Union and the Clerks' Union) challenged the validity of the act and sought to restrain the government from enforcing it. The principal advocate on behalf of the claimants was Dr H. V. Evatt, QC, Deputy Leader of the Opposition. He argued successfully that the Communist Party Dissolution Act constituted a serious interference with the civil rights of trade unions, that the commonwealth had no power to dispense with civil rights to this extent in peace-time, and that to give discretion to the government to take away the civil rights of citizens on a mere say-so of the executive was tantamount to an abrogation of the functions of the judiciary. This latter argument impressed the full High Court, which declared the Communist Dissolution Act invalid on 9 March 1951.

Menzies showed his political resilience by bouncing back from his defeat at the hands of the High Court. He decided to hold a referendum to amend the constitution in much the same circumstances as Labor had before: one party wished to nationalise the banks, the other to proscribe communism, but they both used the same technique. And both met the same fate. The referendum was held on 22 September 1951, and Menzies's aims were defeated: 96 per cent of the electorate voted, and out of a total of 4,754,589 votes cast the overall 'No' majority was 52,082. Most of the electorate agreed with Evatt's denunciation of the referendum as one of the most dangerous measures ever submitted to an English-speaking legislature, contradicting, as it did, the whole nature and purpose of the constitution, and being contrary to all forms of constitutional procedure.

The communists were not impressed by Evatt's rhetoric, and saw the major parties as essentially similar. L. L. Sharkey, a leader of the communists, put the Communist Party of Australia's point of view, saying that the Menzies government represented the interests of the Australian monopolists and American and British imperialism. Nor was the right-wing-dominated Australian Labor Party much different in so far as it was also a party of class collaboration. The Australian Labor Party, said Sharkey, supported the fundamental policy of monopoly capitalism and imperialism, both British and American imperialism, as well as Australian capitalism's expansion in New Guinea and its investments in British colonies. The Australian Labor Party did not interfere with the big monopolies, who controlled Australian industry and finance, by nationalising their companies when the Australian Labor Party was in control of government.

Between the first attempt to ban the Communist Party and the abortive referendum, Menzies showed his political genius by calling a snap election. The ostensible reason for the election was the refusal of Labor senators to pass the government's Banking Bill without serious amendment. But in reality Menzies wanted to see if he could tar the Labor Party twice with the same banking brush, and it turned out he could. The Liberal and Country parties decided to contest the election jointly against the Labor Party; this was the first time that both parties submerged their differences and let Menzies make the major policy speech on behalf of the coalition.

Apart from the banks, the issues were communism and inflation. R. G. Casey, Menzies's most able lieutenant, whose Cambridge education and wartime diplomatic experience fitted him for the role of Foreign Minister, helped the prime minister set the political agenda. Casey believed that inflation was the secret weapon of militant international communism, which forced democratic nations to arm, reduced the volume of consumer goods and raised prices in a ruinously inflationary war. Casey quoted a truism (which he said originated in the Middle East), 'You don't have to cut a man's throat when you have already put poison in his soup.' The poison of inflation was everywhere, said Casey, and the Russians were counting on the democracies collapsing under the strain.

Opening the campaign, Menzies declared that the Labor Party had used its majority in the Senate to obstruct and slow down the government's legislative programme, and in doing so, had refused to accept 'the umpire's decision' after the last general election. The coalition had no new policies other than those given at the 1949 general election, and Menzies asked only that the government be given a fair go in carrying out the policies that had been approved by the electorate then. He singled out and emphasised the problem of communism, and connected the Communist Party with Australia's economic problems. Labor replied that the government was responsible for inflation, but Menzies argued that rising costs, so far as they were controllable, could be attributed to the Labor Party and its 'protected ally', the Communist Party. The principal causes of high prices, he charged, were go-slows, absenteeism and (using Casey's metaphor) the poisons of communist technique which, with inefficiency, a falling-off in individual effort, and deliberate limitation of output, were stifling production.

Labor tried to convince the electorate that what was required was a return to price control. It had given Australia a record of price stability virtually unequalled in the world, but elections resulted in a victory for the Liberal and Country Party coalition, the government having thereafter a majority both in the House of Representatives and the Senate. The coalition gained 69 seats (Liberal 52, Country Party 17) and the Labor Party 54, giving the government a majority of 15, compared with a majority of 27 in the previous House. Although the Labor Party failed to gain a majority, it increased its representation in the Lower House, gaining seats in Victoria, the state later convulsed by a sectarian campaign that was to transform Australian politics.

Near the climax of the anti-Communist Party campaign, Chifley died. A Catholic, he was buried at Bathurst after a requiem mass in the Cathedral: 30,000 people attended his funeral. In London Attlee and Eden made speeches of tribute, as well they might have. The world was not to see again the like of a man who had, at various stages in his career, presented a gift of twenty million pounds to the United Kingdom and driven the Sydney-Melbourne express. The huge crowd underlined the fact that he was not only a man from the masses, but the last truly 'popular' Labor leader.

The 1951 elections were held at a time of mounting anti-communist feeling. Between the shadow of the Communist Party Dissolution Act and the referendum fell the Korean war. In the last week of June 1950 North Korean forces invaded South Korea. The communist attack, spear-headed by tanks and armoured cars, was launched in the area north and north-west of Seoul and combined with sea-borne landings on the east coast below the 38th parallel. Chinese volunteers were in Korea because they feared Japanese rearmament. Menzies could not have faced a clearer example of the need for British and Australian co-operation in support of the United States, and without delay the British and Australian navies participated in the Korean operations. The Minister for External Affairs, P. C. Spender, has published his account of the beginning of Australia's involvement in Korea, which shows that Menzies gave orders against Australian involvement, only to find that his deputies and officials presented him with a *fait accompli*. But once in battle Menzies used every weapon at hand and led the chorus which claimed that Asiatic hordes, under the control of military experts from Moscow and equipped with Chinese weapons, were waging an indirect war.

When United Nations Secretary General Trygve Lie appealed for assistance for Korea, Australia was quick to offer combatant troops. Menzies went to Washington to discuss with the United States government what the precise nature of Australian support ought to be. Philip McBride, the Minister for Defence, subsequently announced that the Australian force for Korea would be recruited by voluntary enlistment. Men in the permanent army, the Citizen Military Forces (militia) and the British Commonwealth occupation forces in Japan were permitted to enlist first. They were to be sent wherever General MacArthur, the UN supremo, directed them. On 27 July 1950, when recruiting offices opened in Sydney and Melbourne, the destroyer *Bataan* and the frigate *Shoalhaven* were already in Korean waters, and an Australian squadron of Mustangs was in action over the 38th parallel.

This was perhaps to be the last heroic war Australians fought in. Labor support for it was no doubt based to some extent on the volunteer aspect of recruiting, but when it came to international communism one had only to scratch a Labor shadow foreign minister to find a jingoist. The Korean war lasted three years: 281 Australian troops were killed and 1,250 wounded before the armistice was signed in July 1953. MacArthur, the hero who had helped Curtin, was at last dismissed by US president Harry S. Truman. 'MacArthur left me no choice – I could no longer tolerate his insubordination,' said Truman, enraged at MacArthur's attempt to make foreign policy by threatening to carry the Korean war into communist China.

The Korean war underlined the relevance and importance of Menzies's campaign against communism and spurred on the government's efforts to obtain defence arrangements with the United States. The prime mover in this direction was Spender, who overcame Menzies's initial hostility to the arrangements which established the ANZUS Treaty. The ANZUS Treaty was ratified by the Australian parliament in 1952. It was supposed to remain in force indefinitely, and was an interim measure until the development of a more comprehensive system of security in the Pacific area and until the development by the United Nations of a more effective means to maintain international peace and security. The most important provision allowed that each party – Australia, New Zealand and the United States – recognised that an armed attack in the Pacific area on any of the parties would be dangerous to collective peace and security, and hence the parties declared that they would all act to meet the common danger. At the same time, the armed attack and all measures taken by ANZUS as a result were to be reported to the Security Council of the United Nations, in the hope that ANZUS action could be terminated when the Security Council had taken the measures necessary to restore and maintain international security. The treaty established a council of foreign ministers who were to hold annual meetings to discuss regional security. At the end of the first annual meeting the communique observed that the ministers had talked about 'the operations of the United Nations in Korea and the problem of assisting the free nations of Asia to resist communist imperialism'. It was Menzies's first treaty with a foreign country, guaranteeing common action against what the prime minister believed was inevitable common danger.

To whip up a sense of insecurity, Menzies relied largely on Casey, who was well suited to the role of scaremonger. Casey, after all, had discovered that there was a 'nest of traitors' in the public service. In October 1954 Casey spoke on the second pillar of international defence: the South-East Asia Collective Defence Treaty. The time had gone, as Casey put it, when Australia could rest securely within its own borders. Instead of living in a tranquil corner of the globe, Australians were on the verge of the most unsettled region of the world. The response to the danger was an Asian version of NATO (North Atlantic Treaty Organisation): at Manila on 8 September 1954 the United States, the United Kingdom, Australia, New Zealand, France, Pakistan, the Philippines and Thailand all signed the SEATO (South-East Asia Treaty Organisation) treaty as a demonstration of solidarity. Casey argued that it was no longer possible for a country to rely for its security on its own strength and resources. This was one of the inescapable lessons of World War II. Throughout the 1950s Australia had been in danger, Casey said, as a result of the aggressive policies of international communism. Casey's view was that Korea was merely the beginning. Armed subversive activities were spreading throughout South-East Asia: in South Vietnam, Laos, Cambodia and Thailand. The Australian government, he concluded, did not attempt to disguise the fact that the primary purpose of the treaty was to combat communism. Communism was an issue which the middle classes were not prepared to take to arbitration.

At home, Menzies's administration encouraged a high rate of immigration, to provide both a large labour force and a reservoir of soldiers. The Minister for Immigration was Harold Holt, whose destiny was vitally connected with the fate of the conservative parties. Like his predecessor, Holt was an excellent Minister for Immigration. He convened a Commonwealth Jubilee Citizens' Convention in Canberra, which discussed the ways in which 'new Australians' might be assimilated. In the period from the foundation of the commonwealth to the outbreak of World War II, Australia's net gain from immigration was just under 600,000, an average of about 15,000 a year, although the actual intake fluctuated widely during the forty-year period. Most arrived in the three years that preceded World War I and during the 1920s. Between 1901 and 1905 and again from 1931 to 1935 the country actually lost population. When immigration resumed after World War II, the flow was at first small because of the shortage of shipping. In 1947 arrivals exceeded departures by 12,000; in 1948 by 48,000, and in 1949 by 149,000. At the beginning of the 1950s Holt's department tried to attract 200,000 immigrants a year. In local terms, between 1945 and 1950, new arrivals exceeded the total population of Tasmania; by the end of 1951 there were more post-war new Australians in the commonwealth than there were old Australians in Western Australia. Holt's efforts had their dark side, the most obvious defect being that many of the new arrivals were unable to find homes. While the building industry could count on an annual demand for 40,000 more houses than the normal requirements of the country, immigrants were forced to live under appalling conditions, by normal Australian standards, in government hostels.

Holt was far-sighted and liberal; it was from the Department of Immigration that the government announced the official banning of the term 'White Australia'. The term was offensive to Australia's Asian neighbours, Holt said; he replaced it with the less offensive term 'immigration restriction policy'.

A feature of respectable Australia was adoration of the English nobility, a quality thought unlikely to outlast the twentieth century. Menzies knew that in Australia members of the royal family were revered as household gods. What was more secure than the British royal family? When Menzies announced a royal tour of Australia in 1954, souvenir mugs and royal family albums were produced in thousands; *Royal Mothers*, *Prince Charles at Play*, *Royal Christening*, and *Baby Prince Charles* were on almost every bedside table. Few books were more popular than *The Coronation of Her Majesty Queen Elizabeth II*. Her Majesty arrived on 3 February 1954, and Menzies announced immediately that there would be an election in May. The prime minister cashed in on society's general enthusiam for blue blood. The Labor Party quickly claimed that the government was trying to capitalise on the reflected popularity that inevitably lingered after a royal visit, but this was a difficult charge to prove, as there were five ALP premiers in six states in 1954. Some of the magic might even have rubbed off on them. On the other hand, the coalition was definitely projected as the more patriotic and imperial party; some socialists in the Australian Labor Party even advocated abolition of the monarchy, an aim reintroduced in the 1990s, with a twenty-first century target date.

On 29 May 1954, Menzies, despite the Labor Party obtaining 50.03 per cent of the valid votes, was re-elected, owing his success less to Queen Elizabeth than to Vladimir Petrov, a Russian spy who defected on the eve of the election. Petrov's first diplomatic experience was as KGB officer in Stockholm, where he successfully spied on his ambassador, the legendary Madame Aleksandra Kollontai, whom Lenin had saved from execution in 1917 when she neglected her duties as commissar for public welfare, spending her time instead with a seaman, Pavel Dybenko. The Petrov case began when Menzies announced to the House of Representatives that Petrov, Third Secretary at the Soviet Embassy, had been granted political asylum in Australia, and that, in consequence of information furnished by Petrov, the government had decided to appoint a Royal Commission to investigate evidence of systematic espionage and attempted subversion in Australia. Menzies could have hoped for nothing more; the Petrov case was to be a clear example of the spread of communist poison.

There were elements of both farce and drama in the Petrov affair. In seeking political asylum Petrov asked for protection for himself – and assistance to establish himself. Transformed by his experience of bourgeois life, he said, 'I no longer believe in communism since I have seen the Australian way of living.' Ejdokia, Petrov's wife, became the central figure when she claimed that Petrov had been kidnapped. Menzies replied that 'we do not go in for that sort of thing in this country'. The next dramatic turning-point was the departure of Mrs Petrov for Moscow. She was carried, drugged, with one shoe missing, to the British Overseas Aircraft Corporation aircraft, accompanied by men described as Soviet couriers and embassy staff. At the airport in Sydney there was a struggle for possession of Mrs Petrov between a crowd of about a thousand right-wing immigrants to Australia (many from Russia, the Ukraine and Czechoslovakia), the police, Australian security officers and the Russian Embassy 'heavies'. This battle, which lasted eight minutes, was, according to W. C. Wentworth, a Liberal member of parliament, punctuated by Mrs Petrov's cries of, 'I do not want to go. Save me.' On the flight to Darwin a BOAC air hostess, Joyce Bull, who subsequently turned out to be working for the Australian security services, talked Mrs Petrov into staying in Australia, and when the plane landed Mrs Petrov was able to telephone her husband. She had in the meantime confessed to Miss Bull in the aircraft lavatory that fear of the couriers had prevented her from speaking out. A senior government officer in the Northern Territory accepted Mrs Petrov on the coalition's behalf, and the Russian couriers were beaten up and disarmed by Australian security police. A series of Russian charges then began, each development assisting Menzies in his forthcoming election. A Polish newspaper reported: 'After the escape of the third secretary of the USSR Embassy Petrov – an ordinary criminal – the Australian authorities let loose a wild anti-soviet hunt and have organised the abduction of Petrov's wife who wanted to return to Soviet Russia. A group of Australian fascists, assisted actively by the police, abducted Mrs Petrov from the airfleld.'

An accompanying picture showed her firmly held by a Russian courier and a chauffeur from the Russian Embassy in Canberra. The embassy then accused Petrov of being a forger and a thief, claiming that he had only asked for political asylum to avoid being punished for criminal offences. The provocative statements made by Petrov were without foundation, said the Russians, and he had no documents as evidence. Two days before Anzac Day, the Soviet government presented a note to the Australian *chargé d'affaires* in Moscow. This note reiterated that Petrov was a thieving forger, said that his wife had been kidnapped, and that it was evident from the public statement of Menzies that the plan for the kidnapping was worked out beforehand by the Australian government. The note stated that the provocative hullabaloo created by the Australian government about the person of the criminal Petrov, the kidnapping of his wife, the assault on Soviet diplomats and diplomatic couriers, and the search of diplomatic couriers by Australian police, carried out with bodily force, formed the most brutal violations of generally accepted norms of international law, and were inadmissible under normal diplomatic relations between states. It ended with a protest against the slanderous campaign against the USSR which the Australian government was waging. The Russians withdrew their Embassy from Australia, expelled the Australian Embassy staff from Moscow and announced that henceforth they would buy no more Australian wool.

There is no doubt that many thought at the time the Petrov affair clinched the election for Menzies. The chain of reasoning was as follows: Australia saw in April 1954 events as portentous as they had seen at Gallipoli in April 1915 (there was no more stirring metaphor open to editors in the 1950s than the Anzac one). As Gallipoli changed the Australian outlook and brought home the horrors of war, so the Petrov case stripped away any illusions that might have existed about the real nature of communism. Australia appeared to be under the observation of a Russian spy ring but, more important, Australians also saw the effect of Russian methods on individuals. Mrs Petrov had been kept in a darkened room at the Russian Embassy in Canberra, she had been brought, bewildered, to Mascot, dragged across the tarmac amid a shouting crowd of 'new Australians', and was not even allowed to retrieve her shoe. This 'horrifying' affair was linked with the Australian Labor Party by a simple statement that its ministers and state presidents had included ex-communists, and that communist unions and communists were part and parcel of Labor politics. Menzies established a Royal Commission that rubbed salt thoroughly into the wounds. If the Petrov defection saw the making of Menzies, the Royal Commission saw the end of Evatt.

Evatt likened the Petrov affair to the forged Zinoviev letter which was used to discredit the British Labour party. The letter, published in October 1924, caused a furore because a general election was about to take place. It was supposed to encourage British communists to cause seditious trouble. But it was Evatt's appearance before the commission that brought disaster for his party, even though he appeared only in a legal capacity, and not in his role as leader of the Labor Party. Evatt spoke on behalf of members of his staff who were summoned as witnesses. He was then refused permission to appear further, because his duties as leader of the opposition conflicted with his duty as counsel before the commission. But by then he was in Menzies's net. In the House of Representatives, Evatt launched a bitter attack on the Royal Commission, alleging that the defection of Petrov had been engineered by Menzies with the 1954 elections in view. Evatt revealed that he had been in touch with the Russian Foreign Minister, Vyacheslav Mikhailovich Molotov, who had assured him that the documents handed over by Petrov were forgeries. Menzies, in a brilliant reply, described Evatt's appeal to Molotov as a new communist technique in which Evatt was against the prime minister of his own country and for the Soviet foreign minister. He declared that the man on trial in the Petrov affair had become Evatt himself. Expanding this theme, Menzies said that the celebrated appeal to Molotov was atrocious coming from a party leader who was an aspirant for the prime minister's office. Public opinion, predicted Menzies, would acquit the Royal Commission, but it would not acquit Evatt, who, from first to last in the matter, for his own purposes, in his own interests, and with the enthusiastic support of every communist in Australia, sought to discredit the judiciary, subvert the authority of the security organisation, cry down decent patriotic Australians, and build up a fifth column of enemies.

Menzies's handling of the events of 1950–54 was applauded by the middle classes. They were reassured by the way in which liberal capitalism in the western world was reconstructing its dominance. The need for security was being met by the conservative administration. An attack on communism was a blow struck for the property of the affluent. Admittedly Menzies was not able to carry the referendum to outlaw the Communist Party. But by force of arms the allies and the Americans were able to save the day in Korea. The 'new Australians' were building up the economy through their impact on the workforce, and with national development went economic progress. Menzies rode on the boom, and the middle class rode with him. There was a shift to secondary industry, and 'people's capitalism' took off shakily as sections of the middle class joined in the investment race. While industrial expansion kept wages up and inflation down automatically, the middle class saw their wealth increasing and were prepared to give Menzies his head.

Finally, Labor was almost irreparably damaged when the middle-class militant Catholic conservatives effectively allied themselves with the right wing of the Labor Party. The destructiveness of the intra-party feud can be read between the lines of a parliamentary leader of the Labor Party's claim that an inordinately large number of his fellow Catholics were fear-stricken, Communist-hating, money-making, social-climbing, status-seeking, brain-washed, ghetto-minded people to whom the Pope was too venturesome, and not sufficiently prudent in his dealings with the non-Catholic world on the one hand and the communist one-sixth of the world on the other. With Menzies providing security, and the Labor Party disunited, there was very little choice for middle-class voters and no incentive to swing to the left.

CHAPTER 4

Beating the Bolshoi

Once a learned Doctor sat down in Canberra,
He was the Leader of the ALP.
And he sang as he watched and waited till election day,
    Labor Must have Solidarity.
Santamaria, Santamaria, Keon and Mullens are faithful to me
And he sang as he watched and waited till election day,
Labor Must have Solidarity.

Down came Petrov, and Menzies was in power again,
The Doctor cried, 'It's a Conspiracy!'
And he wrote out a statement, saying most emphatically,
    Labor Must have Solidarity.
Santamaria, Santamaria, Keon and Mullens are getting at me
And he wrote out a statement saying most emphatically,
Labor Must have Solidarity.

Up came Chamberlain, mounted on Executive,
Down came the Groupers, one, two, three!
Oh, where's that jolly Santa you've got in your Movement,
    Labor Must have Solidarity.
Santamaria, Santamaria, Keon and Mullens and Bourke make three
Oh, where's that jolly Santa you've got in your Movement,
Labor Must have Solidarity.

Up jumped the Doctor and sprang across the stormy sea,
Bound for Hobart and unity,
And he sighed as he sang in that very nearly empty hall,
    Labor has lost Solidarity.
Santamaria, Santamaria, Keon and Mullens are all up a tree,
And he sighed as he sang in that very nearly empty hall,
Labor has lost Solidarity.

Now Keon and Mullens and Bourke are back in Canberra,
In the Anti-Communist ALP,
And they hide behind the skirts of the Leader, Mr Joshua,
    Singing Labor Must have Solidarity.
Santamaria, Santamaria, Keon and Mullens and Bourke make three
And they hide behind the skirts of their Leader, Mr Joshua,
Keon and Mullens with Liberals agreed.

Sung to the tune 'Waltzing Matilda', this student song described
the main stages of the Australian Labor Party's crisis in the
mid-1950s, when the efforts of some laymen in the Roman
Catholic Church, who had been working quietly in cells to
form an intense anti-communist climate, led to the formation of
a new political party.

As far as the conservative wing of the Catholic Church was
concerned, events in Egypt, Malaya, Indonesia, Hungary and
Vietnam had clear implications for Australia. In January 1954
Australia learned that the Vietminh had taken the capital of Laos
after moving down from the north; the 200,000 French troops
in Indo-China had not been able to stop them. The Vietminh
took the capital of Indo-China and also Thatnek on the Mekong
River, which formed the border between Laos and Siam. They
held all the land along the Chinese border north of the Red
River. The French were clinging to the coast, holding only the
Red River Delta, and Haiphong and Hanoi, opposite Hainan
Island, and another short strip from the level of captured
Thathek to Hue further south. This successful downwards thrust
was very perturbing to Australians. In particular, it filled many
Roman Catholic laymen with fear: all that was needed to bring
them into an active, open role was a domestic threat to their
existence, and this was soon provided.

After Evatt's defeat in the elections of May 1954, he was
strongly criticised. He reacted with a violent and abusive outburst
during which he tried to deflect attention from himself to a
group within his organisation – the Labor Party's family ghost –
the Catholic Action section. The ghost materialised to criticise

Evatt on very damaging grounds: he had mismanaged the 1954 election campaign; he had appeared in his private capacity as a barrister on behalf of communist-led unions; and he had appeared, without the party's permission, at the Royal Commission into Soviet Espionage in Australia. Parliament became the killing ground for some Catholic Labor men, who joined with the conservative coalition to depose Evatt.

When the Royal Commission on Espionage Bill was introduced, W. C. Wentworth had led the attack on Evatt, saying that an analysis of the public policy on international affairs of the leader of the opposition revealed the underlying continuous pro-communist bias throughout. The seriousness of the Labor Party's dilemma over the Royal Commission on espionage was clouded by abuse. From the Labor benches R. T. Pollard called Wentworth a 'dirty mongrel' and, when asked to withdraw and apologise, said that he withdrew and apologised to 'the mongrel'. Evatt called Wentworth 'a little lying hound and an *agent provocateur*'. Wentworth yelled enthusiastically, and then, alternately laughing wildly and putting his tongue out, began to jump up and down in his seat. He would then (as the Melbourne *Herald* reported the event) stop jumping, pat himself vigorously on the back, stick out his tongue and then resume jumping, thinking, as one Labor member put it, that he was back at Taronga Park Zoo. Wentworth saw himself as one of the last patricians performing before an electorate that demanded bread and circuses.

The Labor Party and its leader were used to hearing the voice of the Catholic Church. Most of Chifley's ministry had been of Irish Catholic descent. But Evatt did not realise the importance of this fundamental historical truth, for on a day which was to be a turning point in Australian politics, 5 October 1954, he bitterly attacked the Catholic 'tiny minority' who were, he claimed, trying to undermine the Labor movement. Evatt specifically singled out the *News-Weekly* as being the organ of the minority, and announced that he was to bring the matter before the Labor Party's federal executive.

Catholic Action was formally introduced into Australia in 1937. According to the hierarchy, its aim was to counter the typical conditions of industrial society. The operations of Catholic Action were not confined to the factory floors. During World War II, groups or cells of leaders were formed along Catholic Action lines in the armed forces. Catholics were organised and militant in schools and universities. There were Catholic newspapers, a Catholic radio station 2SM (for St Mary), and Catholic spots on television. Between 1947 and 1954 there were nearly twice as many Catholics as non-Catholics among new settlers in the population. But there was a difference between 'Catholic Action' and 'the action of Catholics'. The *News-Weekly* was the official voice of Catholic Action in Melbourne, but neither the journal nor the movement could be taken as the voice of the Catholic Church. Since Cardinal Gilroy and the *Catholic Worker* opposed the actions of the movement, one cannot accept the view of the Catholic Church as a totalitarian structure actively campaigning to bring about a new Catholic Australia. What was important for the Labor Party was the support within the state of Victoria for the Catholic groupers.

When the Victorian ALP executive supported the right-wing Catholics, twenty-one trade unions in the rest of Australia with 250,000 members clamoured for action by the federal executive against the Victorian state branch. Under the federal system the state was able to prove stronger than the whole. The federal executive, comprising two members from each state, decided to investigate affairs in Melbourne, and called for discipline and silence. Three federal MPs representing Victorian seats, M. Mullens, W. Bourke and S. M. Keon, appeared before the executive and made repeated damaging attacks on Evatt, Mullens claiming that Evatt had deliberately revived the sectarian issue to split the party. Keon went further than merely attacking his party leader. He described the Australian National University as a 'nest of communists', and claimed that grants from the Commonwealth Literary Fund were being given primarily to communists. Keon epitomised some of the Catholic middle-class fear of socialism, and in his attack on the literati was following in the traditions of bourgeois philistinism. For his part, Evatt declared that the movement, a secret organisation, was trying to commit the Labor Party solely or primarily to anti-communist activities. It was obvious to Evatt that an outside faction organised to gain control of the Labor movement solely on the basis of extreme anti-communism would destroy the fabric of the Labor Party. At this point Evatt revealed that Bartholomew A. Santamaria was the most prominent spokesman for the movement.

On 3 December 1954 the federal executive found that Evatt had made no specific charges against Keon, Bourke and Mullens, nor had their claims of Evatt's unsatisfactory leadership been sustained. It decided, nevertheless, to order the election of a new Victorian executive at a special branch conference. A proposal that the Victorian executive remain in office, and that the industrial groups be outlawed, was abandoned when the leaders of one of the most important trade unions in Australia, the Australian Workers' Union, threatened to cancel its affiliation with the Labor Party and form an Industrial Labor Party unless the Victorian executive was reformed.

During 1955 there was a step by step formation of a new political party, as the rift between the two wings of the Australian Labor Party became irreconcilable. A special conference of the Victorian branch of the Labor Party met on 26–27 February 1955 and elected a new Victorian executive, but the old executive refused to dissolve itself: it remained in physical possession of the party office, and declared that it would resist all attempts by the new executive to gain possession. Legal opinion was that, because of the traditional strength and earlier origins of the state branches of the Labor Party, the power of the federal executive was limited. This opinion was provided by a boiler-maker's son from Balmain and leader of the Sydney bar, John Kerr, QC. And a second opinion which supported Kerr's was given by Sir Garfield Barwick, QC. These two silks were to reappear again and in agreement over the most momentous political controversy since federation – the dismissal of the Whitlam government.

By February 1955, the Labor Party's critics said that the Australian Labor Party as it had existed from 1921 to 1955 was finished: just as its predecessor had died during World War I and the conscription split, so the second Labor Party perished during the Cold War.

This was an exaggeration. The Labor Party survived in New South Wales and South Australia, to reform and fight back. When the annual conference of the Australian Labor Party opened in Hobart in March 1955, two Victorian delegations sought admission. The delegation representing the deposed executive blockaded the conference room in an attempt to prevent the new executive from participating. The thirty-six delegates to the conference (six from each state) then divided on the question of which Victorian delegation was the accredited one. When the delegates representing the old executive were excluded, seventeen delegates walked out. The seventeen boy-cotters (all six New South Wales delegates, five from Queensland, four from Western Australia and two from Tasmania) met in another hall and decided that the official conference was not valid, on the reasonable grounds that it was a minority meeting at which New South Wales was not repre-sented, Queensland and Western Australia were represented by minority delegations, and the standing of the Victorian del-egation was in dispute.

More significant was the foreign policy debate within the official conference hall, where Evatt, addressing the rump, persuaded them to adopt a policy of 'No Australian Troops for Malaya'. Like the war in Vietnam, the Malayan terrorist campaign was an immediate problem involving Australia's defence. The right wing of the Labor Party was clearly in sympathy with Menzies's stand, taken at the Commonwealth prime ministers' conference one month before, where he had made it known that he would dispatch troops to Malaya. Just after the Hobart conference, Menzies announced that the Australian contribution would include a battalion with support, a fighter wing of two squadrons, a bomber squadron, an airfield construction team and two destroyers and an aircraft carrier. Though not massive, the Australian force would serve as some guarantee to the people of Malaya that their orderly progress towards democratic self-government would not be impeded by communist aggression.

Evatt spoke from a weak position. There were now two Labor parties in the House of Representatives, led by Evatt and Robert Joshua (who led the group of six MPs expelled from the mainstream party) respectively. Evatt said that his party believed that the use of Australian armed forces in Malaya, whether for garrison duty or jungle fighting, would gravely impair Australian relations with Malaya. It would be an act of folly that could easily be misrepresented, and would be resented by the Malayan masses as an act of aggression. He dismissed as unconvincing the argument that Malaya was a good training area, saying that Australian territory extended to the Equator and that troops could be trained there. To establish what amounted to a strategic reserve 2,000 miles from Australian shores was certain to be regarded as a provocative act, Evatt said, and he asked whether it would be right for communist China to establish a strategic reserve in Indonesia to meet possible aggression from Australia. Casey, the Foreign Minister, spoke of 'the red thread of isolationism' that ran through the fabric of the Evatt party's foreign policy. But the crucial break came when Joshua, leading the new Catholic anti-Communist Labor Party, ordered his four supporters into the government division lobby at the end of the debate, observing that the dispatch of troops to Malaya was Labor policy. The split had a cumulative effect once it began. On the surface, the foreign policy issue was to remain the great divider. Beneath, sectarian animosity and personal hatred were to survive until death claimed the combatants. There was no chance of healing the rift.

The coalition was to benefit for another fifteen years. On 28 March 1955, the new Victorian executive decided to expel Mullens from the party and to suspend twenty-four other party members for what was described as a deliberate and defiant challenge to the executive. Those suspended were shrewd, experienced, hard-working political figures. A purge on such a scale led inevitably to the establishment of a new party. The new executive declared bogus seventy-eight of the party's three hundred and twenty branches. On 17 April, Joshua announced that a new Labor Party had been formed, to be called the Australian Labor Party (Anti-Communist). A day later Evatt resigned and Arthur Calwell challenged for the leadership. Evatt was re-elected by a large majority.

The Anti-Communist Labor Party, later called the Democratic Labor Party, was given formal recognition by parliament on 19 April 1955. It was a party that attracted the right-wing anti-communists in the ranks of the middle classes. Joshua and the other defectors said that they were acting at the wish of the rank and file in their electorates in expressing their rejection of Evatt's leadership. Joshua asked the speaker that they be known, for the purpose of distinguishing them from the following of Evatt, as the Australian Labor Party (Anti-Communist). Menzies was first to congratulate Joshua, and Evatt responded by underlining the prime minister's congratulations which, he said, illustrated how the secret alliance between the government and the Santamaria group had now been replaced by an open one.

Unabashed, the government made room on the order paper for a debate on communism, patently designed to damage the Labor Party. Bourke submitted that the house urgently consider the subservience of Evatt and his followers to the Communist Party. Bourke stressed the historical significance of the occasion, saying that parliament had witnessed the end of the Labor Party. In his view it was the result of a cold-blooded plot by Evatt, who was trying to make the remnant of the Labor Party a front organisation of the Communist Party. Bourke alleged that communist trade unionists and Russian Embassy staff had contributed to a 'slush' fund for the Labor Party. Evatt dismissed Bourke's charges as slander and, in an ingenious defence, retorted that the coalition was supported by the great monopolies of Australia. Calwell simply asked Menzies to appoint a Royal Commission to investigate where all parties got their funds. Mullens ended the maiden debate of the Anti-Communist Labor Party by describing Evatt as a 'killer', 'the most dangerous man in public life in Australia', a 'colossal egotist who betrayed the country in the interests of insatiable ambition', a 'millstone around the neck of the party he professed to lead'.

Although re-elected, Evatt lacked the finesse to re-unite the Labor movement. The first result of the split was electoral disaster in Victoria. The Anti-Communist Labor Party gave their second preferences to the Liberal-Country Party Coalition. The Victorian Labor Party was left with less than a third of lower house members. In June 1956, the ALP federal executive decided to purge the right wing of the New South Wales executive. The Assistant Secretary of the New South Wales branch, J. T. Kane, was identified as leader of the Catholic groupers and dismissed. New South Wales branch assets worth $400,000 and a radio station at Newcastle, were confiscated. The wedge was being hammered in.

In Queensland the Labor Party had held office uninterruptedly since 1932. The split began when Vincent Gair founded the Queensland Labor Party. A Catholic conservative who ended his career as the Gair-to-Eire missile, he at first resisted the temptation to join the new political movement. Later, as leader of the Anti-Communist Labor Party in the Senate, Gair held the balance of power in the Senate, and was fond of taunting his parliamentary colleagues in the Liberal Party with such remarks as, 'If it wasn't for us you would not fucking well be there.' Gair and his supporters formed the Democratic Labor Party in March 1957. They followed a hawkish line on foreign affairs by supporting SEATO and by opposing the recognition of Communist China.

Thus, in the mid-1950s, Menzies faced a broken, dispirited Labor Party, destroyed by a small Catholic political movement, and by its own lack of sensitive leadership. Characteristically, the Labor Party was unable to take a trick over the next two crises parliament and the people faced: the Suez crisis and the invasion of Hungary.

While the changes from communism were obvious in Hungary, the Suez crisis was more complicated and difficult for the conservatives to see as a local political issue. Menzies was in America, on the last leg of what was to become his customary post-election overseas tour, when General Abdul Nasser seized the Suez Canal. The Australian prime minister immediately conferred with the Canadian prime minister and with President Eisenhower. Menzies also contacted the prime ministers of India, Ceylon and Pakistan, who were similarly threatened. Menzies saw himself as speaking not only for Australia, but also for the United Kingdom. He behaved as he had in 1939, as if the policies and interests of the British and the Australian governments were identical. Australia was clearly placed in an extremely serious economic and strategic position with the closure of the canal. As the interpreter of Anthony Eden's policy in Washington, Menzies quite overshadowed the British ambassador. Eden, as British foreign minister and prime minister, had often been out of touch with public opinion. Menzies had the task of backing Eden's statement at the conference Eden held in London over Nasser's nationalisation of the Suez Canal.

The Suez fiasco was over in two months. Britain and France withdrew their forces as soon as the precipitate nature of the adventure became clear. Certainly Eden had said on 2 November 1956 that as soon as the United Nations took some effective steps to prevent hostilities on the canal, the British forces would be withdrawn, but it was rather less a pleasure, rather more a humiliation, to keep his word. The final indignity, as far as Australia was concerned, was the destruction of the memorial to the Australian Light Horse, under the eyes of the UN's unprotesting police force.

The war memorial was a magnificent equestrian statue of a light horse trooper, one of the men who transferred the bush ethos into the reality of fighting nationalism. The symbolic importance of its destruction was clear. It showed that the Australian heroes of Gallipoli and the Middle East had been typed as imperialist mercenaries in Egypt, and that the United Nations was as impotent as the League of Nations had been. To Australians, it was of vital importance that a strong military defence force should be kept up, for after Suez and Hungary no one could expect the commonwealth to be shielded by battered Britain or the disunited nations agency.

The Australian prime minister took a leading role in the Suez crisis at some cost. He led a delegation to Egypt, and gained political kudos at home but, in giving Australia's unequivocal support to the British and the French initiatives and actions, Menzies found himself offside with the United States. President Dwight Eisenhower and his Secretary of State, John Foster Dulles, were clearly put out by the British decision to go it alone in the canal zone, Dulles remarking that he could think of nothing that would more surely turn the area to international communism. American unhelpfulness over Suez gave a temporary boost to anti-American sentiment, never far from the surface in Australia, but it also had a positive effect. It forced Australian foreign-policy-makers to face the problems raised by the competing interests of the Pacific and the Atlantic.

When Soviet troops entered Budapest in October 1956 and crushed the Hungarian revolution, an Australian immigration officer was immediately posted from Vienna to the Hungarian border. As a result, after 1956, 15,000 Hungarians were admitted to Australia, fleeing from communist repression. This was a large injection of 'captive nation' *emigres*, and their cohesive national spirit was strengthened rather than diminished by cultural isolation in Australia. Like many of the Croatians, Serbians, Macedonians, Ukrainians, Lithuanians, Estonians and Latvians, the Hungarians came in family groups and immediately set up national clubs, preserving their ethnic singularity, and at the same time contributing to the plurality of Australian culture. Calwell backed the government's policy towards the Hungarian 'victims of Russian aggression', and spoke for most Australians when he declared himself appalled by the bestiality and brutality of the Russians in their attempt to suppress the liberty and independence of the Hungarian nation.

Thus SEATO could meet in Canberra in March 1957, intent to prove that it was an instrument of regional defence, and in an atmosphere of strong anti-communist feeling. A basis for SEATO discussion was a document that argued that the main threat to South-East Asia was an all-out campaign of communist sub-version. SEATO research showed that every device was being used to weaken 'the free nations within', so that the eventual communist domination of South and South-East Asia could be secured. The danger of overt communist aggression, though less apparent, was not to be ignored.

The defence links with America were further emphasised in April 1957, when Menzies announced aircraft purchases that profoundly affected future RAAF development. The government decided to buy from America C130 Hercules troop carriers and American Star Fighters as the basis of RAAF equipment. At the same time, changes in defence planning were announced determining the role and capacity of the Australian military forces for twenty years. Menzies revealed that instead of relying on a large army, Australia would concentrate on the development of a small, cheaper elite corps. In numerical terms the call-up for the army was reduced from 39,000 to 12,000. The selection was to be made by ballot. In training, the emphasis was to be on mobility, equipment and fire-power. Simultaneously, the air force was to be increased by 1,000. As a compensation, the regular army was re-equipped with the Belgian FN 30 rifle, slightly modified and renamed the SLR (self-loading rifle). The strength of the regular army was to be set at 21,000 overall, 4,000 of whom would form a special brigade trained to use the most modern weapons in the western alliance armies.

As if to confirm the growing strength of communism in South-East Asia, the President of the Soviet Union visited Indonesia in May 1957. And in 1958 elections were fought out against an unsettled background. During the year there were military coups in Cambodia, Pakistan, Iraq and the Sudan, all of which overthrew the existing regimes. In Iraq revolutionaries murdered King Faisal, the Crown Prince, and Prime Minister Nur es-Said. British troops moved into Jordan to prevent similar risings, and the United States intervened to protect the *status quo* in the Lebanon.

These events provided some of the compost in which the anti-communist Labor movement could grow. The sound of Mao Tse-tung bombarding the offshore islands of Taiwan was clearly heard in Melbourne's Catholic churches. A general election was held in Australia on 22 November 1958. The Suez crisis was finished, and three months campaigning was over. The Labor Party's chances were severely damaged, if not destroyed, on the very eve of the polls by a vituperative open dispute between Evatt and the Catholic Archbishop of Melbourne, Daniel Mannix. Mannix was no stranger to political controversy. He had been denied entry to his native Ireland by 'the British' because of his support for Irish nationalists during the Easter Rising. On 20 November Mannix accused the Labor Party of trying to use Cardinal Gilroy in their electoral advertisements. A week before, Cardinal Gilroy had declared in Sydney that Christians were free to support any political party in the election except the Communist Party. Evatt had this statement distributed to Catholics outside their churches and published in national newspapers, taking it as the hierarchy's somewhat belated approval of the Labor Party's platform.

Mannix, in a few phrases of block-busting importance, observed that every communist and communist sympathiser in Australia wanted a victory for the Evatt Party. He was issuing a significant warning for every Catholic and every 'decent Australian'. Evatt said desperately on 21 November that he would resign from the leadership of the Australian Labor Party if the Democratic Labor Party gave its second preference votes to the ALP in the election. He had apparently learned, at the eleventh hour, the lesson that DLP second preferences had brought about the defeat of several ALP candidates, and the return of the Liberal-Country Party Victorian state government. Every word he said – by deflecting attention away from the election issues and on to the divided Labor Party – made things worse. Weeping crocodile tears, Evatt said that he did not seek the honour of being the leader of the federal parliamentary Labor Party: he was elected in a ballot of eighty MPs. He had never sought his own preferment in the ALP and he did not do so now. The DLP had claimed that his presence was an obstacle to unity. He was willing to remove that obstacle, that was, to remove himself. Finally, Evatt denied that he was a communist or a communist sympathiser, classifying anyone who claimed he was (this category included Prime Minister Menzies and Archbishop Mannix) among the greatest liars who ever lived.

By the time the polls opened, the actual policy differences were typically obscure. During the campaign, Menzies had recalled his achievements, singling out the successful loans raised in London and New York. He spoke of himself as a trustee of a great estate, in good repair, amazingly developed, sensibly managed, and respected and trusted all round the world.

Menzies directed the campaign under three intelligible headings: job security, higher wages and the standard of living. He said that standards of living rose when financial policies were designed to keep the economy stable. Higher wages could buy more when the country was more productive. A job was most secure when the country was prosperous, and under Menzies Australia was enjoying record prosperity and industrial peace. You were expected to vote Liberal on 22 November 1958 because, taking the mean, Australians were buying more than they ever did, and enjoying one of the highest standards of living in the world.

Even so, Menzies shrewdly did not kill the goose that laid the golden egg. Having been prime minister for nine years, all Menzies could predict was an uncertain economic future for the country, marked by falling wool prices and a shrinkage in world trade. He did not promise security. Menzies offered a government with its eyes set on maintaining Australia's position as a substantial, if not major, trading nation. Evatt simply promised a happier tomorrow under the Australian Labor Party. Wives and mothers were to be given twice their present maternity allowances. Child endowment was to be nearly doubled. Free dental treatment was to be available for children up to sixteen. Sick and aged pensions were to be raised to $10 and wives' allowances to $5. All widows were to have their pensions increased by $1.50. Young couples were to be given financial help to buy homes. Sales tax on essential furniture was to be abolished. There were to be lower interest rates on hire purchase. Ex-service pensioners were to have an allowance of $10 and war-mutilated pensioners were to be given the basic wage.

On foreign policy, Menzies observed blandly that Australia would not recognise communist China, as this would be regarded by the free South-East Asian countries as a victory for communism and would create difficulties with the United States. Menzies expected to see the New Guinea question settled by the International Court of Justice if Indonesia's claim to Dutch New Guinea was based on legal right. Australia would continue to co-operate with the Dutch authorities in developing the native people in New Guinea for ultimate self-government. The leader of the Country Party, John McEwen, nodded his assent.

The election result returned Menzies with an increased majority in the House of Representatives and, for the first time in three years, with a majority in the Senate. Menzies thus won his fifth consecutive general election and obtained his biggest majority in the Senate since he took office in 1949. It was Evatt's fourth defeat. The ALP vote was down to 42 per cent compared with 46 per cent the previous election. The day after the election Evatt attributed defeat to the Santamaria movement and, in so far as Mannix damaged the Australian Labor Party, this was correct. Evatt described Mannix's statement on 20 November as a deliberately timed bomb, and said that it was an illustration of the Menzies-Mannix axis in operation. Pointing out that both Calwell (Deputy Leader of the Labor Party in the House of Representatives) and Senator McKenna (Leader of the Opposition in the Senate) were practising Catholics, Evatt said that both agreed with him that Dr Mannix's views on party politics were governed by his active sponsorship and patronage of the Santamaria movement. Evatt believed that the aims of the Santamaria movement were identical with those of Menzies, whom he accused of introducing into Australia a new political force on the pattern of European totalitarian politics. He asserted that many European immigrants resented the introduction of ecclesiastical interference in free elections: Catholic leaders, said Evatt, like the 'kindly, gentle, charitable Cardinal Gilroy', had frowned upon these un-Australian methods and had insisted upon the right of the people to have a free vote at the polls.

There were new faces in the Menzies cabinet. Although he had been in the senate since 1950, John Gorton was one of the most interesting among them. Gorton was eventually to become leader of the Liberal Party and Prime Minister of Australia, but for the moment he and the other new members and senators in the cabinet were preoccupied with the re-emergence of Japan as a great economic power. The economic strength of Japan was to become a key force in Australian growth. The industrial expansion of Japan demanded Australian primary produce and minerals. And a new version of the nursery rhyme 'Baa Baa Black Sheep' ended with the line 'And one for the Wool Board to sell to the Japs'. Although there was considerable hostility to the Japanese, the Japanese government set up a trade fair in Sydney during January 1959 and followed it up with more trade fairs in other capitals. Japan was already, only eight years after the Allied occupation ended, an economic power to be reckoned with. Japan, short of raw materials, became in 1959 Australia's largest customer for coal and was nearly the biggest wool buyer. Investors hoped to sell the Japanese fuel and iron ore, fish and meat, and some entrepreneurs were quick to appreciate the profit margin in retailing Japanese consumer goods, manufactured with low labour costs but competitive design standards.

In the winter of 1959 the financial situation took a decided turn for the better as wool prices soared because China first bought wool. Although a trade deficit of $40 million had been expected, 1959 showed a surplus of $14 million. This was well below the $54 million figure of the previous year.

Imports for 1959 stood at almost $1,600 million. Exports earned $1,606 million. Annual fluctuations in the national prosperity and in the national balance sheet were attributed solely to the variations in wool prices during the selling seasons. The margin between national happiness and misery continued to depend on the profitability of the nation's sheep.

It also depended on the readiness of communist China to buy Australian primary produce. Menzies spoke with two voices on communism. On the one hand, he attacked the Labor Party for co-operating with communists at home. This issue was kept in the public eye by the simple expedient of a government member asking a minister to comment on 'how to vote' cards used in trade union elections. In making an issue of the Labor Party-Communist Party alliance on the shop floor, the coalition was being hypocritical. The value of Australian exports to China for the eight months ending February 1958 was $14.4 million, goods being exported thereafter at the rate of $20 million each year. At the head of the list was wool. The Country Party leader, John McEwen, told the House of Representatives on 6 May 1959 that goods of strategic importance were not going to communist China – although China was buying wheat, steel, lead, zinc and tin.

Another illustration of the way in which Menzies supped with the Devil was the resumption of diplomatic relations between Australia and the Soviet Union in March 1959 after a break of five years. The Petrov Royal Commission had drawn various conclusions about Soviet embassies: for example, that they were designed to recruit people to sabotage vital installations in an emergency, especially shipping. Embassy staff also recruited communist university students and persuaded them to join the Foreign Affairs Department, and they terrorised Australian migrants who had relatives behind the Iron Curtain.

But the government believed that if the Soviet Union came back into the wool market the price of wool would rise by

20 per cent, and it did. When the Soviet ambassador came to Australia following the resumption of diplomatic relations between the two countries, he said, 'Let bygones be bygones. We will buy wool.' If, said one Labor MP, the government believed the conclusions of the Petrov Commission, no prospect of trade could allow the setting-up of a pseudo-embassy which would become the centre of moral, ideological, political and military warfare. Apparently the new price of wool was so important that the Soviet foothold in Australia, which was so dangerous in the past, was allowed to be re-established. The government provided $158,000 for the re-opening of the Russian Embassy, carefully fixing the re-opening ceremony for after the 1958 elections. Calwell asserted that the coalition was on the point of re-establishing diplomatic relations with Russia as early as 1956, but the Hungarian uprising prevented them going ahead.

Senator Cole, leader of the Democratic Labor Party, believed that the resumption of diplomatic relations with Russia and the re-opening of a Russian Embassy in Canberra 'should have been avoided'. At no great cost to ourselves, said Cole, we rid Australia of a host of espionage agents, but in 1959 we had been foolish enough to allow them to come back. If this was done for trade purposes, it was selling Australia's birthright for a mess of pottage. Cole took a hard line. His speech was not aimed at Labor Party supporters; it was a harbinger of the developing DLP ultra-conservatism.

Although unable at that stage to influence foreign policy, the voice of the movement continued to be heard on domestic issues. DLP Senators spoke on matters affecting moral questions with dogmatic fervour. Senator Cole opposed divorce law reform, for example, saying that its purpose was to destroy the sanctity of marriage. Cole did not even concede that the civil courts had a right to grant divorce: no civil court had the right to break a marriage that had been performed before the altars of the churches. Senator McManus regarded easier divorce as likely to disintegrate the community. And there were many other wedges. Cole asked the Minister for Customs and Excise to assure him that no soft-cover books would be permitted to come on to the market until the appropriate customs officers had read them and were satisfied that they were free of all forms of depravity. DLP concern was increasingly with sexual permissiveness, violence and pornography rather than with the industrial influence of the Communist Party, and the movement's voice took on a clear pastoral note.

Thus by the end of the 1950s a section of the Catholic Church had moved from the wings to the centre of the stage, and then back to the wings. In the course of this political drama, several politicians sacrificed their careers, a new party was formed, another transformed forever, and Australian politics began to polarise around moral and foreign policy issues, with the voice of Catholic conservatism heard in the coalition cabinet room. As far as the Labor Party was concerned, the split had solved nothing; it served not as a purgative but a tonic. It had merely illustrated the ineptitude of the leadership and their ideological unfitness for office. Speaking from the right of the Labor Party, John Kerr stressed the need for the anti-communists to continue to fight, saying that when it disbanded the industrial groups the Australian Labor Party threw out the baby with the bathwater. Kerr was aware that many Labor people felt the need to excise some of the Catholic movement influence from the party. But he believed that if Labor leaders had been willing at all stages 'to give a firm lead in fighting communism', the grip of the movement on ALP affairs would never have developed in the way it did.

The opening of the Russian Embassy provided far less interest than the opening of the Bolshoi Ballet. Wentworth and Killen executed a *pas de deux* as Harlequin and Pantaloon during the visit of the Bolshoi ballet company, choosing the occasion to express their detestation of communism, and to awaken their fellow Australians to the menace of it. Wentworth concentrated on the ballet members' demand for superior hotel accommodation. Killen without humour said that Australians ought to recognise that behind the grace, beauty and the symmetry of the Bolshoi Ballet there was sinister design. The purpose of the ballet was to reach those people who were normally immune from orthodox communist propaganda. The ballet group, he insisted, was a weapon of the international communist movement, and the visit to Australia was pirouetting the country towards disaster. Whitlam described (tongue in cheek) the visit of the Bolshoi Ballet Company as the most insidious infiltration of the Australian community since the visit of the Soviet olympic squad, accompanied, as it was, by hordes of MVD operatives. But when the Russian Ambassador presented his credentials to the Governor-General, the Bolshoi gave a one-night performance in Canberra, and after the show the new Ambassador treated the conservative cabinet to vodka and caviar.

CHAPTER 5

All the Way with JFK

The Australian bourgeoisie was forced to compromise at the beginning of the 1960s, and the compromises were made in many fields. Most spectacularly the Australian government decided to go out from the middle in foreign policy and creep under the wing of the United States. Domestically, the stagnant fifties were followed by a revival of political interest. Symptomatic of the change was the growth of student activism. In Melbourne, students attended Menzies's political meetings with the specific intention of drawing attention to the White Australia policy. They were discontented and unwilling to accept the policies of the government on immigration, and they tried at the same time to focus the press and public opinion on the plight of Aboriginals. The values of middle-class Australians began, in the 1960s, to be eroded by a small group who were cosmopolitan in their outlook. The cosmopolitans lived in Sydney or Melbourne, but they were part of the great society.

In return, local communities often responded with hostility and parochialism. Typical of the challengers was the small group who organised a freedom bus ride through the western outback of New South Wales. This cavalcade was deliberately modelled on American experience with black civil rights workers, and was trying to arouse public sympathy for Aboriginal difficulties in health, housing and education. The results were small, but they were portentous. The small town council of Moree was forced to rescind its resolution banning Aboriginals from the municipal swimming pool. A hotel in Bowraville closed its 'dark room' and served Aboriginals in its main dining-room and public bars.

There were parallel developments at the top. In the next four years Australia was to move perceptibly out of the European orbit, and into the clutches of American foreign policymakers. This development was in part deliberate, in part a reaction to forces that Menzies could not control. The Commonwealth as it had existed in 1949 was clearly breaking up. South Africa's defection was a notable omen. The clear decision of the British government to enter the European Economic Community had enormous implications for the Australian economy. When Menzies and President Kennedy issued a joint statement on the state of world politics the writing was on the wall. The decision to buy American aircraft to re-equip the RAAF was part of the trend away from the British sphere of influence, and into the Pacific and American sector. Indonesian confrontation, support for Malaysia, and the decision to give aid to South Vietnam, which marked the beginning of the mid-1960s, put Australia on a road from which there was no turning back. In February 1960 Evatt resigned from his parliamentary seat to become Chief Justice of New South Wales, and Menzies faced new Labor leaders, Arthur Calwell and Gough Whitlam.

Calwell began his term as party leader in a more difficult situation than Evatt. Hostility to the Democratic Labor Party had hardened rather than softened by 1960. Nor were matters helped by Calwell's insistence that the sleeping dogs of the past be awakened at every opportunity. Calwell worried over the Democratic Labor Party when a more prudent leader might have tried to let it die out.

Menzies won the 1961 election, but only just. The government was nearly defeated because the economy took a dramatic downturn following the lifting of import restrictions.

There was, in 1958–59, a substantial drop in wool income, and inflation. In this depressed atmosphere the treasurer could not strike a balance and injured the middle class by a horror budget that raised the sales tax on automobiles, increased loan interest rates and tightened credit. Unemployment rose, and the Liberals were clearly regarded as acting unfairly. It was his sixth consecutive electoral victory, but the Menzies majority was reduced to only two.

At the dissolution of the House of Representatives, the coalition had a majority of 32. The Australian Labor Party won 15 seats from the government, 8 in Queensland, 5 in New South Wales and 2 in Western Australia. In the new House of Representatives the government parties had 62 seats (46 Liberals and 16 Country Party MPs) and the Labor Party had 62 (including two non-voting members representing the Australian Capital Territory and the Northern Territory). And, as the government had to provide a speaker in the new house, its majority was one. Three cabinet ministers were defeated by ALP candidates. One was Earle Page, eighty-two at the time of the election, and dying. Page's defeat and death were symbolic. When Joseph Lyons died unexpectedly in office in 1939, Earle Page was sworn in and held the leadership post until Menzies was elected. Page belonged, like his parliamentary colleague Casey, to another era. Casey was to reappear yet again in Australian political life as a flamboyant governor-general, driving his wife's Porsche sports car and flying his own light aircraft. But his and Earle Page's absence marked the beginning of a period where American honours rather than British ones were to become important, and an apprenticeship served in the British Foreign Office was to be quite suddenly irrelevant as Asia became the centre of the world's troubles, and Australia's foreign policymakers consequently turned to American for shelter and material assistance.

In the early 1960s, Menzies's views were middle class and

much that affected Menzies's view of Australia's place in the world disappeared. First to vanish was South Africa, from the British Commonwealth. Menzies was in London when South Africa withdrew from the Queen's dominions, a month before Anzac Day, 1961. While the Canadian prime minister saw the withdrawal of South Africa as assuring the future of the Commonwealth, Menzies was in quite a different position. Menzies said that he wanted to keep South Africa in. At a press conference in London on 19 March 1961, Menzies described South Africa's withdrawal from the Commonwealth as a most unhappy affair. While he personally was against apartheid, Menzies said that it was a domestic matter for South Africans.

About 13,000 air miles away by the most usual route Menzies's provocative statements raised a storm. In parliament on 22 March, Calwell described Menzies's remarks as arrogant. Calwell began by saying that the question of apartheid would not have arisen at the conference had South Africa not decided to become an independent republic. Calwell particularly objected, as a former Minister for Immigration, to Menzies's attempt to equate apartheid with Australian immigration laws. This, said Calwell, was a provocative and dangerous observation that ought not to have been made at all. In addition, Calwell said, Menzies had attacked some nations of the Afro-Asian group, including Ghana, India, Malaysia and Ceylon. He had said that in these countries oppression and discrimination were openly practised and that the basic principles of democratic government were flouted. The prime minister, said Calwell, had been poisoning the atmosphere in Asia against Australia and lining up as a junior partner in apartheid. Leslie Haylen said that all Australia had got from Menzies was the complaint 'they have pushed my mate out of the prime ministers' club'. Haylen quoted Menzies's arrogance by referring to a sentence made in his speech, 'If the general public or the people at United Nations don't like it, they can jump in the Serpentine.' Haylen reminded the house that Australians could not be protected by the British government and military forces any more. They had to live in a community in Asia, and belonged to a multi-racial unit. The domestic policy of tyrants, he said, was the concern of the world. Haylen ended his speech, which was limited to ten minutes, by quoting Menzies's remark that he did not mind if ninety-nine nations went on making speeches lasting two and a half hours each, nothing would ever persuade him to identify the exquisite personal relations of the Commonwealth with the debating society that went on in New York. Are we, asked Haylen, to give away the United Nations because the prime minister 'has a comradely pat on the shoulder for the murderer of Sharpeville?'

Following his failure to prevail on this issue, Menzies realistically began to jettison parts of the Commonwealth connection, and to build up the Australian-American alliance in trade, defence and cultural spheres. The process of consolidating the American alliance had preceded the Commonwealth Prime Ministers' Conference: Menzies visited Washington on 24 February 1961 on his way to the conference that was to end South Africa's membership. The meeting with the president and the secretary of state were milestones. After talks with J. F. Kennedy and Dean Rusk, Menzies was in a first class position to interpret the long-range objectives of American foreign policy. The communique issued at the end of the visit was short and followed obvious lines. The President of the United States and the Prime Minister of Australia welcomed the opportunity to reaffirm the traditional partnership between the peoples of Australia and the United States. In their review of security problems, the president and the prime minister reiterated their strong faith in SEATO and ANZUS as bulwarks for the maintenance of peace in the Pacific. And they welcomed the initiative of King Savang Vatthana in proposing a course of action to bring peace, stability and neutrality to Laos, and expressed the hope that his efforts would bear fruit.

There were several important aspects to this communiqué. It was clear that Menzies had gone to Washington precisely to obtain assurances on the validity of the SEATO and ANZUS cloak for Australia. It was obvious that whatever he said about the value of international agencies at after-dinner speeches in London, Menzies was forced to work with the Americans, to make the United Nations a working weapon in the free world's armoury. And the reference to Laos as a neutral country was a harbinger of the importance the American State Department and External Affairs were beginning to attach to the idea that communism's downward thrust might be stopped by establishing neutral zones. Puppet kings and military dictators might be propped up in the name of peace, neutrality and regional stability: indeed, Menzies and Kennedy believed that they could and would be bulwarks against communist China and its military insurgency campaign.

Calwell and the Australian Labor Party, in attacking Menzies over South Africa, completely missed the boat. Menzies was able to deflect the opposition's attack on his apparent excessive sensitivity to the problems the South African government was having in running a multi-racial society, and turn attention to the much more crucial and continuing issue, Australia's relationship with SEATO and its defence priorities in the early sixties. Menzies gave a lengthy account of his talks with President Kennedy and Dean Rusk which, he argued, were much more important than the South African affair. Menzies stressed that Kennedy had 'a most alert interest in Australia' and its problems. In particular, the trio discussed the problems of SEATO and its relationship to the struggle for Laos. The president outlined to Menzies the state department's view of the state of tension between the democratic world and the communist powers, and in return Menzies briefed the Americans on the Australian government's policies and activities in Papua and New Guinea. A dispute with Indonesia over West New Guinea was seen by Menzies as the same sort of issue which the Americans were concerned with in Laos. Menzies was impressed by Kennedy. He described him in warm, rather than formal terms, paying tribute to his lively mind, vigorous approach, energy and desire for results, and forceful personality. He could only report that there was no likelihood of immediate developments as a result of the meeting, but he hinted that Australia's interests would be well taken care of once Kennedy had ascertained the facts.

Apart from Laos and Vietnam and South Africa, Menzies was confronted by the possibility of war with Indonesia. Relations with Indonesia would remain edgy. There were a series of crises involving Papua New Guinea and Timor that continued to plague Menzies's successors, especially Whitlam, Hawke and Howard. On 19 December 1961, President Sukarno called on all Indonesians to be ready for general mobilisation to liberate West Irian from the claws of Dutch imperialism. On 3 January 1962, Sukarno proclaimed West New Guinea an Indonesian province. Subsequently the Dutch Navy sank an Indonesian motor torpedo boat and Dutch marines fought Indonesian paratroops in crocodile-infested swamps, marshes and jungles around Fak Fak.

Two days after Sukarno's call for liberation, Menzies condemned the Indonesians as warmongers and liars. He recalled that Sukarno had given categorical assurances that Indonesia would not resort to force in West New Guinea. He asserted that Australia stood firmly on the principle of self-determination for the people of both halves of New Guinea, Australian and Dutch. He ended by saying that Holland's proposal to transfer sovereignty over West New Guinea to the United Nations was in full accord with the principles of the United Nations.

On 3 January, Calwell finally said what was in the minds of the coalition ministers: if Sukarno were to succeed with his annexation of West Irian by force, who would guarantee that he would not produce border incidents with the Australian

Territory of New Guinea as an excuse for further annexations? Not only Australian New Guinea, but Malaysia, particularly Borneo and Sarawak, would be coveted by Sukarno. It was certain, said Calwell, that Sukarno would not be satisfied with one victory, because, like all dictators, he had to divert the attention of his people from internal troubles by engaging in foreign forays.

When Indonesian paratroops landed in West New Guinea in May 1962, Menzies said that if that was not aggression he did not know what was. The following month Menzies said that the coalition had every natural desire to live on terms of friendship with Indonesia, but it was necessary for him to once again stress two points. One was that the war action was inconsistent with statements publicly and repeatedly made to Australians that Indonesia would not pursue its territorial claims in New Guinea by force. The other was that the negotiations begun in the presence of the American diplomat Ellsworth Bunker, after initiating action by the UN Secretary-General, had yet to be resumed and concluded. Australian foreign policy was to hope for and respect a peaceful settlement arising from negotiations. Sir Garfield Barwick, on the coalition's behalf, visited Indonesia in July 1962, when he was told by General Subandrio that Indonesia had no claims or design on any Australian territory. Sir Garfield also talked to Sukarno, who assured him that the Indonesians desired a peaceful settlement in West New Guinea, that the prospects for such a settlement were good, and that military force was to be eschewed in the future.

The long-standing dispute between Indonesia and the Netherlands ended on 15 August. The Dutch and Indonesian governments signed an agreement that provided for UN administration of West New Guinea from 1 October 1962 until 1 May 1963, the transfer of administration to Indonesia on the latter date, and a plebiscite in West New Guinea in 1969, when the population could say whether or not they wished to remain part of Indonesia. The West New Guinea Agreement ended nearly three hundred years of Netherlands rule in the Territory, apart from the Japanese occupation in World War II, the first Dutch landings having taken place in 1678.

Both the Indonesians and the Australian government kept up military and diplomatic pressure till the last moment. The seriousness of the situation was underlined when, while the cease-fire and treaty negotiations were being concluded, Indonesian paratroops landed within forty miles of the ill-defined Australian border. Barwick lost no time in making a strong protest to Indonesia against the landings, and told the House that he could not understand why the paratroops had been sent in at a time when the Indonesian negotiations were virtually completed.

The Indonesian-Dutch conflict was a crucial factor in causing a re-organisation of defence expenditure. Before 1963 Menzies had calculatingly cut down defence expenditure and built up domestic welfare spending, especially on education. This was carefully disguised by political rhetoric. It won elections. But after the landing of Indonesian paratroops in a successful anti-colonial action, Menzies went forward with a re-equipment plan to replace the obsolescent hardware that had served in the Pacific and Korea. The RAAF was the key arm in the strategic war plan of the 1960s. French Mirage fighters were the frontline aircraft. In May 1963 Menzies foreshadowed a Mirage complement of 100 aircraft.

The real turning-point came when the coalition decided not to buy British and instead to order its new bomber from the United States. When Menzies announced the government's decision to replace the British-made Canberra bomber, the aircraft was still in service with NATO and Menzies had a personal affection for it. Had he not been invited to go to an English aerodrome to name the Canberra, and to see it taken up by a test pilot on a demonstration flight in 1951? The coalition's decision to spend $82,000,000 extra on defence over the 1963–68 period was easy. How to spend the money was not. By buying more Mirages some of the money could be accounted for, but the Mirage did not replace the Canberra. Australia was equipping its aircraft with a strong fighter arm, but lacked any strike-reconnaissance bomber. The Mirage was selected only after an on-the-spot evaluation by a team of qualified experts. The minister himself flew a Mirage at 1,500 miles an hour. When the Canberra had to be replaced the Chief of Air Staff was sent on the shopping expedition. The team left and returned. Menzies reported to the house in October 1963 that the evaluation team had selected the United States TFX, subject to what he called, in an unwitting understatement, 'problems of the timetable and of payment'.

Once the coalition had decided upon the TFX, Menzies sent the Minister for Defence, G. A. Townley, to the United States and to the United Kingdom. In Britain, Townley explained to the government that the British reconnaissance bomber, the TSR2, had been given the thumbs down. In Washington, Townley found the TFX renamed the F111A, but no nearer delivery. At the same time it seemed much more important to remember that by buying American he was able to extract a package deal that involved an American contribution to Australia's defence. The purchase was an indication of mutual goodwill. It showed that the United States had a high opinion of the capacity of the Australian armed forces and the reliability and importance of Australia as a nation in its area of the world. As Menzies put it, Townley discussed the F111 in context with strategic needs and had close political consultation with the United States administration. Townley and McNamara (the United States Secretary of Defense) agreed that the government of Australia would buy from the United States two squadrons of F111s, which would give the country up-to-date strike aircraft designed to carry nuclear weapons. Menzies then made a number of embarrassingly inaccurate predictions, all of which turned out to be extremely costly and wrongly optimistic calculations.

The F111, Menzies said, would be available in Australia at the same time as deliveries were made to the United States armed forces. It was not. Delivery would be from 1967 onwards. He stressed that date because rumours had made it a couple of years later. He should have investigated the rumours. Most astray, Menzies declared that financial arrangements were entirely satisfactory to Australia. As far as escalating costs were concerned, the F111 was to be a flying version of the Sydney Opera House. The United States had agreed to supply the aircraft on the basis of a purchase price that included one year's initial spare parts, including engines, ground handling equipment, training aids, and the initial and operational training of crews, which would be carried out in the United States. Menzies had been told that the coalition would secure its first deliveries in 1967. He looked forward to the arrival of the two-man bomber which could fly at two and a half times the speed of sound and well above supersonic speed at sea level, could take off and land from short and rough air-fields, and fly to any part of the earth within twenty-four hours. Townley had also obtained the promise of a loan of two squadrons of B47 aircraft until the F111 was delivered: this was never taken up, however, and the government decided in June 1964 to do without them.

For the opposition, Whitlam asked what the cost and financial arrangements would be. Whitlam had the assurance of the British Ministry of Aviation and the British High Commission in Canberra that the Vickers prototype TSR2 would fly from Weybridge in Surrey to Woomera for missile tests by the end of 1963. The prototype F111 was due to fly in 1965. Why was the house not told why it was preferable to wait for the American aircraft instead of taking the British aircraft?

On the B47 stopgap, Whitlam pointed out that it was even older than the Canberra, and was, in a comparison intelligible to laymen, slower than the Boeing 707, could not fly as high as the Boeing 707, did not have the range of the Boeing 707, nor the lifting capacity. Finally, Whitlam concentrated on the purchase price omission. What financial arrangements had been made?

The decision to buy the F111 and not the TSR2 is all the more striking when one remembers that Menzies was dealing with a Conservative British government. But, in this matter, stereotypes of Menzies's attitudes were quite different from the reality. It is sometimes thought, for example, that the coalition neglected to prepare Australia for Britain's entry into the European Economic Community. On the contrary, the trend towards an increasing reliance on the United States, and a move away from the British orbit, was noticeable in 1962, when the federal parliament discussed at length the entry of Britain into the Common Market. By January 1963 the French veto ended the debate, but in the meantime the Minister for Air, Leslie Bury, was sacked for saying what most Liberal ministers came to believe to be true, that Australia would have to cut its losses and look elsewhere for markets and alliances. Bury was pressured out of the ministry after a speech he made to the Australian Institute of Management in July 1962, during which he asserted that the overwhelming majority of Australians would not notice any material change or be materially affected. The only shadow Bury anticipated was that certain rural industries would have to forgo plans for expansion and that, he indicated, would be insignificant, as the aggregate of their output was only a minor element in the total economic scene.

Bury's view was, of course, heresy to the junior partner in the coalition, the Country Party, whose primary industry-based organisation was going to be the one to suffer most when Kangaroo brand butter vanished from the co-operative supermarkets of the British Isles. McEwen, the Country Party leader, was shocked: that a ministerial colleague should completely undercut the strength of Australia's negotiating position by declaring that Australia had little to lose by Britain's entry, irrespective of terms, was monstrous. McEwen said that it was the accepted cabinet view that virtually all the primary industries would be grievously affected if Britain were to join the EEC without making special arrangements for countries such as Australia which had built up industries on the assumption of favourable access to the British market. Menzies made a less colourful remark to the same effect and forthwith sacked Bury from the ministry. There was, said Menzies, only one cabinet policy and it was the one voiced by McEwen and himself: the dangers to Australia were very real. Calling for Bury's resignation, Menzies observed that it was impossible for him to remain a member of the ministry with whose policies he disagreed on such an important matter.

Menzies remained on the surface as Anglophile as ever. When the Queen visited Australia for four weeks in February and March 1963, she admitted the Prime Minister of Australia to the Most Ancient and Noble Order of the Thistle. The Order was limited to sixteen persons chosen by the Queen personally and not upon ministerial advice. Sir Robert Menzies, as he then became, was the first Australian to be admitted to such high distinction among the chivalric orders.

Not distracted or deflected by the Thistle from his Australian-American bent, Menzies continued to cement the alliance with the Kennedy administration. One of the most significant features of the 1960s was the establishment, on a firm footing, of American military bases in Australia. In September 1960, the first mention was made in the federal parliament of the proposal by the United States that a communication base be established in Australia. In 1961 and 1962 there were occasional questions about the base, but it was not until the construction plans reached the blueprint stage that the issue took fire. There were two interesting features to the following decision-making processes of both the coalition and the Labor Party. Both Calwell and Menzies blundered over the stage management of the affair from a party political point of view. Menzies decided to submit the issue to parliament when, in reality, there was no need for him to do so. In Australia the power to contract treaties with a foreign power was the prerogative of the crown, there being no need to submit the treaty to parliament for ratification unless the treaty affected the existing rights of citizens, or modified law, or involved a cession of territory, or required the vesting of extra powers in the crown, or necessitated extraordinary expenditure. But for the proposed American base, the commonwealth acquired the land from Western Australia under existing statutes. No cession of territory was involved, the United States being the lessee of 28 square miles of Australian territory. Even so, Menzies brought the matter before the House of Representatives. Albeit unwittingly, Menzies scored a notable success, as the resulting conflicts between the various sections of the Labor Party were thus more readily brought before the electorate.

Calwell convened a special federal conference of the Labor Party, which in March 1963 thrashed out rather too publicly foreign policy and defence questions as they related to the proposed base. From 1955 to 1962 successive conferences of the Labor Party had called for the establishment of a nuclear-free zone in the southern hemisphere. The group which continued to believe in this ideal argued that to allow the creation of the North-West Cape base would be to make nonsense of Labor's aim to achieve a nuclear-free zone. It involved Australia in a total commitment to United States policy. The minority report continued that the base would impair Australia's relationship with Asia and prevent regional agreement with Asian countries, and that it would make Australia a prime target in the event of nuclear war. This, they said, was the final and decisive point:

the base would close the last link of complete encirclement in the strike strategy of the United States and thus would place Australia and its cities in the first category of attack and destruction targets.

The report of the ALP Foreign Affairs Committee was rejected by the party executive. Most agreed that the Cape was a grim and awful necessity (in Gough Whitlam's words). Whitlam's side contended that a defence radio communications centre, connected with submarines, operated by an ally, was not inconsistent with party policy if Australian sovereignty was maintained. The party majority also laid down that Australian citizens working at the station were to be subject to Australian law. The radio communications were to be under joint control of both governments and the facilities open to Australian forces. They also declared that Australia's involvement in war was a matter for Australia alone to decide at all times and under no circumstances and under no agreement should Australia automatically become involved in war. The party concluded that the radio communications centre ought not to become a base for the stockpiling of nuclear weapons in time of peace. In parliament Labor accordingly did not oppose the bill, but tried to secure amendments designed to secure joint control and to stress the point that Australia should not be dragged unknowingly into war behind the chariot wheels of the United States. On 22 May 1963, amid the cry that government MPs were 'a pack of dingoes', the House of Representatives approved the bill, incorporating the text of an agreement between the United States and Australia. So the United States gained a toehold, or perhaps rather a bootprint, in Western Australia.

A naval communication base at North-West Cape was established, and its strategic importance was enormous, even if this was not publicly demonstrated until the 1990s, when the defeat of Saddam Hussein in the Gulf War was in part attributable to Australian-American defence communication links. The base was an essential link in America's nuclear defence system and made North-West Cape a prime target in the event of war between the East and West. The clear purpose of the base was to provide communications with Polaris submarines. North-West Cape gave an unsurpassed field of fire covering the crucial seas, straits, oceans and waters contingent upon southern Africa and Asia. The Polaris submarines, euphemistically described as mobile second-strike bases, could thus be directed on their targets from Western Australia and wipe out whatever had to be wiped out, without having to surface from the depths.

The machinery of agreement between the United States and Australian governments was curious, to say the least. This agreement was made at ambassador/minister level. The Australian foreign minister, in an exchange of letters, tried to give the impression, for it could be no more than an impression, that the use, access and control of the base would be divided equitably between the United States and Australia. Agreement was made that the two governments would consult each other over the station and its use. More important, it was laid down that, except with the express permission of the Australian government, the station would not be used for purposes other than defence communication. Appropriate Australian authorities nominated by the Australian government were at all times to have access to the station.

'Equitably' meant different things to different people. So far as the American ambassador was concerned, it was not intended to restrict the government's right of consultation; but it had to be spelt out that consultation did not carry with it any degree of control over the station or its use. The Australian foreign minister agreed with the American ambassador's memory in which, so the ambassador said, it was clearly understood that consultation connoted no more than consultation. It was not intended to establish Australian control over the station nor to give any government use of the station for defence communications, including, for example, communications for Polaris submarines.

Menzies decided to hold a general election in November 1963, in the wake of the Cape base controversy and the clear divisions of opinion within the Labor Party on matters of foreign policy. This was to bring forward the date by twelve months. No election was due under the constitution until the end of 1964. Menzies's courage was justified. One minor problem was that the decision to have an early poll moved the House of Representatives elections and the Senate elections out of phase with each other, the simultaneous occurrence of the elections to both federal chambers having been restored in 1955. In the outgoing parliament, Menzies had a majority of two. He argued that an election had become necessary because the country needed an authoritative government, one whose strength in the chamber was unequivocal. Menzies tried to trick the electorate into thinking that they were really deciding between two parties separated by foreign policy differences. He was in all probability motivated by the fall in unemployment. In October 1963 the number out of work had fallen to 59,000 (the lowest figure since December 1960), an indication that the country had moved out of the slump which had nearly led to the government's defeat in 1961. The coalition favoured the establishment of an American base in Western Australia and a close alliance with the new state of Malaysia, which was, at its birth, threatened by communist terrorists.

The Labor Party, for its part, had no clear voice. Calwell was in a cleft stick. If he berated the government for its economic mismanagement, he could not also afford to draw attention to its greatly improved economic performance in 1963 by charging Menzies with cynicism in bringing forward the election date. Nevertheless, supremely inept, Calwell did both. A typical statement was this rhetorical question: was Australia to be governed for another three years by the same government which only three years ago struck such a blow to the Australian economy that it had taken three years to recover? If the middle-class voters could not think, they could at all events count. The answer was yes. Menzies, with a bronchial sneer, accused the Labor Party of trying (rather offensively, he thought) to buy the electorate's votes with grandiose election promises, and often proceeded to make some bribing overtures himself. The only difference was that Menzies's bribes had to be paid. The coalition promised to give married couples (one or both of whom was under thirty-six years of age) a $500 handout towards the cost of their first house, and new funds were to be given to assist the teaching of science in non-government as well as government schools. Secondary and technical school schol-arships were to be created. Child endowment was to be increased to $3 for a third and subsequent child. The government also promised to proceed with its plans for ending restrictive trade practices and to provide a separate section of the Department of National Development which could be charged with looking at the economic problems of the Northern Territory.

During the election campaign there were the symbolic deaths of two major political figures – one abroad, one at home – who had exercised a marked influence on Australian development. When President Kennedy was assassinated and Archbishop Mannix died, two phases in Australian history were closing. Mannix was ninety-nine when he died, and Melbourne was preparing for his hundredth birthday. As the archbishop lay in state, the *deus ex machina* was finally laid to rest. When Mannix was buried, B. A. Santamaria immediately disappeared from his regular spot on Catholic television programmes in Victoria. Just as quickly after Kennedy died, the president was inserted into one of Menzies's television election commercials. Calwell claimed that the coalition were ghouls trying to make capital out of the president's death. He was wrong: they had already realised their investment during Kennedy's lifetime.

Guest appearances at the 1963 polls were made by Aboriginals, all of whom were eligible to vote for the first time. Before this, they had had to enrol as electors and voting was compulsory for them only if they were on the lists. As a result of the election, the coalition's effective majority was increased from 2 to 22. Menzies, on announcing the dissolution, had predicted half that margin and he was at that time being optimistic rather than conservative. The most remarkable change occurred in New South Wales, where the Liberal Party won five seats from the Australian Labor Party, and the Country Party won another two. The Liberals also regained three Brisbane seats which it had lost in 1961. In Western Australia the Country Party captured Canning from the Liberals, there being no electoral truce between the two parts of the government coalition in that electorate. The Democratic Labor Party's primary vote was down from 8.5 per cent to 7.3 per cent, but even so there was no doubt that DLP preferences had helped to decide the issue in favour of the government, especially in Victoria. The new ministry was announced in December 1963. It was increased by 3, bringing the total of 25. All twelve cabinet ministers retained their former portfolios, except for Paul Hasluck, who was promoted from Territories to Defence. Bury was reinstated, as was Alan Hulme (who had lost his seat in 1961). The rising stars of the coalition were Billy Snedden, the Attorney-General, and Douglas Anthony of the Country Party.

One of the first acts of the new parliament was to introduce the Decimal Currency Bill, and even in this there was a symbolic clash between the Anglophiles and the Americanists. Menzies knew that all Australians, once it was explained to them, could see the merits in a system of a decimal coinage. It was obviously preferable to one where twelves and twenties, pounds, shillings and pence, all jostled each other in a confusion of cash registers. Well knowing also that he was under siege for dropping yet another British institution (the visible trappings of the monetary system), he disingenuously suggested that the new coinage should be called 'royals' after the ancient coin-tokens, the 'real', a suggestion which was laughed out of court. The word 'dollar' was inserted before the bill was debated.

One of the new ministry's most serious and pressing tasks was to deal with Indonesian confrontation. The clash between Indonesia and Malaysia, right on Australia's doorstep, was of great importance. Not for nothing, as it turned out, had Australia formed a close link with the United States administration, and happily it was able to use its new forceful presence in the interests of a Commonwealth ally. When Indonesia attacked Malaysia, the Malaysian prime minister appealed to Menzies, and his cry for help was heard. It was Malaysia's right, Menzies believed, to ask for help in the dispute from any fellow member of the Commonwealth. The most promising sources of military aid for the Tunku were the British Army (the country's traditional shield) and that of Australia (Malaysia's nearest and most powerful Commonwealth ally). Menzies made it clear that Australian sympathy was, on the whole, not with the Indonesians and, having said this, realised that this could conceivably involve the government in confrontation itself, to such an extent that the ownership of an advanced bomber would not be without its diplomatic as well as military value. The Indonesian Ambassador, General Saudi, did not conceal his government's dislike of Australian intervention, issuing a friendly warning that confrontation was an Asian problem to be solved by Asians in an Asian atmosphere and in an Asian way.

Nevertheless, in January 1964, Australian assistance to Malaysia began to grow. The cabinet decided to send a mission to Kuala Lumpur, where, after a two-week stay, Paul Hasluck, as Minister for Defence, was required to organise the dispatch of ammunition, engineering equipment, general stores and seagoing craft, including minesweepers. In addition, Malaysian forces were trained by a small number of seconded Australian

Army instructors. Relations with Malaysia were much better in the 1960s than thereafter, when diplomatic misunderstandings reached crisis point over the execution of Australian drug peddlers and the perceived disrespect of the Australian Broadcasting Corporation for the Muslim state demonstrated through the television series 'Embassy'. In April 1964 the Australian government decided to assist in the prevention of sea-borne infiltration of insurgents along the coasts of Sarawak and Sabah and to provide engineering constructions in Borneo. Helicopter support was given in security operations against terrorists along the northern border of Malaysia and air transport was provided. In June 1964 the aircraft carrier *Sydney* dropped off one hundred and eighty engineers, who had been ordered to shoot back if fired upon. The attack on Indonesian confrontation was planned by Garfield Barwick (the Foreign Minister) and Hasluck. In the middle of Australian escalation Barwick was dropped from the ministry, having made some rather undiplomatic but nevertheless true remarks to the effect that Australia could count on American defence under ANZUS if Australia was attacked by Indonesia.

The June events in Malaysia did not represent the furthest limit of Australia's forward defence policy. There was a price to be paid for going all the way with JFK. There were by then thirty Australian instructors in Vietnam and there were likely to be more: the government received from the United States an *aide-memoire* which indicated various directions in which additional aid to Vietnam would be welcome. Previously the annual SEATO conference had agreed, on American request, that SEATO members consider giving further help to South Vietnam. On 8 June, Hasluck's replacement as Defence Minister, Senator Shane Paltridge, announced that Australia would double the number of its advisers to sixty, to be employed in the field at battalion and lower levels. Then, at a press conference in Kuala Lumpur, Hasluck said he believed that the Vietnam and confrontation conflicts were connected; he added that he considered that if one could get peace and stability in South Vietnam, it would be much easier to deal with Indonesian confrontation and vice versa. More he would not say. These ruminations were private. Hasluck's thoughts, however, were rather important and ought not to have been allowed merely to seep out and then be blotted up. Hasluck, who had helped plan the Malaysia confrontation attack, believed that subversion was infectious.

Australia jumped into the Vietnam war in August 1964. On 4 August, the United States made retaliatory attacks on North Vietnamese patrol boats, bases and installations, following incidents in the Gulf of Tonkin. On 5 August, the Australian Foreign Minister described the American policy as completely justified: he gave more details in the House on 11 August, spelling out in full the views he had declined to elaborate in Kuala Lumpur. Hasluck said that he hoped that the actions of the United States would have a strong deterrent effect. He believed that there was, at that time, no reason to expect that the conflict would extend. The Australian government, nevertheless, saw no alternative to using force against the southward thrust of militant Asian communism in Vietnam. Calwell sounded a morbid note on Vietnam. If we are to be committed, he said, we ought to know the extent of the commitment. The commitment cannot be made piecemeal – 23 men to South Vietnam as instructors one day, 50 another day, and so on, as we 'do not desire to see another 8th Division of Australian troops sucked into an Asian jungle or swallowed up by the quicksands of Asia'. The crucial point was that Asian communism was to be met by the introduction of selective conscription. The future divisiveness of Vietnam can be easily understood against the background of an arbitrary and capricious 'lottery of death'.

CHAPTER 6

Wizened Warmongers

The last half of the 1960s saw the beginning of an end for the Liberal-Country Party government. The conservatives were rapidly becoming sociologically inappropriate. The leaders failed to tune in to the changes in the community, and to remould their policies in conformity with the new society about to crystallise in the 1970s. There were several physical pointers to a convulsion in the community. One of the most obvious was the development of vast shopping centres. These became a feature of Australia's urban landscape. Roselands and Chadstone began to have smaller spawn as Coles and Woolworths spread into the hinterland of suburbia. The contribution of the centres to community living was negligible. The first shopping centres were built in 1957, but in the late 1960s the rate of growth gathered momentum. The weekly shopping expedition was born, made possible by the huge volume of car ownership.

By 1967, Australia had 3,000,000 registered cars, not including commercial vehicles. At the same time delivery services declined, and refrigerator ownership increased. The shoppers in the new centres, despite the promotional efforts of the entrepreneurs, were not easily tricked into believing that life was better the new way. In the late 1960s touring holidays boomed in Australia. By 1966 the population of Australia was enjoying a relatively large increase in income, which was expressed in family car ownership. They had greater leisure, especially since most workers enjoyed three weeks annual leave and long service leave. With better roads, more efficient vehicles, and improving accommodation, Australians set off for Ayers Rock, the Dandenongs and the Snowy Mountains, and away from the shopping centres and the suburbs.

The new material prosperity in the period 1965–69 was the result of an upturn in Australia's balance of payments position rather than the increased productivity of industry and primary production. The decision of investors in the United Kingdom and the United States to put their funds into Australian companies was the real basis of the increased money supply in the last years of the 1960s. Entrepreneurs in the United Kingdom led the investment race, spurred on by the potential strength of the new Australian mineral boom, and also by the possibility that the pound sterling would be devalued. The pound was devalued in November 1967 and the investors realised the capital gains expected.

This funk money seeking protection coincided with an extraordinary mineral boom. As the well-known Australian companies involved in mineral exploration investment were listed on the London exchange, investment was technically easy. After the devaluation, some of the 'funk money' went back to the city, where it earned high interest rates, but in the meantime the injection of overseas funds had a dramatic effect on the Australian economy. The year 1967–68 saw a 66 per cent jump in the Sydney share-price index. Brisbane saw a 189 per cent jump in oil stocks, and the pace of Western Mining and Hamersley Iron investment in nickel and iron ore kept the market bubbling. The non-mining investment industry rose by 26 per cent in 1967–68, led by BHP, which provided one-third of Sydney's index rise after oil was struck. In the wake of the mineral boom, pastoral, transport and automotive industry stocks led the rise in the industrial-commercial sector. By September 1967, Hamersley and Goldsworthy were operating and supplying iron ore to meet Japan's increasing demands. Mt Newman was under construction and the mining magnates, Sir Maurice Mawby, chairman of CRA, Hamersley's parent, and Lang Hancock, were leading the battle for the government to relax its guidelines on contract prices.

Personal share-buying also picked up because of institutional and multinational investment. In the mining market and elsewhere, investors looked for stocks. Journalists cautioned the unwary. October was a particularly dangerous month for speculating in stocks. The others were July, January, September, April, November, May, March, June, December, August and February. Female investors were advised not to cry about falling prices but to learn the difference between bulls and bears. Federal Hotels were recommended by *The Bulletin*'s 'speculator' because of the way in which 1967 would see regular beachheads of American servicemen down from Vietnam for their battle breaks. When these boys hit Sydney, Melbourne and Surfers' Paradise, Federal Hotels, said the speculator's diary, would 'get a shot in the arm that should help it make dollars, not cents'.

The Department of National Development encouraged investment by pointing out that Australia's mineral industries were going to provide a significantly increasing amount of national income. Official figures showed that on the basis of signed contracts for the faster developing projects like iron ore, total mineral exports were going to jump from $384 million to $830 million between 1967 and 1971. The impact of such growth on Australia's balance of payments was to be significant. And the mining company profits were likely to be phenomenal. The buying was wild. It was called the charge of the nickel brigade. Office girls in Melbourne rushed to Little Collins Street where they plunged on oil search stocks. Great Boulder's board was warned by the stock exchange not to issue inflammatory reports that suggested nickel discoveries that were unproven. The boom led to a rush build-up of stockbrokers' staff. Books were written on how to make a million on the stock market.

The Indian summer of the mineral boom was marked by the fortunes of Poseidon shares, which between September and December 1969 rose from about $1 to $100 each. Poseidon started nickel drilling at Windarra, in Western Australia's spinifex country, in September 1969. Although the directors of Poseidon said only that nickel and copper sulphides were found, the people on the spot sparked a boom by jamming telephone lines to brokers in capital cities asking them to buy Poseidon. For many investors it was a rags to riches opportunity. Profits from the boom were not confined to Australia. In London a shop assistant in Harrods was discovered with stock worth $120,000, having bought Poseidon shares at 4 cents each in 1966.

The Poseidon boom was a reflection of more than the avarice of the punting investor. It was a mark of confidence in Australia's mineral prospects. Poseidon was floated largely on hope, but it was pointed out early that a railway 200 miles long would have to be built, that a concentrating plant would have to be made, and that the price and quality of nickel assayed would have to stand up. Poseidon touched $100 in Perth in December 1969, but by then the bubble was about to burst.

In the late 1960s, the search for personal and national identity became both more critical and more difficult. A major Australian movie project, 'They're a Weird Mob', was shot entirely on Sydney locations between October and December 1965. Its three central characters were said to be 'as Australian as kookaburras'. But by 1966 it was necessary to be more than just identifiably Australian: the electorate was beginning to demand reasons and alternatives. The birth of *Oz* magazine, the *Kings Cross Whisper*, and the Adelaide Festival of Arts were all part of the search for new directions. Barry Humphries was not joking – indeed he spoke for many – when he said that he was developing a new view of Australia, and that he had been awakened by artists like Patrick White, Manning Clark and Alan Moorehead.

The Liberal-Country Party was not able to harness the new creative spirit and identify a political programme with the changing mood of Australia. Even so, it must be admitted that the high-water mark of Liberal-Country Party popularity was the success of conservative candidates in the 1966 elections. Thereafter it was impossible to be idealistic about the Liberal principles that Menzies had pronounced in 1949. In a symbolic moment during June 1966, a woman smeared with red paint brushed against parading troops in Sydney. The troops were veterans returning from the Vietnam war zone; the woman was protesting against Australian involvement in Vietnam.

The period 1965–69 saw both enormous changes in Australian society and, at the same time, a continuation of the themes of the 1950s and early 1960s. On the surface, there were many obvious watersheds and incidents that pointed to the development of a new type of community that would demand new leaders capable of dealing with new pressures. But Menzies resignation on 20 January 1966 was not immediately the end of an era. His successor, Harold Holt, merely trod in Menzies's steps. The attempt to assassinate Calwell was not a usual feature of Australian life, and was, many thought, an unwelcome manifestation of American influence. The visit by President Johnson in October 1966 and the increase in Australia's role in Vietnam were others. The first Australian infantry battalion was sent to Vietnam in June 1965. The force was trebled within twelve months by the inclusion of national servicemen. Although all eras are times of change and uncertainty, the late 1960s were particularly so: Australians had to face a devaluation of sterling, a unilateral declaration of independence by Rhodesia, the beginnings of a black power movement among Aboriginals, claims for independence by Papua New Guinea, and all this with conspicuously untried leaders, both in government and in opposition.

Calwell retired from the leadership of the Labor Party and was replaced by Whitlam. Holt drowned, and the coalition chose the wrong man to lead the Cabinet and the country: J. G. Gorton. Gorton was not merely the wrong man: the fight between him and the others seeking power in the Liberal Party was so open that for a time it destroyed both him and the party. By the end of the 1960s it was only a matter of time before the coalition internecine fighting so upset the running of government that change was inevitable. Gorton was able to win the 1969 election, but the spectacle of his quarrels with William McMahon damaged the party irreparably, and the administration's incompetence became increasingly obvious and all-pervasive. When the battleship *Melbourne* sank its second friendly destroyer, the omens could hardly have been worse.

The most significant political issue of the late 1960s was Vietnam. Opinion polls at the time put other things higher. But the Vietnam war divided society in Australia in the same way that it split America. The decision to become heavily committed in Vietnam was a part of the process begun by Menzies in his admiration for Kennedy. Australia sent a single battalion of 800 men to Vietnam in 1965. They could not comprise an independent command and so were incorporated into the US 173rd Airborne Brigade. The Australian battalion, 1 Royal Australian Regiment, had to conduct its operations in strict accord with the US methods, and to abandon Australian techniques, which had been developed during the Malayan emergency. Only when the first national servicemen had completed their basic training were the Australians able to conduct autonomous operations by committing a task force of two battalions and a regiment of gunners. Phuoc Tuy Province was the area chosen. The Australians were based at Nui Dat, fifty miles south of Saigon, and comprised at first two battalions with supporting troops: a total of 3,000 men.

When Menzies announced his retirement, he had been prime minister for sixteen years, during which, he said unconvincingly, he had never had a real holiday. After pointing out that he would be seventy-two at the time of the next lower house elections in December 1966, Menzies admitted that all his years and tasks in office had taken their toll. He was depressed at the thought of another election campaign, another political speech. He was not up to handling the complexities of modern government, domestic and international, which had grown enormously. But neither were his first three successors, Holt, Gorton and McMahon.

Harold Holt, the crown prince, was elected unopposed as Menzies's successor. He had been ten years in the Liberal Party as deputy leader under Menzies. Holt swore in his new Cabinet on 26 January 1966, remarking that it was Australia Day 'and this I feel has some happy symbolism for us all'. The press pointed to what they saw as the obvious difference between Menzies and Holt. Holt preferred the Australian-American alliance, Menzies preferred the Union Jack. Was not Sir Robert leaving to become Lord Warden of the Cinque Ports, and had not Holt chosen as his first grand tour a visit which would take him off to Washington? The truth of the matter is that Holt was a grandstander and, apart from that, the two men's policies were continuous.

During his first visit to America as prime minister, Holt spoke as Menzies would have done. At the White House in Washington, Holt explained that Australia's involvement in Vietnam was much more important and significant to the Australians than American involvement to the Americans. Australia, claimed Holt, was not in Vietnam because America was there; Australia was involved far more directly than the Americans. If the Vietnam area went, asked Holt, where did one attempt to hold the line? In Thailand, or in the neck of the Malay Peninsula? He did not think that anyone would attach greater confidence to a capacity to hold the line in those places than to a capacity to hold it in Vietnam. In the meantime, there would have been more people overrun, and more destruction. The Americans, he concluded, were right to be there, and Australia was right to be with them.

On the eve of the 1966 federal election, President Johnson decided to attend the meeting of the heads of government of America's East Asian and South Pacific allies in Manila in October 1966. He subsequently decided to visit Australia and New Zealand on his way to Manila, being the first American President to visit Australia while in office. The Labor Party was quick to point out the ways in which Johnson's tour was in Holt's interest. Calwell claimed that the government would exploit the president's visit in much the same way that Menzies had exploited Queen Elizabeth's visit in 1954. Johnson's visit would be used, said Calwell, to cover up the coalition's short-comings on wage justice, failure to stop rising prices and to improve depreciated social services, and refusal to face the problems involved in working out how to abolish the means test.

During his sixty-five hours in Australia President Johnson made speech after speech that defended Holt's line on defence, Vietnam and foreign policy. Johnson made his most pointed remarks in Victoria, saying that Melbourne was much closer to the trouble spots of South-East Asia than was San Francisco. He hoped that it would not be necessary for another Hitler to gobble up all the little countries and march into Poland, or for another enemy to be on the other side of the Owen Stanley Ranges in New Guinea, before people realised where their national interests lay. Eleven hundred American pressmen were accredited for the visit to Canberra. School children by the thousands were bussed out over the president's motorcade routes. Lunch-time shopping crowds cheered him as if he was a member of the royal family. The visit was a resounding triumph for Holt: it was in line with Holt's policy of high-level hob-nobbing in the glare of press and television. The media naturally welcomed the chance of selling more papers featuring the newest example of presidential charm: the visit was almost as good as an assassination.

The final boot in the Labor Party's direction was delivered by Senator John Gorton. It marked the entry of Gorton into the limelight, which was to glow sufficiently brightly for him to overshine the rest of the parliamentary party. In answer to a rhetorical question, which sought to exploit the fact that, while government organised the visit, the Labor Party was hostile, Gorton said that if any bad image of Australia were projected in American newspapers in connection with the visit of President Johnson, it would only have been presented by a concentration of a small, violent, bearded, undemocratic, extreme minority who screamed hatred until they were drowned out by the hundreds of thousands who screamed acclamation. Such demonstrations, concluded Gorton, ought not to be permitted, for they were a denial of democracy. Amid uproar he added that the demonstrations had probably been encouraged and incited by the calls for demonstrations made by the President of the Australian Labor Party.

The first policy speech in the 1966 elections was delivered by Senator Gair on 7 November. He pledged, on behalf of the Democratic Labor Party, generous social services, national service of two years for all young men, a peace corps, one per cent of gross national product to be spent on foreign aid, an ombudsman, and more for defence. Holt's policy speech was broadcast the following day on television. Holt's main emphasis was on defence. He claimed that the commitment in Vietnam was a commitment for peace, a shield behind which free Asia could grow strong; his government wanted peace and a peaceful solution to all conflicts, and it was prepared to be on friendly terms with countries having different ideological systems, provided that they did not try to impose their ideas on Australia by force, subversion, or other means. If support for South Vietnam were abandoned, then the whole of Vietnam would fall to the communists. The consequences of this would be felt throughout South-East Asia, and Australia would also come under threat. Australia had a vital interest in the effective presence and participation of the United States as a power in Asia and the Pacific. Australia had obligations arising from treaty relationships and the country's role as an ally, and from the fact that Australia's own international interests were directly involved in preserving South-East Asia from aggression and communist domination. Country Party leader 'Black Jack' McEwen assured the farmers that economic growth at the rate of 25 per cent every five years would continue. Then, not surprisingly, as national service call-up was high from country areas, he too turned to foreign policy, explaining to the primary producers that Australian aid to Vietnam was an insurance policy rather than a matter of good versus evil. As Australia would expect help if in need, Australians in 1966 demonstrated that they were willing to extend their help to a free people under attack. Australians wanted to so conduct themselves that the US would not hesitate to stand between Australia and an aggressor, America being the one country that could do this. Thus Australian troops in South Vietnam earned for Australia the right to the protection of the US and other treaty allies, should Australia be threatened.

The Labor policy boiled down to an expansion of Calwell's charge that Holt was 'a wizened old war-monger'. The Labor Party's election promises were costed by a conservative daily press, which set the sum needed in the event of a Labor victory at about $700,000,000: McMahon predicted that if this happened, income tax would have to be raised by 30 per cent to pay for it. In the closing days of the campaign there was some conflict between the coalition parties over several matters of regional importance. McEwen claimed that there had been an attempt on the part of the Liberals to saddle the Country Party with the responsibility for the rejection of stage two in the Ord River Scheme, when the decision had been the collective responsibility of the coalition cabinet. McEwen subsequently revealed a division within the cabinet over the dismissal of Bury, saying that he (McEwen) had advised Menzies against dismissing Bury, but Menzies had persisted, arming himself with the support of four Liberal ministers, McMahon, Barwick, Spooner and Paltridge.

The result of the 1966 election was never in doubt. Holt, warmonger perhaps, but wizened never, won the greatest triumph the Liberal-Country Party had experienced since 1949. There was a substantial swing to the government in the four largest states. The new House of Representatives contained 61 Liberals, 21 Country Party members, 41 members of the Australian Labor Party and one Independent. There were then 123 members with full voting rights – the status of the ACT members having been changed before the election – and one seat with limited rights, that being (it seemed appropriate enough, in view of the Aboriginal population living there) the Northern Territory.

Holt's response to election victory might have been different. He did not understand that his party, the Liberals, were on the verge of obliterating the Country Party, and in a position to govern the country alone. He might have emphasised the Liberal Party's new power by refusing to continue the tradition of appointing a Country Party man deputy leader of the government coalition. He might have reshuffled his cabinet and settled the scores of the Western Australian feud once and for all. Without cabinet representation at the most, or the deputy leadership at the least, the Country Party would have suffered a blow that would have hampered it for a generation and saved the conservatives from the embarrassment that was to recur over the questions of party leadership, international trade, tariff and currency strength.

As it turned out, Holt lost his chance at a critical moment, and the Country Party, from a position of great weakness, was able to rewrite its platform (for the first time since 1958) and include national centre party ideas as well as crude rural protectionism. The Country Party no longer insisted on a 'White Australia', stressed Australian independence and not the British connection, dropped the plank that the Communist Party ought to be banned, reasserted that there should be a 20 per cent loading in favour of country electors, said that it was in favour of the creation of a national investment corporation (which would preserve Australian equity in rural development) and came out against integration of Papua New Guinea with Australia in post-independence days.

In terms of electoral support, the Australian Labor Party took a step backwards, indeed a long jump backwards, to the situation which it held in 1932. Sectional factors helped Holt's victory. In South Australia the Labor administration was performing poorly. In Tasmania there were problems over the refusal of the federal government to subsidise a Dutch shipbuilding company which would have employed 2,500 men, and it appeared that the responsible minister, Gordon Freeth, was trying to divert the project to his home state. In Western Australia the coalition squabbling, and the debate over the Ord Scheme – combined with the refusal to extend television services to Kalgoorlie and Geraldton – reinforced the idea that Australia's western third was being neglected. Calwell had not improved Labor's chances by his spiteful and random attack on the vulnerable family life of Holt. Holt's stepsons were accused of 'chickening out' of the Vietnam war, in the same way that their stepfather had avoided the 1939–45 conflict.

As a result of the 1966 election Calwell fell into the category of dispensable leader, as Evatt had before him. The danger for the Liberal-Country Party during 1966 was that while Evatt had had no dynamic successor, Calwell could be replaced by a man with a pleasant appearance. Calwell belonged to that Labor tradition in which culture was camouflaged in public. Gough Whitlam looked different: he appeared to have the intangible stamp of leadership, and to be a man of calculated vision. No doubt the coalition was hoping that the left wing of the Australian Labor Party (who supported Calwell as leader) would triumph over the right, and leave the opposition in the shaky hands of an over-emotional demagogue whose leadership style was also appropriate to the early thirties. And for a time it seemed that Calwell might survive: Bill Hartley, the Victorian state secretary, warned his branch not to attribute defeat to Calwell. Hartley's Western Australian counterpart, F. E. Chamberlain, took the same view, and attributed defeat to lack of party loyalty to the principles and policies of the leader. In New South Wales, on the other hand, the state executive congratulated Calwell for past services in terms clearly expressing their belief in the inevitability and desirability of his retirement and called for a prompt solution of the leadership question. The New South Wales state president, C. T. Oliver, proposed a block vote on the party leadership, and attributed the party's defeat to a public image associated with both communism and an unrealistic degree of anti-American phobia. Dougherty and the AWU made similar points, and Calwell, in his turn, counterattacked, describing the Australian public as selfish and stupid – charges which, even if true, could scarcely be expected to help his party achieve office – and complained that Whitlam, Oliver, Dougherty, the ACTU and the Catholic Church had not given him their undivided help. He was a Lear without a Cordelia. Edward Gough Whitlam was elected leader in Calwell's place. Whitlam was to win the first Labor victory since the Pacific war, to strike out to give Australia a more distinctive domestic and international image, and to be the first prime minister sacked in two hundred years.

That, however, was in the future, and depended, as it turned out, upon a chance impulse of Holt, who, at the time of the 1966 elections, was clearly intending to set up an American presidential style of leadership in Australia. He grafted a southern White House on to the unresponsive State of Victoria, and he equipped himself with a battery of aides. He augmented his personal staff by appointing a former editor of the *Age* as a part-time special consultant to the Prime Minister's Department, and he increased his hold over foreign policy by appointing a liaison officer – P. H. Bailey, First Assistant Secretary of the Cabinet and the foreign relations division of Foreign Affairs – to keep him informed of developments in the foreign relations field. In a clear break with tradition, Holt spent considerable time on personal diplomacy: in February 1967 he visited New Zealand, at the end of March, Cambodia, and during April, Laos, Taiwan, Hong Kong, Okinawa, the Philippines, Singapore and Korea. At the same time Hasluck was dispatched to Japan for a meeting with the Economic Commission for Asia and the Far East, and for consultations with the Japanese government.

On 23 December 1966, Holt revealed that Marshal Ky, the Prime Minister of South Vietnam, might visit Australia. This visit was, as it turned out, a complete success for the coalition, and a bright nail in the coffin of Labor's electoral prospects. Calwell produced some memorable epithets to describe Ky – 'a quisling gangster', 'a butcher', 'a moral and social leper', and 'a pocket Hitler' – but the marshal's behaviour bore no resemblance to his caricatures. He was mild, thankful and a polished television interviewee. Holt had wisely counselled against any attempt to repeat Johnson's barn-storming among the people. Ky came not to seek further military intervention, but to thank Australians, saying that if anything was needed it was civil, not military, aid. One man sent a congratulatory telegram to Calwell, in which he described Ky as a 'fascist dictator' – the postmaster having excised 'ratbag' in favour of 'fascist' – but on the whole the visit was generally regarded as one of the greatest public relations coups Australia had seen. Calwell was summed up by the head of the South Vietnamese Embassy in Australia as a desperate old politician, who was running down, and who could not keep up with the progress being made in unveiling the devil's intentions and the subversion of the communists. This was an appropriately coloured blend of Christianity and the red-peril syndrome, and it received no rebuke from the Australian government.

All the omens seemed to be symbolic of the growth in the Australia-America alliance, not only in the positive events, such as the visits of Johnson and Ky, but the negative role Great Britain played. The United Kingdom government produced the timetable for its withdrawal from South-East Asia in mid-July 1967: a White Paper made it clear that the British government was going to be out of its bases in Singapore and Malaysia by the middle of 1970. The precise timing of withdrawal was to depend upon progress made in achieving a new basis for stability in South-East Asia, and in the resolution of other (unspecified) problems in the Middle East. Holt and the cabinet reacted to this with mixed feelings. On the one hand, Australia's dependence on the United States had been steadily increasing, and the country no longer relied on the United Kingdom for a shield. On the other, the withdrawal of the British from the area seemed certain to add to the problems of regional stability, and thus to the likelihood of a series of serious guerilla outbreaks. The wisest thing, as far as Holt was concerned, was to try to obstruct rather than assist British withdrawal (by refusing to take over bases, for example) while at the same time putting on as brave a face as was possible. In spring 1967, the Australian government put out its policy statement on defence issues which noted, in typically ambiguous and vague terms, that while they were disappointed over some aspects of the British decision, they had found considerable satisfaction that Britain had decided to play a continuing military role in the area and to honour its obligations within its financial competence.

The Australian-American link became even closer and more popular after the British Treasury devalued the pound sterling. Australia had considered the possibility of a sterling devaluation for years, at least since 1964. Menzies had steadily and unobtrusively reduced the proportion of Australia's reserves held in sterling. On 19 November 1967, sterling was devalued by 14.3 per cent to equal $2.40. On 21 November 1967, Holt announced that Australia had decided, in company with ten other major trading nations, not to devalue. It was, as Holt said, an historic decision, and a difficult one also, and one that in a sense showed, as Holt said (and as many before him had said on other occasions), that Australia had come of age as a nation. Australia was not a large nation in terms of population, but it loomed large through its international trade. Australia ranked among the twelve largest trading nations of the world. At the time the decision was taken, the cabinet knew that of the other eleven, while Britain had devalued its currency, the remaining ten had decided to maintain their currency values undisturbed. The cabinet believed that while some Australian exporters would have gained a temporary increase in their income had the country devalued, the long-term outlook over the whole area of the economy and Australia's international trading relationships would have been heavily to Australia's disadvantage. Australia certainly would not have helped Britain had it followed her down. There was, Holt concluded, a mutual interest for Australia in seeing sterling regain its strength, and Britain had looked to Australia to do precisely what it had done. In the long term, a growing British economy was likely to offer larger market opportunities for world traders.

It also had to be said that the decision to hold the dollar at its 1967 level avoided additions to budgetary burdens. Australia's indebtedness in US dollars was, at the time of sterling devaluation, for example, approaching $800,000,000. If the country had devalued to the same degree as Britain, it would have added in effect $100,000,000 to this debt immediately. Certainly, Australia lost $90,000,000 on its sterling balances, but this was offset by much the same amount in official sterling indebtedness in the United Kingdom.

The Australian Labor Party and commercial manufacturing interests agreed with the decision to hold the Australian dollar, but naturally it placed a considerable strain on the coalition. Difficulties were inevitable for the dairy farmers, meat producers and fruit growers who exported to London, and some wheat farmers under existing contracts faced considerable losses. McEwen was out of Australia during the devaluation crisis, and his henchmen Doug Anthony and Ian Sinclair were clearly not at the same level of political expertise. It was little use carping after the event, as they did; what was required from the Country Party point of view was resolute determination to break up the government unless the Country Party got its way in the cabinet room, determination which had not been lacking before November 1967 or after. Rather belatedly Anthony informed a sympathetic audience of journalists who wrote the agricultural columns of the Australian press that the country ought to plan its future as an exporter of cheap food, fibres and minerals, because it lacked the manpower and output for anything else.

W. W. Pettingell, the President of the Associated Chamber of Manufactures, correctly characterised Anthony's remarks as being based on a narrow and out-dated philosophy. He went further to say that Anthony by these comments had proven himself unacceptable to the manufacturing sector of the country as a future Minister for Trade, as manufacturers believed that manufacturing was the cornerstone of Australian prosperity and growth. The wool-growers' and graziers' pressure groups in turn expressed their horror at Pettingell's interpretation of events, and Anthony was forced to try to take the heat off by calling a meeting of Country Party members in order to publicise the provision of safeguards for rural industry that had accompanied devaluation. McEwen returned to Australia and showed that he was made of sterner stuff than Anthony or Sinclair. He used the technique of making ministerial comments without consulting Holt. McEwen said that it was a matter of principle for the Country Party to find steps to protect primary and secondary industry from damage. The effect of devaluation on some industries would not be ascertainable for months. The Country Party needed a more precise and binding policy statement than the general intimation that these industries would be looked after. He explained that he had deliberately made his statements before he saw Holt because he wanted to make it clear that it was the policy of the Country Party and not of the coalition. McEwen's responsibilities were dual. He was the leader of a great national party dedicated to looking after the rural industries that had been affected by the government's decision; he was also Holt's partner in the government. Holt replied that McEwen ought to understand that he was very definitely the junior partner, and, worse, quite often the absent partner.

Holt disappeared in the middle of the devaluation crisis, when the coalition was looking towards a split, and the touch of success seemed to have deserted him. His last exit was so dramatic that it is difficult to find a parallel, except perhaps the sudden blow to America as a result of the assassination of J. F. Kennedy. About midday on 17 December 1967, Holt went swimming in heavy surf off Cheviot beach on the Nepean peninsula, near Portsea, sixty-three miles from Melbourne. The waves were fifteen feet high. Holt was an enthusiastic skin diver but, mysteriously, he was not wearing flippers and underwater equipment, or carrying a spear gun. He was fit and, although he was being treated for muscular soreness in the shoulder, he played tennis on the afternoon before he disappeared. Holt was hoping to catch a glimpse of Alec Rose, the British green-grocer from Plymouth who was completing his lone voyage from Britain in the ketch *Lively Lady*.

Holt has not been seen since. Police, servicemen and volunteers searched the beach near Portsea in a hunt that began about an hour and a half later. Cheviot was well known to Holt, who had a holiday house at Portsea. *The Times* promptly said, in its leading article, that the disappearance of Mr Holt in the inshore waters that are the joys, but can be the death-trap, of Australian swimmers, would be a shock to Australian politics as well as to public feeling. By nightfall on 17 December, no one held out much chance for Holt, except perhaps the Deputy Prime Minister, John McEwen, who said that he was going to pray. The Queen was extremely distressed. President Johnson asked the US Embassy in Canberra to keep him advised. The helicopter crew taking part in the search reported sighting a huge shark in the area where Holt was last seen alive. A macabre joke at the time ended with two fishermen finding Holt at sea, and one saying to the other, 'It's only the prime minister, throw him back.' Certainly, the search for Holt was brief: it did not last two days. By 22 December the memorial service had been held. This gathering saw tribute on a scale usually reserved for monarchs: it was attended by Prince Charles, President Johnson, Harold Wilson and Edward Heath, and the lesser heads of state from South Vietnam, the Philippines, South Korea, New Zealand, Singapore, Malaysia and Thailand. Holt was sent off with a memorial service, not a state funeral, as his body was not recovered. This omission led to speculation that Holt might have been done away with: it was one thing not to find the body of a missing surfer, but quite another not to recover a drowned prime minister, even one rumoured to be a Chinese spy.

There were, when Holt disappeared, three obvious candidates who might have been prime minister: William McMahon, Paul Hasluck and John McEwen. There were also John Gorton, alone in the middle rank, and two outsiders, Billy Snedden and Leslie Bury. McMahon was officially Deputy Leader of the Liberal Party, having won a closely contested ballot for the post after Menzies retired. And McMahon was the most likely candidate; his prestige was at an all-time high following his success in coping with the devaluation of sterling, his voice being loudest among those who decided not to devalue Australian currency. The thinking man's prime minister would have been Hasluck, the Foreign Minister (journalist, diplomat, historian, author) who was defeated by McMahon in the ballot for deputy leader. Naturally people in the country would have liked to see McEwen, leader of the Country Party minority in the coalition, succeed. McEwen, Minister for Trade, was strongly critical of Britain's move towards the Common Market and was an expert at selling wheat to the Chinese communists and at coping with Japanese business interests. But McEwen was a non-starter. Gorton was simply leader of the government in the Senate. His supporters suggested that he be given Holt's old seat of Higgins. This would allow him to leave the Senate and so become the Leader of the Parliamentary Liberal Party in the Lower House.

In a dramatic error of judgment McEwen announced that he would not serve in any ministry headed by McMahon. He did not say why, so one can merely deduce it was because of McMahon's implacable opposition to devaluation of the Australian dollar. McEwen's dog-in-the-manger attitude was to have disastrous results: McMahon was to be too old for the task when he did achieve party supremacy, but at the time of Holt's disappearance he was an able treasurer and a popular figure. McMahon stood aside and bided his time. All eighty-one Liberal members of the House of Representatives and the Senate took part in the election, for which four candidates put up: Hasluck, Snedden, Bury and Gorton. Gorton was elected on the second ballot in a straight fight with Hasluck, after Snedden and Bury

had been eliminated. The election of Gorton was not a surprise: it was a shock. John Grey Gorton was to shake the Liberal
Party to its foundations, but he was the only man with sufficient
vigour to give it a long-term chance of survival in the 1970s.

One of Gorton's first problems was with the Democratic
Labor Party. The new Foreign Minister, Gordon Freeth, alienated
conservative Catholic voters when he let slip that Australia had
been negotiating with the Soviet Union on Russian proposals
for involvement in Asian security. Freeth, reckoning without
the Democratic Labor Party, said that it was unthinkable that
Australia should take any comfort from the hostilities between
Russia and China. He announced a new conciliation policy
towards the Soviet Union's presence in the Indian Ocean and
looked forward to Russian co-operation for Asian regional
development. Freeth said that the talks between the two
governments represented a new era in Soviet-Australian
relations. The Soviet Foreign Minister, Andrey Gromyko, had
told the Supreme Soviet in July that the prerequisite and
potential for an improvement in Russian relations with Australia
existed. Leonid Brezhnev, the Secretary of the Russian
Communist Party, had at the same time spoken of the need
to create a system of collective security in Asia. To Freeth two
and two made four. It appeared to the Foreign Office that the
Soviet Union was exploring the reactions of other countries
in the area before trying to convert the idea into a detailed
proposal. Contact had been made in both Canberra and Moscow.
Freeth warned that any realistic plan for South-East Asian
regional security would have to take into account the possibility
of oppression from outside: the most likely source of aggression
being China. This was likely to be, as *The Bulletin* said, a
remarkable and possibly historic departure in government
policy if it was followed up. Senator Gair, the spokesman
for the Democratic Labor Party, was aghast. Freeth had been
caught red-handed selling Australia down the drain to the

communists. The Santamaria-Gair statement after the 1967 Senate elections was dusted off. During the 1967 Senate elections the Democratic Labor Party had improved its position, and the DLP leader, Senator Gair, said that he was determined to use DLP strength as a lever on the Liberal Party. On 7 October 1968, the federal executive of the Democratic Labor Party met and said that at the next federal election it would express dissatisfaction with the policies of the Liberal Party. Senator Gair warned the prime minister that the Democratic Labor Party would operate by not nominating candidates for certain seats, or by advising their candidates to give the vital second preference vote to non-government candidates. B. A. Santamaria, of the National Civic Council, said that the Democratic Labor Party would switch its preferences in a carefully selected number of seats. The switches would be few enough to ensure that the Australian Labor Party was not returned, unless by accident, while at the same time allowing Whitlam to clean out pro-communist influences in the party and inflicting a painful blow to the government's majority. Gorton, aware of the strength of the Democratic Labor Party, completely backed down, disowned Freeth's statement, and said that Australia was not considering the possibility of any defence arrangements with Russia.

Nor was the Gorton ministry able to handle the administration of New Guinea competently. Here he was hampered by having C. E. Barnes as responsible minister. Barnes's handling of Australian colonial responsibilities was disastrous: didactic, patronising, constantly nodding his head, Barnes had frequently cast doubts on whether Australia was really prepared to give New Guinea independence. Coalition tradition is that the Liberal leader chooses his own ministers, and naturally the Country Party leader decided how to allot his portfolios. Possibly, if Barnes had been a member of the Liberal Party, he would have lost his office immediately on Gorton's assumption of power, but as he belonged to the increasingly powerful Country Party, all that the prime minister was able to do was to take away some of Barnes's responsibilities. One cannot, of course, blame all Papua New Guinea policy on Barnes. Which other member of the cabinet had a different view?

Gorton seems to have grasped the symbolic importance of New Guinea at a very early stage. It was clearly his ministry's policy that the destiny of Papua New Guinea was to become a self-governing country. It was to become independent when it was clearly demonstrated by most of the indigenous population that that was what they wanted. New Guinea became a powder keg when Conzinc Rio Tinto began to exploit copper deposits on Bougainville. When a group of seccessionists, who styled themselves the 'Mataungan Association' opposed capitalism, the brawls, killings and bashings to be marked the emergence of a revolutionary elite, bent on turning Australians out of Papua New Guinea by force. Australians left, but lawlessness remained, and civil disorder became endemic in Papua New Guinea.

Thus Gorton was up against it when faced with his first election as prime minister on 25 October 1969. The natural growth of public interest in politics was illustrated by the record number of candidates: 499 stood for 125 seats in the House of Representatives. Gorton successfully beat off a rebellion among Liberal back-benchers: the visible sign of this being that Edward St John failed to retain his seat. St John, shortly before parliament dissolved, had criticised Gorton's leadership, and left the party to stand as an Independent. The 1969 election returned the coalition, but with a greatly reduced majority, from 38 to 7. But more significant than the party losses in the election were the signs of dissent within the party. Even before the result was announced, the Minister for National Development, David Fairbairn, said that he would not serve in any cabinet headed by Gorton and on 2 November 1969 announced that he would stand for the party leadership. It then became clear that there was a fight for power within the Liberal Party between

McMahon and Gorton: the treasurer and deputy leader announced that he intended to stand for party leadership too. Gorton was, nevertheless, elected leader of the Liberal Party on 7 November, and McMahon, deputy leader. Then followed a development for which McEwen must share responsibility. Gorton chose the occasion of election victory to settle scores and purge his opponents within the party. No longer, as in the days of Menzies and Holt, was the front bench a 'ministry of talent': it was a cabinet of henchmen.

Gorton reformed his cabinet with the air of a president of France. He banished and downgraded the Deputy Leader of the Liberal Party; Billy McMahon, protesting that he did not want to be moved, left the Treasury for Foreign Affairs. Gorton then sacked three members of the cabinet, Charles Kelly, the Navy Minister, Dudley Erwin, Minister for Air, and Senator Malcolm Scott, the Customs Minister. Scott and Kelly went quietly. In a moment of pathos Kelly sold his ministerial suit, foreseeing no further use for his striped pants. But Erwin decided to make a series of damaging attacks on Gorton that were to reduce federal Australian politics to a personal level unknown in the 1950s and 1960s. Erwin said that he had been tossed out by Gorton on account of 'a shapely political manoeuvre that wiggles', Ainslee Gotto, the prime minister's secretary. Erwin did not elaborate save to say that Gotto had denied him access to the prime minister and was ruthless and authoritarian. Erwin made clear what St John had suggested: that something was rotten with the state of the Liberal organisation. He said that six months before Holt disappeared the Liberal Party was looking for a replacement: the party machine approached Fairhall, but he would not accept the leadership, and Gorton was decided upon. Gorton promptly denied that he knew anything about the attempt to pre-elect him prime minister before Holt's disappearance: if he had known, he said, he would have informed the prime minister. It was much more difficult to deny the last of Erwin's allegations: that Gorton led a faction within the party called 'the mushroom club'. The members of this club were all in the 1969 ministry. They referred to Gorton as 'chief spore', and took as their motto regarding the back-benchers 'Keep 'em in the dark and feed 'em bullshit'. Mushroom club members who had supported Gorton were Leslie Bury, the Treasurer, Malcolm Fraser, Defence Minister, Nigel Bowen, Minister for Education and Science and Phillip Lynch, who assisted the Treasurer and was Minister for Immigration. A personification of the new man was junior minister Andrew Peacock. Peacock was thirty years old and had only been in the House three years but he was given the Army portfolio and was assistant to the prime minister. For the coalition to survive the next decade both loyal ministers and capable administrators were needed. Some were loyal, some were competent, but few were both.

CHAPTER 7

The Pygmy Chief

'What is a nice country like us doing in a political mess like that?' asked *The Bulletin* in March 1971. By that autumn, morale had sunk to its lowest ebb since Pearl Harbor. William McMahon torpedoed Gorton and took over Australia's political leadership. William McMahon, however, proved unable to woo the emerging urban middle-class voters who were strong on social concern but weak on the bread and butter economic issues motivating the trade unions and the traditional ALP voters.

During 1970–71 the conservative coalition went from bad to worse. Although they were to some extent victims of their own lack of forward planning, Gorton and McMahon, the two rivals, shared one misfortune: allegiance to President Richard Nixon. A series of about-turns by Nixon cut the ground from beneath the feet of his antipodean conservative allies: the decision to get out of Vietnam and into Red China enhanced the reputation of Nixon and Henry Kissinger (President Nixon's principal adviser on foreign policy), but cut the ground from beneath both McMahon and Gorton.

Before these dramatic diplomatic reversals, Gorton, as prime minister, faced trouble at home. At the top level the Labor Party stepped up its campaign of civil disobedience. Whereas a strong leader like Menzies could have turned this to his advantage by characterising it as a drift towards anarchy, Gorton was made to look vacillating and unsure of himself. Old certainties were questioned, and the issues were too momentous to be shrugged off. In order to govern oneself, said one Labor leader, Dr Jim Cairns, one had to exercise power where power was, and parliament was not the only place where there was power. Power also existed in schools, in universities, in factories, in government departments, in banks and everywhere else. Australians had won their democracy by breaking laws, by campaigning in the streets. Cairns was speaking as chairman of a moratorium committee that had organised street parades of 100,000 people who opposed the Vietnam war. Gough Whitlam, leader of the Labor Party, added soon afterwards that conscripts ought to give written advice, that if they were ordered to go to Vietnam, they 'would not obey the order'.

Conservatives did not want to govern themselves; they wished to be governed by Gorton. The left doubted whether it was possible to carry out Cairns's hopes, and the country seemed to be drifting into anarchy as the press described opposition leader Whitlam as sanctioning law-breaking. At this time of crisis, strong government was essential if the Liberal-Country Party was to survive, and Gorton was not able to provide it. Middle-class Australia demanded that domestic life, in the long run, should be allowed to proceed uneventfully. The bourgeoisie could hardly agree with Cairns's slogan: 'Authority has had its day'.

Gorton had to deal with difficult international and domestic policies: New Guinea sought independence, the states asked for more power over mineral exploration royalties, some of the reporters of the Australian Broadcasting Commission attacked the establishment, a huge mining company created a scandal by allotting preferential shares to state and federal cabinet ministers (most of whom declined them), immigration levels needed reassessing, the F111 delivery was delayed, and the

Vietnam war entered a new phase as the US reassessed its commitment. All of these issues demanded loyal support. And Gorton had to face not only these problems but internal manoeuvres within his party to depose him. Wool prices fell, Canadian diplomatic recognition of communist China immediately affected Australian wheat sales, Cambodia was falling, but within the Liberal Party economic issues were ignored and sections planned Gorton's removal.

In April 1970, President Nixon delivered a blow to Gorton's Cabinet. Nixon announced the fourth stage in the American withdrawal from Vietnam: the president undertook to remove 150,000 American troops from Vietnam during the next twelve months. Gorton followed suit and withdrew 1,000 troops from the Australian task force by November 1970. A regiment and its support were to leave Vietnam in November, and the cabinet decided not to replace them. Gorton explained, amid government shouts of approval and Labor cries of 'Withdraw them all now', that the decision to begin to withdraw Australian troops followed the increasing self-reliance of South Vietnam under the Vietnamisation programme. It was impossible to phase further Australian troop withdrawals into the plan because the future situation was uncertain. The cabinet had decided to help the growth of South Vietnamese self-reliance by providing a small mobile army team of 130 men to carry out training functions with the regional and popular forces in Phuoc Tuy province – the advisers would act on a pattern similar to that developed by members of the Australian Army Training Team, which would also continue to work in Vietnam. On the site vacated by the regiment Australia was to provide instructors and other aid for a South Vietnamese training centre for junior leaders, and instruction was to be given in jungle warfare.

Gorton strongly repeated the concept that Australia was helping a small country attacked from without by invaders, and added that no one should say that because there was a modification of the Australian role, therefore it should play no role at all. Gorton was on thin ice. There were simply too many ambiguities in the coalition's Vietnam policy. Cabinet ministers were divided among themselves, the Minister for Defence disagreed with the Minister for the Army, the regimental officers in Vietnam disagreed with their commander-in-chief.

The Minister for the Army, Andrew Peacock, for example, made an exhaustive tour of Army bases in Vietnam in January 1970, and talked to Vietnamese military and political leaders. The Vietnamese made it clear that the Australian government could safely send home a battalion of troops. They believed the Australian task force could operate out of its base at Nui Dat with two battalions instead of three. This view of the military situation was based on the assumption that there would be no upsurge of enemy activity in Phuoc Tuy province. But Australian regimental officers did not agree with the assessment of the leaders of South Vietnam: many field commanders believed that it was a political decision to send troops to Vietnam, and that it would be a political decision to send them home. Nor was the military situation stable. No one in the officers' mess at Nui Dat thought that the Australian job in Phuoc Tuy was finished. More than 340 diggers had lost their lives in clearing the Viet Cong main force from the populated areas, and in opening up the roads. The South Vietnamese Army was generally considered unreliable, and many feared that to withdraw prematurely, to hand over to the South Vietnamese more responsibility too quickly, would ruin years of effort.

Gorton was a flexible leader. His critics called him a weather-vane. But he was able for a time to keep pace with changes in international affairs to a degree that his chief rival, William McMahon, could not. In September 1969, Gorton announced that there was no immediate withdrawal of Australian troops intended. By April 1970 he was forced to devise 'a phased withdrawal', which began in November. The withdrawal from Vietnam was followed by the boil-over in Cambodia. When a *coup d'etat* toppled Prince Sihanouk and war began between the Vietnamese and the Cambodians, McMahon tried to thrust his views forward. It was a moment of potential disaster for the whole of South-East Asia. On behalf of the cabinet, McMahon endorsed an Indonesian proposal that a conference of Asian and Pacific countries be called to discuss the problems of Cambodia. Australia recognised the post-Sihanouk regime in Cambodia as a *de facto* government.

Despite the heat generated by a moratorium campaign of street demonstrations, which began before American troops officially crossed the Cambodian border, Gorton was calm and quiet over Australia's attitude to the Cambodia question. Gorton considered Cambodia for a week before making an eight-minute statement in the House of Representatives. The central issue was, of course, whether or not Australia would join the allies in Cambodia. Gorton said no. Australian forces were not engaged in Cambodia and he could see no prospect that they would be. The reason for the prime minister's week of silence must be a matter of speculation. But it seems that the decision not to follow America over the border marked a turning-point in Gorton's reading of Australian foreign policy needs.

It was an important departure that gave clear notice that Australian involvement in Vietnam was no longer merely a copy of Washington's views, but was based on a regional appreciation of local needs. America could – as Nixon put it in May – be in and out of Cambodia by the end of June. America could withdraw equally easily from the whole region. But Australia could not, and Gorton's decision seems to have been taken in the hope that no Australian act would harm the talks in Indonesia by South-East Asian powers on the Cambodian question. Gorton was not prepared to go all the way with the USA, but he was certainly prepared to shout encouragement across the Cambodian border, not least because this was sound political fuel for the coming domestic Senate elections. In a most adept performance which was designed to antagonise neither Americans nor friendly South-East Asians, Gorton explained that the Australian government understood the reason for the US-directed military action in Cambodia as a course designed to protect the lives of allied servicemen. He accused the Labor Party of showing a willingness, even a desire, to accept the defeat or a surrender of the allied forces in Vietnam. Gorton said that he wished to see a neutral Cambodia – a country that was not used by anyone as a battle-ground or a base, and safe from North Vietnam's oppression. With considerable enthusiasm the Labor Party characterised Gorton as pledging the government's support for the violation of Cambodia.

Lance Barnard, the Deputy Leader of the Opposition, pounced on Gorton's delay in making a statement. The old ring of confidence surrounding the government's philosophy on Vietnam had been dissolved; the impression was unmistakable that the government was re-assessing its Indo-China policy. It realised that America may have gone too far; the period of unquestioned commitment might be nearing an end. Gorton's statement on Cambodia had an ironical twist, when members of his party were forced to vote in the House of Representatives to defeat an opposition amendment supporting the prime minister's call for all foreign troops to be removed from Cambodia. While visiting Japan, Gorton had said that all foreign troops should be withdrawn from Cambodia, and that the Cambodian people should decide who should run their country. Gorton went further than Barnard by calling for the withdrawal of US troops from Cambodia. He hoped that the Jakarta Asian-Pacific conference on Cambodia would urge the complete withdrawal of all outside forces, saying it would be in the interests of the world if the North Vietnamese, South Vietnamese, Viet Cong and all those who were in Cambodia were to withdraw. But he did not believe that the withdrawal of US and South Vietnamese troops would help to achieve Cambodian neutrality if the North Vietnamese troops remained. Both Gorton and Sato, the Japanese Prime Minister, agreed on the need for Cambodian neutrality.

In the last analysis it was personal grievances that shattered the Liberal Party. The technical issue was the question of state versus federal rights to control the commonwealth's offshore minerals. The governor-general, in his speech opening parliament in 1970, announced that the government intended to acquire mineral rights over the continental shelf outside the three-mile limit. Gorton's ministry was put in jeopardy when Liberal back-benchers combined with the Labor Party. Gorton was forced to deny in the House of Representatives a statement by David Fairbairn, the former Minister for National Development, that there would be consultation with the states before the commonwealth introduced bills on mineral rights. No such undertaking had been given, said the prime minister. Gorton spoke in some detail on meetings and correspondence between state ministers, Fairbairn and himself. His remarks were intended to lay a smokescreen in which Fairbairn could be dimly seen as confused and inaccurate. Evidence was lacking: there were only brief transcripts of the discussions. The records did not support accusations of governmental dishonour. All the transcript showed was that there was an agreement to further discuss offshore mineral legislation; it did not show a government commitment to refrain from announcing federal legislation before the discussion had taken place.

As soon as Gorton had finished, the Labor Party moved a censure motion charging that Gorton and his Cabinet had failed to honour an undertaking made by Fairbairn, when he was Minister for National Development, that he would consult again with the states before he introduced offshore legislation. Dr Rex Patterson, who moved the censure motion, said it was absurd and naive to expect parliament to swallow the view that the prime minister did not know the meaning of statements he made, and that the six state ministers did not understand the undertaking that they had been given and had accepted. Gorton's attempt, said Patterson to justify the breach of confidence from stubbornness and annoyance was disgraceful. The prime minister and cabinet were grossly incompetent. Their action was high-handed. The cabinet was unfit to govern the country, and the prime minister, the principal of the sordid affair, had shown that he was not fit to be premier of the nation.

Gorton could stand Labor's criticism. His Achilles' heel was his own back bench. The prime minister's vulnerability was closely connected with his relationships with David Fairbairn and Jeff Bate. Fairbairn had previously been sacked from the conservative ministry over his part in the leadership crisis between McMahon and Gorton; and he had shown considerable animosity over Gorton's friendship with Ainslee Gotto. Jeff Bate had married Zara Holt, the former prime minister's wife. Fairbairn certainly ought to have known the details of the offshore mineral agreement. But he said that he was completely unconvinced by the prime minister's statements and complained that state ministers did not know what the Gorton government intended, until they were informed by telegram on the eve of the governor-general's speech. Fairbairn concluded that although he considered that the opposition was 'a herd of hyenas', he would vote with them as a matter of honour. He said that there was no doubt at all that there had been a commitment by the commonwealth government to respect state rights, which had been broken after last year's election. Jeff Bate and

Peter Howson, outside parliament, made it clear that they were considering crossing the floor. The government Whip, E. M. C. Fox (who appropriately was a leading wild-life conservationist), feared that there were seven possible defectors, sufficient to cause the defeat of the ministry and Gorton's resignation. The whips on both sides of the house had a hectic period rallying their parties. Many members had left to return home early, anticipating (quite wrongly) a quiet session until the weekend break. Gorton was forced to cancel his plan to fly to Brisbane to meet Canadian Prime Minister Pierre Trudeau. Trudeau was instead met, not inappropriately, by several koalas and Mrs Gorton. During the afternoon a deal was made between rebel members and the cabinet, by which time the government agreed to postpone the legislation for six months, during which further consultations could be held with the states. The rebel leaders, Bate and Howson, introduced the amended motion amid Labor cheers, and cries of 'the surrender terms'.

Gorton failed to keep up with Whitlam who, in the 1970s, repeatedly took the initiative in creating policy discussions on important matters. Whitlam went to New Guinea. Gorton followed later. Neither man emerged from New Guinea with enhanced stature, but clearly Gorton, as prime minister, had a larger reputation to lose. University students had greeted him at the airport with a squealing pig, protest songs, and placards demonstrating against alleged racism in the Territory.

The prime minister was most unwelcome in Rabaul. When he stepped from the VIP plane, Gorton was met by a roar of hate, as Mataungans waved their fists and shouted at him to go home. It was the most hostile crowd the prime minister ever faced, and he was protected by only two hundred and fifty police, shoulder to shoulder against the airport fences, supported by one hundred and fifty riot squad trainees, as they were described, armed with clubs, shields and guns. An evacuation plan was made. A helicopter and a fast launch stood by. The crowd were whipped up by their chief spokesman, John Kaputin, whose impromptu delivery of an impassioned anti-imperialist speech was recorded in Australian daily newspapers. The kernel of Kaputin's remarks was that the native people of Papua New Guinea provided only a pool of cheap labour for the Caucasians and Asiatics who controlled the country, a situation not good enough for his people. Kaputin's attack had no effect on the prime minister. On the contrary, he afterwards announced that law and order would be maintained as the first prerequisite to a stable society. On the Gazelle Peninsula Gorton warned the rebels among the Tolai that it was impossible to permit land bought by the administration to be occupied illegally by squatters. If squatting were permitted, it would retard the chance of orderly economic development, said the prime minister, therefore illegal occupation of land had to, and would be, stopped. The Tolai squatters, supported by radical Mataungans, refused to leave the land that the administration had acquired for distribution to other people as part of its attempts to ease land shortages in the area.

Thus Gorton slid down the slippery slope. He was to be deposed as leader as a result of many forces, but a crucial weakness was his failure to protect his position when handling the New Guinea situation as it reached explosion point. It was to be the Minister of Defence, Malcolm Fraser, already suffering from a sense of grievance following his dispute with the Army Minister over Vietnam, who was to be the catalyst to bring Vietnam, cabinet solidarity, New Guinea's independence and the question of state security together to oust Gorton.

As the intra-party feud developed, blows were struck with any weapon that was at hand. By the end of 1970 it was clear that the Liberal Party was in the process of destroying itself in much the same way that the Labor Party had in the mid-fifties. Coalition ministers and back-benchers did not seem to be conscious of public opinion. Their complacency seemed bound-less. In crisis after crisis they turned their backs on their critics. The coalition was on flimsier ground than it realised. To ignore the bourgeoisie and concentrate on political internecine warfare was to run the risk of being ejected from office. Once roused, the humdrum middle class was prepared to run a straight course away from the Liberals and towards Labor. Gorton, like Holt, had clearly proved to be a mistake in the eyes of a large number of Liberals. It was only McEwen's resolute opposition to McMahon's becoming the parliamentary leader of the coali-tion that kept back the assassins' knives. And on 1 February 1971, McEwen resigned as deputy prime minister, and from the House of Representatives, after thirty-six years. Gorton was unsteady as he announced the cabinet changes brought about by McEwen's departure. Douglas Anthony became leader of the Country Party and deputy prime minister. The way was then clear for a putsch: Anthony had no objection to serving under McMahon.

Thereafter, in Gorton's words, there was a definite attempt to destroy him. The missile was Malcolm Fraser, Minister for Defence, who precipitated a crisis by resigning. Gorton was the first parliamentary leader Fraser unseated but not the last. In an amazing burst of political legerdemain 'the prefect' was able to depose his own party chief Billy Snedden and, on 11 November 1975, without so much as an election shot, Prime Minister Whitlam as well. When Gorton knew that Fraser was going to resign he called a party meeting on his own initiative to try to obtain a vote of confidence, before his other opponents – the Labor Party – could organise themselves. The meeting was due to start at 11.30 AM but Gorton postponed the opening for an hour, during which he offered Fraser some sort of package deal reconciliation. During the morning Fraser and Gorton both made much the same points that were later to be heard in parliament, with the exception that Fraser kept an ace up his sleeve. After the two men had spoken, Senator Marriott called a vote of confidence, which he later withdrew under pressure from Peter Howson, John Jess and Henry Turner. This triumvirate said that they might cross the floor and vote with the Australian Labor Party if the Marriott motion was put to a vote. The reasons they gave were that they had not had time to consider all aspects of the Fraser resignation. The Liberal Party then trooped from the party room to parliament.

Gorton found himself in the stickiest situation since obtaining office on a slightly humid early autumn day. After prayers at the opening of business there were a handful of petitions to be presented. The first order of the day was about grants for flood mitigation: the flood of disapproval about Gorton would not, however, be stemmed. God was asked to vouchsafe His blessing, the Lord's Prayer concluded. After a few coughs Whitlam rose to ask immediately that the house suspend standing orders, and that the petitions be stood over, and that routine business of the house be stopped. Everyone knew that Fraser was about to set the cat among the pigeons. Then Fraser made a ferocious attack on the prime minister. Choking with emotion, Fraser said that Gorton, since he had been elected prime minister, had seriously damaged the Liberal Party and cast aside the stability and sense of direction of earlier times. He had a dangerous reluctance to consult the cabinet, and an obstinate determination to get his own way. He ridiculed the advice of a great public service unless it supported his own view.

The example Fraser took to illustrate his point was one of great moment. It involved the most sensitive area of Australian domestic and foreign policy, the call-out of the Pacific Islands Regiment during the mid-year riots in 1970 on the Gazelle Peninsula of Papua New Guinea. During the Gazelle Peninsula riots, there was the possibility of a clash with the Mataungan Association and it was likely that the police might not be able to control the situation. Gorton therefore asked Fraser to call out the Pacific Islands Regiment, but did not wish this issue to be discussed by cabinet. The prime minister's attitude was, 'This is the course I want, and that's all there is to it.' The first Fraser heard of the matter was when he was asked to arrange for a call-out of the Pacific Islands Regiment on 14 July 1970. He then sought advice from his department that showed that the legal requirements for the call-out had not been fulfilled and, according to Fraser, told the prime minister that he would not sign the order until the cabinet had been consulted and the legal considerations fulfilled. Fraser concluded by underlining the points to be stressed: the Pacific Islands Regiment could have been reinforced from Australia; Australian troops could have had to fire on people from Papua New Guinea; the prime minister did not believe that cabinet discussion was warranted; the prime minister fought to prevent cabinet discussion.

Amid yells of 'Hear! Hear!' Fraser concluded, 'Because of his unreasoned drive to get his own way, his obstinacy, impetuous and emotional reactions, [he] has imposed strains on the Liberal Party, the government and the Public Service. I do not believe he is fit to hold the great office of prime minister, and I cannot serve in his government.'

Without being announced, Gorton immediately replied that Fraser could not claim that at any time he had been interfered with, obstructed, or not supported in carrying out the functions of a Minister for Defence. He puffed his way quietly through a detailed refutation. Gorton's reply was reasonable, but it was not enough to save his office.

Without exception, the daily press in Australia predicted the outcome. In the event there was a three-hour meeting of the party on 10 March 1971. Gorton declared that the situation was the most serious that the party had ever experienced, and that he wanted the leadership issue settled before parliament met that same day to hear a Labor Party motion of no confidence. Alan Jarman and Leonard Reid moved and seconded a motion of confidence in Gorton, and immediately Fairbairn began a long, hostile speech, during the course of which he criticised the prime minister for his handling of commonwealth/state relations, and pointed out how many 'unfortunate experiences' the party had known under Gorton. These were elaborated on in all Australia's morning newspapers: Hasluck's departure to the governor-generalship, McMahon's removal from the Treasury, quarrels with Ministers Fairbairn, Howson, Fairhall and Erwin (all of whom were sacked, or moved from their portfolios), and the difficulties arising from Gorton's imperious secretary, Ainslee Gotto, to which were added the St John, Wood and Fraser quarrels. Jarman then pointed out – it was a crucial point, which the ALP was able to make with great effect in G. M. Bryant's speech on the matter – that the opposition to Gorton came from the press, and the press alone. When the vote was taken it stood at a deadlock negative: 33–33. The Liberal Party was not only divided, it was split down the middle. At that point Gorton cast his vote against himself. In a leadership ballot held immediately after, McMahon, as expected, defeated the Minister for Labour and National Service, Snedden.

McMahon was the first prime minister from New South Wales for twenty-two years, and the first New South Wales non-Labor prime minister since W. M. Hughes was defeated in 1923. Gorton successfully contested and won the post of deputy leader of the party and immediately took up the defence portfolio vacated by his assassin, Fraser. The Adelaide *Advertiser* commented, wrongly as it turned out, that there was little doubt that McMahon possessed qualities in which Gorton was deficient, being less impulsive and less addicted to the one-man-band style. The Liberal Party postponed the moment when it was to face a motion of no confidence. Parliament rose to give McMahon a chance to select his ministry, and sat again on the Ides of March. But by that stage the ministry had still not been selected, probably because it seemed prudent not to give Whitlam any concrete appointments to criticise in the course of the no-confidence motion. In the absence of information about ministerial changes, Whitlam found it difficult to establish the point that the new government was the same as the old. The ground was also cut from beneath him by McMahon's tactic of using the occasion of a no-confidence motion to announce that the government had decided to increase the pension rate. Certainly public opinion was more interested in the details of the new pension rate than in the debate on the no-confidence motion.

Whitlam and the Labor Party used their time discussing Gorton in a most uncharacteristic fashion: they came to praise him, not to bury him. Gorton had, Whitlam believed, a vision of sorts, vague and incoherent as it was. But he could not think it through, or follow anything through, so he was dragged down by the very hands that raised him. To give him his due, he had raised expectations among the public, and Whitlam acknowledged that it would be easier for the Australian Labor Party to tackle some of the overdue problems in Australia because Gorton was one Liberal who acknowledged their existence. In the first of a series of backhanded compliments, Whitlam said that Gorton had committed the unforgivable sin in the Liberal code, he had made the establishment uncomfortable. As a result, the order went out that he had to go, and his severest critics, his most constant critics in the government, were clearly, visibly and audibly members of the establishment. It was Whitlam's view that the change in leadership had not altered the tensions, dissensions and selfishness of the Liberal Party. His view was that the issues were still utterly unresolved and could be resolved only by an election which would allow Australians to pass judgment on the extraordinary events of the past week by giving their vote on who should govern them.

The most telling speech of all was made by Kim Beazley, who argued powerfully and with a good deal of effect that the prime minister was destroyed by Sir Frank Packer and other press barons. He produced evidence to support his claim that the destruction of Gorton was planned by the press proprietors, and not by the working journalists. Clyde Cameron described Gorton as a great, strong, tough and courageous man if ever there was one: he had come into parliament as only John Grey Gorton could, and announced that his party had stabbed him in the back and that they had appointed 'this little pygmy'. Cameron withdrew his remark after complaints to the Speaker about the term 'pygmy', immediately pointing out that parliament could hardly fail to recognise the likeness. *The Times* described Gorton as a larrikin, pointing out that it was inevitable that a larrikin king of an establishment party would be deposed. Gorton unconvincingly described the week's events as a complete surprise. He thought that the charges that he had dominated the cabinet were absolutely ridiculous. Rarely had there been a cabinet with so much cabinet discussion; he did not think that he had ever ridden roughshod over his colleagues. His last remarks, on leaving the prime minister's lodge, were that he did not feel bitter, but he felt disappointed: he thought that the coalition could have won the 1972 election. Gorton clearly believed that it had little chance with McMahon as leader.

From the time McMahon became prime minister, the Labor Party began to pick up ground strongly. The coalition lost the first crucial initiative over China. When the Canadians recognised Mao's China, there were ominous developments for the Australian economy that could not help but affect the hip-pocket nerve of the bourgeoisie. Two weeks after Canada announced that it intended to recognise the government in

Peking, not the regime in Taiwan, the Canadian wheat board sold 98,000,000 bushels of wheat to the Chinese, the biggest sale ever made to a single country over a twelve-month period by the Canadian wheat board.

Whitlam was able to take the initiative over China as he had over New Guinea. The Labor shadow minister, Rex Patterson, was asked by the Labor Party to visit China in order to explain that when the socialists became the government in 1972, the conservatives' policy would be reversed. This move proved so popular that Whitlam decided (it was a decade before the use of the fax machine) to telegraph the Chinese leader, Chou En-Lai, to ask for permission for a full-scale party delegation to visit China. The telegram ran:

AUSTRALIAN LABOR PARTY ANXIOUS TO SEND DELEGATION TO PEOPLE'S REPUBLIC OF CHINA TO DISCUSS TERMS ON WHICH YOUR COUNTRY IS INTERESTED IN HAVING DIPLOMATIC AND TRADE RELATIONS WITH AUSTRALIA. WOULD APPRECIATE YOUR ADVICE WHETHER YOUR GOVERNMENT WOULD BE ABLE TO RECEIVE DELEGATION.

McMahon was sure that there was no chance Chou En-Lai would agree to the visit. He taunted Whitlam about the delay the Chinese made in replying. But it was less than a month before Whitlam received a telegram from the Chinese People's Institute of Foreign Affairs, which announced that an ALP delegation would be welcome to China in mid-June, the purpose of the visit being for discussions on questions concerning relations between the two countries. Immediately McMahon announced a government about-turn: the Australian government had noted the rapid succession of events that suggested a marked development in the willingness of the Chinese People's Republic to deal with the rest of the world, and decided on 11 May 1971 to explore the possibilities of establishing a dialogue with the Chinese government.

The Chinese Prime Minister met Whitlam on 6 July 1971. Whitlam had a particularly difficult task. On the one hand, he had to appear in the Australian press as the potential radical prime minister; on the other, he had to give the impression of conservative solidarity to the middle-class Australians who would have to vote him in at the 1972 elections. The tone of the meeting was very much like that of the past occasions when the west tried to charm the Chinese who held the whip hand. Chou En-Lai asked questions, Whitlam provided answers. The most touchy issue was the role of Japan in Asia. Chou En-Lai asked if Whitlam intended to go to Japan on 14 July. Chou next asked whether the ALP advocated the withdrawal of all Australian forces in Vietnam, and the withdrawal of foreign troops from other countries. Whitlam continued his catechism by responding that the ALP from 1965 had consistently advocated the withdrawal of United States and Australian troops, and the foreign troops in Korea and Czechoslovakia. Why, asked Chou En-Lai, did Whitlam not include Japan? Chou then asked whether the ANZUS Treaty was, in the eyes of the ALP, directed against Japanese militarism. Whitlam then entered into a shadowy area where public opinion was uncharted. Casting caution to the east wind, he recalled how Australia had only been attacked by one country in its history – Japan. Australian cities were bombed; territories for which Australia was responsible were invaded; Australians fought the Japanese through South-East Asian islands for three and a half years. So Australians at that time had a fear of the Japanese, the same fear of the Japanese that Whitlam believed the Chinese had in 1972. Chou observed that both the Chinese and Australian people had similar sentiments. On mutual ground, Whitlam added that China had had a longer struggle. Australia, said Whitlam, had always led a peaceful life until the Japanese attacked.

Whitlam emerged from his trip to China as a national leader of international standing, and in a formidable position to contest the 1972 elections. His position was reinforced when President

Nixon announced that he intended to visit Peking. Both McMahon and Whitlam were taken by surprise. A few hours before Nixon's statement, McMahon was in Devonport, Tasmania, explaining to the Tasmanians that Australia would have to look forward in the long term to normal relations with China. McMahon argued that China's new interest in the outside world did not reflect a change of heart. From the content of McMahon's Devonport speech it seems that all McMahon knew of the Nixon plan to go to China was that the president was to make a statement on China. Obviously the need for secrecy was a prime one in Kissinger's negotiations, so it is unlikely that McMahon was given any hint of what was in the wind. But although he had been by-passed by the US government, he promptly released a statement in which he said that he welcomed without reservation President Nixon's statement on the United States relationship with the People's Republic of China and Nixon's intention to visit China in 1972. Whitlam was jubilant and no doubt correctly so. While McMahon could claim that the ALP trip to China was an awful farce, Whitlam could point to the rapidly growing queue to meet Chou En-Lai that McMahon would have to join. McMahon tried (rather unconvincingly) to stress that the president's purpose of normalising relations with China had been the publicly announced policy of the Australian government for some time. Indeed, argued McMahon, Nixon's anxiety to seek normalisation of relations and exchange views of questions of concern precisely described what the Australian government itself had been seeking to do through diplomatic channels in Paris.

The Deputy Leader of the Labor Party, Lance Barnard, in a few sentences, pointed out that never had an Australian prime minister been so humiliated by the rapid evolution of international diplomacy as had McMahon; never had an Australian prime minister had to eat his words so abjectly.

While Whitlam and Chou En-Lai were engaged in a dialogue in Peking, Kissinger was waiting in the wings. Nixon and Kissinger delivered the *coup de grâce* to the fatuities McMahon had mumbled about the ALP delegation to China. Barnard recalled how McMahon had jibed at Whitlam, saying that Chou En-Lai had Whitlam on a hook and had played him as a fisherman played a trout. Was McMahon now to argue that Chou En-Lai was angling in the same way with Nixon and Kissinger? To borrow the fishing parlance that McMahon was so fond of, it appeared to Barnard that the prime minister's status was that of a stunned mullet. McMahon had said that Chou En-Lai had made his meeting with Whitlam into an international propaganda exercise. Did McMahon claim that Kissinger's presence in China and his dialogue with Chou En-Lai amounted to the same thing? McMahon had said that Chou En-Lai advised Nixon on how to run his administration and had said that this was an impertinence to Nixon which would not be forgotten. If this were so, why was Nixon going to China to meet an impertinent Chinese leader who was so rude to him? This, he concluded, was typical of the legion of absurdities and inaccuracies in McMahon's words.

There were, nevertheless, consistent positive policies carried out by the coalition despite the leadership change, and the post-Gorton period saw some of the usual divisions within the opposition. An illustration of both aspects was given by the debate on immigration. The 1970s saw a re-examination of Australia's traditional views on the desirability of a high level of immigration. The Minister for Immigration, Phillip Lynch, was in part making a virtue of necessity when he called for a five-point study to evaluate the current Australian migration policy in July 1970. He had just returned from an overseas immigration drive, no doubt aware that rising standards in Europe were more likely to attract Europeans from Australia than to it. Lynch said that Australia would have to contrive to attract migrants at a high level in the 1970s, but increasingly the implications of immigration would have to be related more closely to total progress, including non-material and environmental considerations. Five new studies would be begun to review the benefits and costs to Australia of immigration, investigating the desirable future population level, and conducting a survey of up to 10,000 people on the experiences of migrants during their first years in Australia. Authorities on urbanisation and environment were to be appointed as consultants to the immigration programme, and there was to be closer liaison and mutural exchange with the country that shared Australia's problems most nearly, Canada.

Ironically the coalition paid the penalty for its success: the Liberal-Country Party had given the country economic prosperity and from a secure vantage point Australians began to look more closely at social issues. The Children's Hospital at Alice Springs, for example, investigated Aboriginal mortality. Women's organisations lobbied for reforms affecting their status in society. Child-minding centres were needed for working mothers. Abortion law amendment was in the air. There was a growing reluctance to accept the official view that secrecy was in the national interest where internal security organisations were concerned. A country with both wealth and leisure wanted to see the establishment of a film and television school for the masses. Popular culture was preferred to an opera house elite. Both government and independent schools vociferously demanded additional Treasury assistance. Conservationists were not prepared to accept that the commonwealth had no power to protect the Great Barrier Reef from pollution, and they sought the preservation of native flora and fauna. There was no repercussion when, during 1964, Alan Moorehead deplored in the magazine *Animals* how one could buy tinned kangaroo meat in San Francisco, Valparaiso and Hamburg. But 1970 was conservation year in Europe and by 1971 many Australians were calling for an end to intraparty bickering.

The 1970s saw the boom in business. Multinational corporations battled in Australia for the spoils of progress. Examples of multinational takeovers were easy to see. One was in the field of confectionery. Australians supplemented their enormous consumption of tranquillisers, bowel-openers and analgesics with confectionery. In 1970 Australia produced 226,000,000 pounds of confectionery. On a per tooth basis Australians were third in the consumption after the United States and Britain. In the 1960s, takeovers completely changed the structure of the industry. In November 1971 the Australian firm of James Stedman Ltd was the subject of a takeover bid by the British based Rowntree-Mackintosh, which was opposed by the Australian firm Life Savers, sweetening their offer with outbursts of patriotism. In other spheres the takeover by multinationals was equally disturbing. British Tobacco, as part of its diversification programme, moved into frozen food. Philip Morris took over Lindeman Wines. Dunlop Australia, with assets of $39,300,000 in 1971, moved into the takeover field after its profits sagged in 1966 to $3,400,000. By 1971, it controlled most of Australia's clothing industry: 60 per cent of its profit in 1970 came from shoes, pantyhose, stockings, lingerie, bras and girdles, raincoats, knitwear, socks, shirts, sportswear, suits, fashion and furnishing fabrics, mattresses, sheets, dinghies and pillowslips – the other 40 per cent came from its traditional base of rubber and industrial products.

The Liberal-Country Party seemed to have no answer to the multinationals, and the general air of confusion and dissolution was caught by Bruce Petty's *See It My Way* and *Australian History*, a pair of animated cartoon film glimpses of contemporary Australia. *See It My Way* and *Australian History* were sophisticated and relevant, audacious, sharp, innovatory. They surrounded social issues with wit and satire. They gave more than Petty's personal vision of contemporary Australia – it was a vision shared by influential sections of the middle class.

Prime Minister McMahon, when interviewed on television by the visiting British television personality David Frost, revealed that he prayed to God frequently, and that he considered election victory a suitable subject for intercession. Australians tried to avoid watching political broadcasts, but Frost was entertainment – no one seems to have missed McMahon's gaffe. McMahon was extremely unfortunate to fall into the trap. It is doubtful whether this *faux pas* even represented his real views. In 1963, for instance, the editor of *The Bulletin*, Peter Coleman, interviewed McMahon and asked, 'Which theologians influenced you most?' McMahon answered, 'I think William Temple. His *Christus Veritas* and *Christ's Revelations of God* can be read and re-read. Also Moss's *The Christian Faith* and Cyril Garnett's *Church and State*. But my reading has been pretty cosmopolitan, including G. S. Lewis [sic], J. B. Phillips and lately John Robinson's *Honest to God*. My own view is that religion is intensely personal and it's unwise to try and mix it with politics. The dangers of insincerity and hypocrisy are too real.'

Those who did pray for a Liberal-Country Party election victory were unsuccessful. The successful economic policies of the conservatives, and the massive inflow of foreign capital, had sparked an optimistic and confident air in the business world. Despite the beginning of an ominous economic downturn in 1972, with affluence went confidence, and sufficient members of the middle class chose to upset the *status quo* and give Labor an opportunity to redistribute wealth and power in the community. It was a slim chance. In reality, the bourgeoisie could be confident that there were no deep dark schemes for nationalisation laid behind the wall of The Lodge in Canberra when Labor held office in the 1970s. The only serious threat – if threat it was – of social reform came from the extra-parliamentary Labor movement. 'When Labor speaks who is really talking?' asked the New South Wales Liberal Party, showing a photograph of the charismatic trade union leader Bob Hawke holding a mask to Whitlam's face. Hawke (who at that stage held a positive public image) was after all a graduate of Oxford University, a Rhodes scholar, and a product of middle-class meritocracy.

The attempt to draw Hawke as a bogey man failed. The myth of trade union militants dominating a puppet government was not swallowed. Labor was believed to be reformist and liberal, not radical; Whitlam's own image was that of a capable moderate. The new prime minister's dilemma was how to introduce policies that were sufficiently new and nationalist. These needed to be sufficiently attractive to make it worthwhile upsetting the post-war balance, while at the same time representing a continuity of development, so that the electorate could be sure that there was no red flag behind the scenes. And this he had to accomplish with a cabinet elected by caucus containing mavericks, critics, even socialists, who would not hesitate to rock the boat in much the same way that Gorton had rocked the establishment. Moreover, Whitlam had to get his crypto-radical measures through a conservative Upper House in which the Democratic Labor Party was prepared to commit suicide in order to bring the Labor Party down.

By the middle of 1972 it was clear that 23 years of Liberal-Country Party rule were likely to come to an end. Labor hoped to bring McMahon down with a two-pronged strategy: it involved a defensive operation to maintain the status quo in Western and South Australia, and an offensive to break through in the east.

McMahon tried to make the campaign a low-key one. It was the first election for years that was fought without emotive calls to arms against external threats. As the campaign wound down, Labor concentrated on education reforms, McMahon trying to project his vision of a wholesome society. Both leaders were confident. McMahon's policy was dictated by what he considered was the state of public opinion. Since women's liberation was a social issue, he promised to establish a Royal Commission into the status of Australian women, and said that the government would make more money available for education. He promised a pension increase, and help for the states to develop their transport systems. Since Aboriginals were an obviously cantankerous minority, and justifiably so, he proposed to establish a national centre for Aboriginals under an all-Aboriginal advisory council elected by Aboriginals only. His policy speech was unimaginative and less dynamic than the Labor Party's. Whitlam had some concrete proposals, but only one of these might be described as mildly socialist. He said that he would begin a nation-wide health scheme, aimed to cover both hospital and doctors' fees, and under which 350,000 families would be exempt from contributions. The rest of Whitlam's ideas reflected a realistic appraisal of international affairs. Projected foreign policy changes included recognition of communist China, the withdrawal of an Australian troop garrison in Singapore, and the effective end of Australian participation in SEATO.

Labor suggestions were not different enough to encourage a voting swing from the conservatives to the socialists. What made the electorate move was the clear ineptitude of Billy McMahon as prime minister. Symptomatic of his unsuitability was his attack on his cabinet on the eve of the poll. They were too slow in making decisions, McMahon said, so all too often he had to make policy decisions on behalf of tardy ministers who could not make up their minds. Billy Snedden, the Treasurer and Deputy Leader of the Liberal Party, tried to paper over the crack. He protested that he had supported McMahon, who must have been misreported. McMahon had always worked with a loyal and energetic ministry. The Country Party leader, Doug Anthony, agreed with Snedden. The Foreign Minister, Nigel Bowen, was dusted off and appeared on television to give a more pleasing smile and a better polished performance in the campaign. But the damage was done. The cat was out of the bag. McMahon had shown that his style of government was really no different from Gorton's. It was impossible not to be disillusioned by this revelation. To what extent the disillusion would be fatal was not known, but it was clear that the years of Menzies's autocracy had sapped the coalition's will and ability to act collectively.

Why did Labor win? Was it a party victory or a personal triumph? Did McMahon simply lose? Or was Whitlam responsible for the greatest shake-up of national political life since 1949? The answer lies in a set of circumstances similar to those which existed in 1949. As *The Times* editor said, the pledges of both parties were competitive, so it was natural for the electorate to entrust their implementation to fresh rather than tired leaders' arms. Nevertheless, the government was turned out by a swing only half as big as that in 1949, when the coalition began its twenty years of unbroken power, and the narrowness of the margin was not without its effect on Labor policy. The *Age* believed that the people had voted for a vision of the future, for new ideas in government, for new initiatives and for new directions. Menzies caught the spirit. He sent Whitlam a telegram of congratulation, wishing him mental vigour and physical health, and observing, 'You have been emphatically called to an office of great power and responsibility.'

The Times, in a massive overstatement under the headline 'Another Labor Victory down under', said that both Australia and New Zealand were at turning-points in their history. With Britain's entry into the EEC many of the old certitudes were gone, leaving Whitlam with the task of finding a new role for Australia as neither a client of Britain nor of the United States. *The Times* was behind the times: Menzies had begun that process over a decade before.

CHAPTER 8

Stuffed

Historians agree that in the twenty-five years following World War II Australia became an affluent society. The economic policies put into effect by the wartime and post-war Labor governments, and followed generally by their conservative successors, had a stabilising influence on the economy and also some positive effects in encouraging growth. There was no attempt to redistribute the new affluence until the 1970s when, for a period, the middle class found its conscience and voted in a reformist administration. The efforts of the reformers came up against the world-wide general economic downturn, of which the oil crisis was the most dramatic illustration. Aspirations were directed to ends which the nation could not supply.

The years 1949–72 saw the radical left tolerate the conservative power bloc, because the working-class base of Labor politics was 'embourgeoised', that is to say that while blue-collar workers were gradually moving upwards in society they were content to rely on peaceful and reformist strategies. When the workers saw, in 1972, that the gradual upward movement of the blue-collar class meant nothing in terms of relativity to the middle class, they were prepared to try harder to defeat the conservative government. But blue-collar pressure was not sufficient: it had after all been exercised throughout the

1950s and the 1960s, with various degrees of distraction from the Catholic anti-communist wing of the party.

What really counted, and what withdrew first the conservatives' mandate, and then in December 1975, the Australian Labor Party's, was the changing sensibilities of a small section of the middle class. This new group of cosmopolitan 'trendies', as they were described in a pejorative description of their propensity to adopt new fashions, was prepared to give the underprivileged a go. But when the dream of the good society soured under the pressure of economic realities, the middle class withdrew their mandate to govern again, just as capriciously as they had done in 1972. While the middle class had been pathfinders in the search for a new society, in the 1975 election they were the cork on the tide of popular disapproval. The conservatives did not win the 1975 election, Labor lost it.

Whitlam conceded defeat on 13 December 1975, shaken and bewildered. He took office, jubilant, on 5 December 1972. Since he wished to deal immediately with what he considered urgent domestic and foreign policy issues, Whitlam took immediate responsibility for thirteen portfolios and his deputy, Lance Barnard, assumed fourteen until caucus elected a full ministry. Whitlam said that his intention was to develop a more constructive, flexible and progressive approach to foreign policy issues. He wanted an Australia that would be less militarily orientated and not open to suggestions of racism, an Australia that would enjoy a growing standing as a distinctive, tolerant, co-operative and well-regarded nation, not only in the Asian and Pacific regions, but also in the world at large. The rest of Whitlam's remarks might have been made by Menzies in 1949: they were the politicians' stock-in-trade, with the difference that where Menzies spoke of standards, Whitlam spoke of standing. Whitlam's victory was a victory for the bourgeoisie, not the workers. The prime minister's wife,

Margaret, epitomised the middle-class values she and her husband and the swinging voters swung for. Her expressed concerns were trivial and domestic, and her first thoughts were on the issue of whether she would still be able to put her leg of lamb in the oven on Sundays. Gough and Margaret Whitlam represented the solid virtue of the middle class, and the narrowness of their horizon.

The Liberal-Country Party changed their leader after electoral defeat. At the beginning of his last party meeting as leader, Billy McMahon said that he would stand aside. Nothing became him in office so much as his leaving of it. He was succeeded by Billy Snedden, who was elected in inauspicious circumstances. Snedden had to face no less than five ballots, and beat the eventual runner-up, Nigel Bowen, by only one vote. The other leadership candidates were all connected with the downfall of the post-Menzies Liberal Party: Gorton, Fraser and James Killen. In the first ballot, Jim Killen, Minister for the Navy in Gorton's cabinet, was eliminated; in the next Gorton, who had been prime minister from 1968 to 1971, was put out. Third to go was Malcolm Fraser, the pneumonic master of 'Nareen', whose triumph was a bare three years away. In the first ballot between the survivors, Nigel Bowen and Billy Snedden, one of the fifty-nine Liberal MPs neglected to vote, and the vote was tied. In the second and final ballot, Snedden won by a single vote.

Robert Southey, the federal President of the Liberal Party, attributed defeat to the party organisation's lack of control over its parliamentary members. Southey, who ought to have known, admitted that the personal ambitions and feuds inside the parliamentary Liberal Party since the death of Harold Holt had been deadly and destructive. That sort of conduct had to be buried with the past. If it were not, the organisation's authority over the endorsement of candidates might have to be employed ruthlessly. The interests of the party transcended those of the individual; the party as a whole, and not any section of it, had to shape the party's future. The Labor movement spoke of 'the machine', Liberals of 'the organisation'. But both saw the lesson of 1972 to be that party discipline was essential if the electorate was not to be disillusioned.

Whitlam's first reforms were piecemeal. He instructed Governor-General Hasluck to remit the prison sentences on the seven young men who had failed to comply with the National Service Act. He cancelled the commonwealth list of new year's honours. He declined to follow tradition and become a Privy Councillor, as all other Australian prime ministers had been. But he did not follow through and cancel the vice-regal link with the monarchy by abolishing the office of governor-general – a mistake he was to regret. On the contrary, he was proud to call Hasluck an intimate friend, one with whom a prime minister might be happy to drink a bottle of champagne. Whitlam protested about the French nuclear tests, and ineffectually threatened court action in The Hague to stop them. But, while the Australian Ballet boycotted French make-up and perfume as a practical gesture, Whitlam and Hasluck sipped French and not Australian champagne together. This extravagance was one of the first signs that Whitlam was going to antagonise the bourgeoisie by ostentation. His purchase of a white Mercedes with the special number '1' was in the same vein. A more sensitive minister would have driven an old FJ Holden, as one of them did.

Whitlam's recognition of communist China might be considered a break with tradition. Both Australia and New Zealand returned social democratic governments at the end of 1972, and together Whitlam and Norman Kirk, the New Zealand Prime Minister, were agreed that recognition was logical and sensible. The Chinese and Australian ambassadors in Paris arranged the establishment of diplomatic relations. On 21 December 1972, Alan Renouf and Huang Chen signed a joint communiqué. The two countries had decided to establish diplomatic relations immediately. Australia recognised the People's Republic as the sole legal government of China, acknowledged that Taiwan was a province of the People's Republic and agreed to remove its ambassador from Taiwan before 25 January 1973. Whitlam appointed Stephen FitzGerald Australian Ambassador to China on 9 January 1973. By establishing relations, Australia was merely coming into line with the rest of the world, as was the case when Whitlam decided to follow Canada into recognition of North Vietnam. This was a heart-breaking decision for the many Australians who had for almost a decade considered the countries at war, and agreed with the coalition's projection of Hanoi as an aggressor and a dangerous tool of Mao Tse-tung.

One of the most crucial areas where foreign policy differences might have been expected was in Australia's relationship with the United Kingdom. At first sparks flew when Whitlam chose John Ignatius Armstrong as the new Australian High Commissioner in London. This post was traditionally not given to career diplomats, as the Australian High Commission was used as a sounding board for government policy initiatives. Almost immediately John Armstrong predicted the establishment of an Australian Republic and the breaking up of the Commonwealth. He spoke of bad friends and feelings being made at the time Britain decided to join the EEC, and said that malevolence had been exacerbated when the British handled Australians like aliens. With a resentful smile Armstrong noted that Britain had put Europeans in a position where Britain's former rivals and enemies were in a better position than their friends who fought with them.

Attorney-General Lionel Murphy was rather more conciliatory than the new high commissioner. He stressed that Australia's new socialist government was looking forward to a period of intensive co-operation with Britain, and assured the British government that immense amounts of goodwill towards Britain existed in Australia. This reassurance was necessary, as it was Murphy's task to supervise the ending of the constitutional and legal ties between Australia and Britain. While appeal to the Privy Council was irritating, Murphy stressed the continuity of policy and institutions within the Commonwealth framework. The prime minister had considered it was undesirable that the Australian states should constitutionally remain British colonies where governors flew the Union Jack. The objectionable feature of the Privy Council was that its judicial committee judges were appointed by the British government, and that it sat in the United Kingdom. Murphy admitted that Privy Council powers had fallen into disuse over the years, but argued that their presence was demeaning. He was sure that Britain would be as anxious as the new Australian government to get rid of the last continuing relics of colonialism. Much as both protested to the contrary, the policies of socialists and conservatives at that time boiled down to the same thing. In 1968 the Liberal-Country Party government itself limited appeals to the Privy Council to those against the Australian High Court on matters that did not involve the exercise of federal jurisdication, such as, for example, the test case on whether a child could claim damages for injuries suffered while in its mother's womb. The commonwealth actually terminated appeals to the judicial committee of the Privy Council from September 1968. The former attorney-general, Ivor Greenwood, said that Murphy was challenging the crown and the governor-general. Labor had cause to rue that it did not follow through and consign the viceroy to oblivion with the Privy Council link.

In practical terms, the first indication of how the wind was blowing came over the knotty question of British immigration. Whereas Australia had touted for British migrants after the war, by 1972 the situation was dramatically altered. Whitlam's Minister for Immigration was Albert Grassby, whose first task was to reduce the number of migrants to be admitted to Australia from the figure of 140,000 fixed by the coalition to 110,000. Promotional advertising for migrants overseas was replaced by the establishment of small task forces in Australia's capital cities who would be co-ordinated with welfare organisations and relevant government departments.

Under Grassby, immigration was synchronised with Australia's labour needs and planned in close co-operation with regional planning bodies. Eligibility for assisted passages was reviewed. Until the unemployment situation improved, careful control of the types and numbers of immigrants was necessary and changes in the national pattern of employment were to be considered in shaping future immigration programmes. A new emphasis was placed on family reunion and sponsorship. Since too many migrants were leaving Australia, Grassby proposed to improve selection techniques overseas and give more help to newly arrived settlers. Grassby claimed to abolish racial consideration in the selection of migrants and described the coalition as having an invidious white Australia policy. He made great play with the decision to allow coloured New Zealanders, and natives from the Cook and Polynesian islands, into the country.

The essential similarity between Liberal and Labor policy was revealed when Grassby pointed out that 'non-Caucasians' would be judged on their qualifications (economic potential, medical fitness, ability to resettle and stay in Australia, and character record), and on their likelihood of blending into Australian society. Grassby was working in a tradition of liberalisation that had begun in 1945. The coalition, without publicity, had modified the racial ban in stages. The non-whites allowed in were permitted to become Australian citizens after extended residence. Holt reduced this from fifteen years to five. By 1972 the coalition was admitting about 4,000 blacks and 6,000 people of mixed blood a year. Nevertheless, both parties had their diehards who were criticised as being racist.

Grassby's changes to immigration policy were more psychologically than legally significant. The words 'British subject' were dropped, leaving only the description 'citizen of Australia': this might have been done in 1948 after the passage of the 1948 British Nationality Act. Grassby had not proposed, as he might have, that assisted settlers would have to take out Australian citizenship after a set period, because the number of returning British settlers was already embarrassingly and uneconomically high. Immigration had only been slowed to help stop inflation. It would reduce pressure on housing and education expenses, and reinforce the effect of the upward revaluation of the dollar. In conformity with the refurbished racial policy, which promised a new deal for Aboriginals, colour was not to be a criterion for immigration. Technically it was not, anyway. But it seemed racist that coloured British immigrants, even when accepted as migrants, could be refused the subsidised fare.

Whitlam's first month showed more innovations of style than of matter. It had to be admitted, however, that, under Grassby, the political beliefs of migrants were no longer to be a criterion for admission. Yugoslavian separatists and members of the communist parties were to be allowed into Australia without a security veto if they fulfilled the other necessary criteria. The trend was away from special treatment for United Kingdom migrants, and it was deliberately sponsored by the Labor government. The search for a new national anthem and the deletion of the reference to the Queen in the Australian oath of allegiance were part of the same phenomenon. On Australia Day 1973, Whitlam revealed that a small group of established writers and composers, and some members of the public, would be invited to compose a new national anthem. Since federation, 'God Save the Queen' had been sung whenever a national anthem was needed. Whitlam said that a new national anthem was long overdue, and that he had no doubt it was fervently desired by most Australians. As in the heats of the Eurovision song contest, the final choice was to be made by popular vote after television and radio had played a selected group of entries. A prize of $5,000 was to be given and a decision was to be made by Anzac Day. Whitlam's suggestion was not new. Gorton had expressed a preference for 'Waltzing Matilda' as a national anthem, and McMahon also thought that 'God Save the Queen' might have been replaced by a more appropriate lyric. In a typical compromise, Whitlam noted that 'God Save the Queen' would continue to be sung when the Queen was present, or when it was especially necessary to establish Australia's link with the crown. No doubt such an occasion arose when Whitlam unsuccessfully asked British Prime Minister Alec Douglas-Home for his support in the ineffectual attempts to stop French nuclear bomb testing in the Pacific.

On 26 January 1973 Whitlam also announced that the government had decided to establish an Australia Council for the Arts which would administer government support for the arts. The new council was divided into seven boards, which were responsible for the theatre, visual arts, music, literature, crafts, film and television, and Aboriginal art. The beginnings of this trend were made by Menzies with the establishment of the Australian Elizabethan Theatre Trust. With the exception of television, organisations already existed that would have continued to perform their functions adequately, and without the additional expense to the Treasury that this new bureaucratic superstructure involved. The infrastructure generally existed. In sponsoring a television academy, Whitlam was following the lead set by Gorton, whose support for a national television school was one of the first projects scrapped by McMahon when he came into office. Gorton was the favourite of Australian thespians (was he not prepared to appear on the Norman Gunston show?) and Whitlam might justly be characterised in this reform, as in many others, of carrying on the policies that Gorton would have carried on if he had been given the chance by the more conservative members of the coalition cabinet.

It might have been thought that Frank Crean, Australia's new treasurer, was adopting a new progressive policy when he revalued the dollar immediately after the elections. But Crean was following in the footsteps of McMahon and Holt. Crean had first become interested in economics as an income tax consultant. He had been elected to the Victorian State Parliament in 1945, and six years later to the federal house. He was an accountant rather than an economist. Revaluation was not quite election policy. It had been necessary to adopt a low profile on this to avoid both speculation and the antagonism of the country electorate who depended on export income. But it was almost Labor policy, and the Country Party did not fail to use the possibility of a Labor revaluation in their appeals to the farmers. Labor said that revaluation had become necessary because the Liberals had consistently undervalued the currency as a concession to their partners in the coalition. From 1 July to 31 December 1972 the provisional trade surplus amounted to $941,800,000. The balance of payments had changed from a deficit of $94,000,000 in 1968–69, to a surplus of $900,000,000 in the 1971–72 financial year. But the new revaluation was, even so, the third since Holt's historic decision in 1967. At the time of the December 1971 international currency realignment, McMahon had revalued the Australian dollar upwards by 8.57 per cent against the United States dollar. Frank Crean sent it up another 7.05 per cent.

In January 1973 Gough Whitlam and Norman Kirk met for the first time since their respective Labor governments unseated the conservatives in Australia and New Zealand. They gave the highest priority in their discussion to concerting a plan of action against the French. Whitlam and Kirk called upon

France to abandon its nuclear test programme in the Pacific. They anticipated that France would go ahead nevertheless, and were planning a co-ordinated opposition to the tests with other countries in the Pacific region. To find and endorse a relevant policy which had been held by previous Labor Ministers was difficult but not impossible: the two prime ministers reaffirmed the principles of the 1944 Canberra pact, which had pledged the closest co-operation between the governments of Australia and New Zealand in political, economic, defence and social matters, and they agreed to meet informally at least once a year. With an eye to France, they stressed the value of the South Pacific forum, which offered to heads of governments of the self-governing and independent states in the Pacific opportunities to explore common problems, consider priorities and plan co-operative programmes. Whitlam and Kirk declared that they would maintain friendly relations with the United States in a spirit of mutual respect and trust. They characterised the ANZUS treaty as symbolising a community of interest and outlook among the three partners in many fields other than defence. By strengthening the security of Australia and New Zealand, the treaty helped them to contribute to peaceful progress in Asia and the Pacific.

A month later Whitlam flew to Indonesia. There he addressed the Indonesian Parliament, explaining that Australia saw great merit in the formation of an organisation genuinely representative of the South-East Asian region, free from ideological differences and the taint of great power rivalry. In June 1973 he convinced Indian leader Indira Gandhi that Australia under Labor was even more determined than it had been to be not merely an outpost of western influence, but a truly Asian nation. The most dramatic diplomatic breakthrough was made not by Whitlam, but by the Trade Minister, Dr Jim Cairns. The biggest trade agreement between Russia and Australia since 1965 was signed by Cairns and

Nikolai Patolichev, the Soviet Trade Minister, in Canberra on 16 March 1973. Never had such a high-ranking member of the Russian establishment visited Australia. Russia wanted to exchange its technological expertise in massive civil engineering projects for Australian alumina and bauxite. The agreement provided for the setting up of a joint commission, comprising government and business representatives, who would explore the ways of increasing trade between the two countries. Cairns and Patolichev had in mind drawing-up long-term contracts for grain, alumina and bauxite, and they hoped that there would be a huge expansion in trade between the Soviet Far East and Australia. The chief beneficiaries of the trade boom between the Soviet Union and Australia were the entrepreneurs who seized the opportunity to create and expand new organisations to act as go-betweens. Thinking along these lines was the former naval frogman who had unsuccessfully searched for Harold Holt's body, Laurie Matheson. Matheson left the Navy with the rank of Lieutenant Commander shortly after Holt's disappearance, joined the Department of Trade, and was First Secretary at the Australian Embassy in Vienna before being posted to Moscow where he helped to organise bilateral trade.

As part of the apparent trend towards better relations with the communist world, the Prime Minister of Yugoslavia, Dzemal Bijedic, visited Australia in March 1973. Cairns's coup over Soviet trade was in the economic tradition of entrepreneurial Australian capitalism. But Bijedic was in an entirely different category. Australia's relations with Yugoslavia were at a low ebb. Croatians had been openly training in Australia since 1964. It was a case of Daniel in the lions' den. The most serious Yugoslav protest came in June 1973, after nineteen Croatians had entered Bosnia. Six of them had been Australian citizens and three others lived in Australia. Military training camps were periodically discovered and bombings within the Croatian community were too common for Bijedic not to be heavily guarded. A bodyguard of thirty Yugoslav security men surrounded him, a thousand Australian police were drafted to protect him, and a helicopter with police marksmen went wherever Bijedic travelled. The Croatian communities were turned upside down by police searching for evidence of a projected assassination plot and naturally this turned the Yugoslavs off Whitlam as well as Bijedic.

The largest collection of Yugoslav migrants was at Port Kembla, seventy miles south of Sydney, but there were so many Croatians among them that Whitlam decided it was unsafe to walk abroad there while Bijedic was his guest in Canberra. Whitlam was supposed to have opened a new extension to the BHP steel factory at Port Kembla, but decided not to visit the works. Instead he opened the extensions from the safety of the nearby Wollongong Town Hall. Threats against Bijedic were naturally taken seriously. About half of the 165,000 Yugoslavs who had emigrated to Australia in the days of the coalition were Croatians. Whitlam was able to reassure Bijedic that his government would not allow Australia to be used for terrorist activities against friendly countries. Whitlam told Bijedic that McMahon had not been firm enough and had not taken sufficient action on detecting, suppressing and expelling Croatian extremists known to be operating in Australia. Under the coalition, Australia was clearly the centre of an anti-Yugoslav movement. Bijedic was able to tell Whitlam personally how concerned his government was that Croatian extremists were being harboured in Australia.

During Bijedic's visit, the Australian Broadcasting Commission released the contents of a memorandum which the Liberal-Country Party government had been given by Vladimir Rolovic in February 1970. Rolovic had at that time travelled to Australia with the Yugoslav Minister of Labour, and held the post of Assistant Secretary for Foreign Affairs. Rolovic had come to Australia to sign an immigration agreement.

But, with fatal results to himself, he also gave out a memorandum that described the organisation of the Croatian
Revolutionary Brotherhood. This world-wide organisation was
directed from Australia after it was banned in West Germany in
April 1968. It had cells in Wollongong and all the capital cities.
It was organised into groups responsible for terrorism, intelligence and propaganda, and practical instruction was given in the
use of firearms and explosives. The memorandum gave the
names of six Australian leaders. In April 1971 Rolovic was
Ambassador to Stockholm: he was assassinated there by two
members of the separatists, allegedly because of what he had
revealed in the memorandum. Ivor Greenwood, the attorney-
general in the McMahon government, who was responsible for
security, at first said that he had no evidence that Croatian
extremists were being trained in Australia, and subsequently he
claimed that ASIO had withheld information from him.

So that he would not be in the same position, the Labor
attorney-general, Lionel Murphy, led commonwealth police
in a raid on the headquarters of ASIO in Melbourne. He carried
away files, including presumably the memorandum that the
Broadcasting Commission published. Murphy was accompanied on the raid by the Director-General of Security, Peter
Barbour, who watched as the commonwealth police sealed fifty
cabinets to preserve their contents. Murphy said that in future
the security headquarters would be located in Canberra, not
Melbourne, and that legislation would be introduced to give
the federal police power to deal with crimes affecting national
security. Murphy led the federal police into the security headquarters when he suspected that his department was not being
given sufficient information on the activities of terrorists. In
his dramatic assault on the security headquarters Murphy
was no doubt killing two birds with one stone. He was protecting
the Yugoslav prime minister and taking over control of an
organisation that irked the party's left wing. The ASIO-Murphy

affair then turned into a prolonged party dispute which became, as the *Age* said, 'the Blue Hills of Australian politics'.

Relations with the communist world, diplomatic recognition of China, trade with Russia, amity with Yugoslavia, were inextricably tied up with the demands of the left-wing segment of the party. Indeed, Whitlam had only been in office six weeks when his boat was rocked by Tom Uren and Jim Cairns. Uren, Minister for Urban and Regional Development, made a bitter attack on Nixon, whom Whitlam was trying to placate, calling the president an arrogant, double-dealing hypocrite. Cairns, who for seven years had led street demonstrations against the Vietnam war, refused to trim his cloth; in January 1973 he deplored the renewed American bombing of Vietnam and forced Whitlam to gag him: Whitlam announced that thereafter there would be no more statements on foreign policy except by the Minister for Foreign Affairs.

But even so, the radicals did, at first, make some headway. Clyde Cameron, the Minister for Labour, said that he would introduce legislation to abolish penal sanctions against strikers, and to ease the rules concerning the amalgamation of trade unions. Under the Liberal-Country Party, amalgamation of unions was not allowed unless half of those entitled to vote supported it; under Labor, Cameron proposed that all that was necessary was a majority of half those who actually voted. A committee of enquiry was appointed to investigate the arbitration system, after taking evidence in Britain, the United States, West Germany, Sweden and Canada. Unions and union officials would be protected against any actions for tort, breach of contract or conspiracy which might arise during industrial disputes. Protection would naturally not be given to any criminal act involving physical assault or damage to property. Cameron tried to end the confusion that affected unions subject to five or six separate acts of parliament under state and federal legislation. Typical of the result of this was the oil strike in

New South Wales following a demarcation dispute between the Federal Transport Workers' Union and the Transport Workers' Union of New South Wales. Cameron said that his ministry's approach would be to emphasise conciliation, help and amicable agreements. Opposition Leader Snedden retorted that Cameron looked for a virtual sell-out to the demands of the left wing of the Australia Labor Party and to the trade union movement. He particularly deplored the proposal to grant immunity to unions and unionists from civil action in respect of their conduct during a strike.

In the event, Snedden worked through the Senate to defeat Cameron's legislation. The Senate rejected the Industrial Law Reform Bill on 6 June 1973. This was a crucial blow in what became a systematic refusal by the Senate to follow the lead of the House of Representatives. Lance Barnard, the Deputy Prime Minister, said that the government would have to look very carefully at the situation resulting from the Senate's rejection and amendment of government legislation. The situation remained poised nevertheless. Whitlam clearly did not wish to go before the electors on such a controversial issue as increasing the powers of trade unions.

Whitlam faced the same sort of problems as had his predecessors in office. He was successful in some matters, and failed in others. The largest and most galling failure was over the French nuclear test programme. At The Hague on 21 May the Australian Attorney-General, Lionel Murphy, summarised the Australian case. Natural conditions made inevitable the deposit on Australian soil of radioactive debris from the French nuclear explosions at Mururoa atoll: the debris would enter the body of every member of the Australian population, subjecting them to additional ionising radiation, which was inherently harmful to human life. There was a serious danger that any addition of ionising radiation, however small, was harmful. The prudent scientific approach was to assume that there should be no exposure to ionising radiation from artificial sources without a compensating benefit. Murphy claimed that every man, woman, child and foetus in Australia had in his or her body radioactive material from French as well as other atmospheric tests. The bones, lungs and other vital organs of every Australian had been invaded by France's radioactive nuclear debris.

Australia was joined by other Pacific nations. Indonesia lodged a protest to the French government against its plan to continue nuclear tests in the Pacific on 21 May 1973. But France boycotted proceedings of the International Court and declared that it would take no notice of the judgment. France's refusal to recognise the court's competence to deal with Australian and New Zealand complaints was set out in two letters handed to the court's registrar by M. Jacques Senard, French Ambassador to the Netherlands. By May 1973 ships flying the French flag had been banned from Australian ports. The Seamen's Union imposed the embargo for an indefinite period, and it applied to ships serving French territories in the Pacific. The Australian Academy of Sciences and the Atomic Weapons Safety Committee provided evidence that there had been biological effects from the fall-out of the French atomic explosions in June and July 1972. Tests had shown that the bombs had caused radioactive fallout and had contaminated the Australian environment to such an extent that the tests could cause one death every ten years, and fifty to one hundred deaths or disabilities in subsequent generations. Other scientists produced equally convincing evidence that the effects of the French tests were, and would be, negligible.

But the international court contest between the Pacific nations and France was a quixotic case. New Zealand was the nearest industrial country to Mururoa atoll. Norman Kirk said that as a last resort he would send the country's most modern frigate, the *Canterbury*, into the French bomb test zone. Whitlam agreed to refuel the *Canterbury* as it could not sail to

Mururoa atoll non-stop. Every nation shared the high seas, said Whitlam, and no nation had the right to close them. The Duke of Edinburgh had expressed his willingness to carry a banner down the Champs-Elysees if he thought it would influence French policy on nuclear testing in the atmosphere. But this offer was as useless as Whitlam's legal action, for the French were determined not to suspend their nuclear testing programme. M. Aynar Achille-Fould, the Secretary of State for the Armed Forces, said in the National Assembly at Paris on 2 May 1973 that the French government felt it necessary to endow France with a nuclear deterrent because the big powers had not limited their nuclear potential. The reaction of a French nuclear force required that tests be carried out. Achille-Fould added that Britain, the United States and the Soviet Union had made such tests in the past, and that China was making them concurrently. He dismissed the protests as being political, and hoped that a special commission of the United Nations had come to the conclusion that the French tests did not constitute a threat to the Pacific population.

The Labor programme was said to be the most comprehensive in Australian history. But the important changes in Whitlam's era were those with long histories: they were a response to existing evils rather than novelties. Inflation justified the establishment of a Prices Justification Tribunal and measures to curb restrictive trade practices and to protect consumers. Whitlam told the state premiers that Labor had been elected on a programme of social change. It had promised the people a programme of wide-ranging and overdue reforms of the social structure. But inflation could reduce the commonwealth's capacity to pay for social change, and thus he appealed for co-operation from the states.

Whitlam wished to end the depopulation of rural Australia, and Uren, the Minister for Urban Regional Development, was given the task of reversing the trend. Between 1953 and 1973 the rural population of Australia had dropped from 31 per cent to 14.6 per cent of total population. The solution was to consolidate the towns of Albury and Wodonga into a city. Albury (in New South Wales) and Wodonga (in Victoria) stood on opposite sides of the great River Murray, on the main rail and road crossing. Their joint population when Whitlam took office stood at 43,000: Labor hoped to raise it to 300,000. There ought to have been no difficulty in attracting people to the area where the Murray River left the hills and began to meander through the Riverina flats. The country was among the richest and most attractive in Australia, and a centre for fruit, wheat, sheep and cattle-raising.

The Labor victory seemed to be most significant for women and native fauna. In response to the demands of nationalism and ecology, the Labor government banned the export of all kangaroo products. In December 1972 Whitlam prohibited the import and export of crocodile products. In January, Senator Murphy listed 310 other species which faced extinction, of which 46 were indigenous, and trade in these species was banned. Not only the crocodile and the kangaroo were thus given a chance of survival, but the new ecological spirit helped to save the swamp tortoise, the helmeted honey-eater, the western whip bird, parakeets and parrots, wallabies, kangaroo rats, Tasmanian tigers, bandicoots and wombats.

Despite the appointment of Elizabeth Reid as a special adviser to the prime minister on women's affairs – a 'super woman' – women were not so unequivocally fortunate. They were immediately involved in two feminist legislative and industrial proposals, one to grant them equal pay and the other abortion on request. Two Labor MPs introduced a bill to provide abortion on request for a woman up to twelve weeks pregnant, and, with the consent of two doctors, up to twenty-three weeks. All twenty-three supporters of the private member's bill were Labor members, and ten were ministers, including the prime minister and the treasurer. But the five hundred demonstrators who came to Canberra to oppose the bill might as well have stayed at home: the Catholic centre of the Labor Party remained to give it a solid core of social and moral conservatism.

Women were more fortunate in the Arbitration Court than in the House of Representatives. Clyde Cameron and his Department of Labour supported the case for equal pay, which was accepted in principle in December 1972. The McMahon government had opposed the unions' claims for equal pay and under the coalition only about 18 per cent of working women were paid the same wages as men. The court believed that the election results reflected new views within society. Judge Moore said that, in the commission's opinion, the Australian community was prepared to accept the economic consequences of the decision. The changes were to be phased in slowly; not until the end of 1975 were all women in Australia to be paid the same as men doing the same jobs. The president of the ACTU had been conspicuously quiet before and after the election. Hawke was vulnerable to charges that he was going to run the country in the event of a Labor victory, and to rumours that he was bidding for parliamentary power himself, would shortly accept a safe seat, supplant Whitlam, and transform Australia into a workers' paradise. But he was moved to express his disappointment that the Arbitration Court was going to take so long to change the system, and disheartened by the court's ruling not to give a national wage rise at the same time.

In the last analysis all Labor legislative proposals had to run the gauntlet of the Senate. By 18 May 1973 the Senate had shown its strength. Behaving in much the same way as the Tory House of Lords had done in Edwardian Britain when faced with liberal social reform legislation, the coalition senators threw out measure after measure. Perhaps the most important bill to go was the government's Electoral Bill. This provided that the number of eligible voters should not be more than 10 per cent

above or below the average number of voters in each electorate, and that electoral commissioners should no longer consider disabilities arising from remoteness or sparseness of
population. The Electoral Bill would have placed the Democratic
Labor Party and the Country Party at a disadvantage. It was
defeated by 31 votes to 27. The Australian conservative Senate
majority was not content with emasculating the bill by amending
its provisions, they refused its passage outright.

Whitlam abused the senators as arrogant, fearful, recalcitrant and reactionary and threatened them with the prospect of
a double dissolution, saying that Labor did not intend to put up
with such a humiliating situation. The government lost even
more face on 6 June 1973 when the Senate rejected Cameron's
Industrial Law Reform Bill. This rejection set the stage for
a double dissolution of both Houses, but Whitlam was a realist.
He knew that just as it was no good breaking off diplomatic relations with France, it was useless to call for an election that
might lose him his Lower House majority. He was a man who
bluffed, and could not afford his bluff to be called. R. G. Withers,
the coalition Senate leader, knew that the conservatives had
everything to win and nothing to lose if there was a double dissolution. Withers said that the huffing and puffing and ministerial grand-standing ought to stop, and an election be called.
Billy Snedden still hoped to see the Labor Party break up because
of conflict between the parliamentary party and the trade
unions. He tried, as was usual, to show how there was
a great and fundamental difference of opinion between the
prime minister and the president of the ACTU. Hawke and
Whitlam were on opposite sides of the fence on the French
nuclear test issue, said Snedden, and the trade union movement
would insist on a double dissolution if the Senate threw out the
Arbitration and Conciliation Amendment Act – a key piece of
industrial legislation designed to increase trade union powers and
freedom of action.

The sequence of events following which Whitlam lost his office began when he appointed Vincent Gair Ambassador to Ireland. The appointment of Gair created a vacancy in the Senate, where Gair's party held the balance of power. The Irish invented the political 'job', so there was singular aptness about Whitlam's ploy. He was removing a long-term opponent from the Senate and at the same time improving his own party's chances of representation. Gair left Parliament House by a side door, disowned by his friends of the movement and the industrial groups. Ostensibly shocked by Whitlam's breach of the constitution, the Leader of the Liberal-Country Party, Billy Snedden, threw down the gauntlet. He instructed his Senate colleagues to prepare themselves to vote against the appropriation bills that would have supplied Whitlam's administration with $170 million to run the country. The DLP Leader, Frank McManus, believed that Gair's appointment was part of Whitlam's plan to gain control of the Senate by stealth. The Democratic Labor Party therefore joined the conservatives in threatening to defeat the money bills. The Senate's action was unprecedented and, although the money bills were never voted against, Whitlam took his chance and treated the deferred consideration as failure to provide supply. He asked the governor-general to call a double dissolution election, and the people went to the polls in May 1974.

Snedden led the Liberal-Country Party opposition for the last time. Gair's parting shot, that Snedden was a lightweight who could not go two rounds with a revolving door, proved true. Snedden was to lose the election and be replaced by Malcolm Fraser, the man who had torpedoed a previous leader, John Gorton. Snedden campaigned on the issue of inflation. He pointed out the crippling price rises that had occurred since 1972, the severity of taxation scales, and the high interest rates which were discouraging home buying and investment confidence.

Whitlam began his 1974 campaign on a shaky note. Normally

unruffled, he answered journalists with slurred juxtapositions and Freudian slips. He said in the House of Representatives that he would wait upon the attorney-general to request a double dissolution. He said on an ABC current affairs television programme that he had appointed Gair to an academic post. Attorney-general for governor-general, academic for diplomatic – these mistakes were signs of a new lack of sureness.

The Labor leader was particularly attacked by voters in the rural sector. He was pelted with fruit by young farmers in Perth. He was also vilified by the ethnic press of the Baltic nationals. Estonians, Latvians and Lithuanians did not share the middle-class enthusiasm for social democracy. An Estonian migrant woman was used by the New South Wales Liberal government in an election television advertisement during which she explained why she was not going to vote Labor: 'Today I can see Labor is disguised socialism, but for me it is disguised communism'. The 'reffos' with their 'DP' mentality were to be punished for their part in the conservative campaign when Whitlam won the election.

Whitlam had foreseen that he would not have a majority in the Upper House after the 1974 elections. But he had the numbers to command the floor in a joint sitting of both houses of parliament. This joint sitting was provided for under the constitution. It had to take place so that the bills that had been the occasion of deadlock might be passed. In a mood of optimistic jubilation, the Labor Party put on the statute books legislation setting up Medibank, allowing for electoral redistribution by providing extra seats for the Upper House in the Australian Capital Territory and the Northern Territory and bills dealing with industrial development and mineral exploration. For win he did, by five seats in the House of Representatives. To Labor's satisfaction the old splinter party, the Democratic Labor Party, was swept out of the Senate. Into the Upper House came Steele Hall, a former premier of South

Australia, whose Liberal Movement catered to the new breed of middle-class Liberal reformers.

Between the election and the August joint sitting Sir Paul Hasluck retired. Whitlam replaced him with another distinguished Australia, Sir John Kerr, QC. Sections of the party demurred at Kerr's elevation. He had been active in the anti-communist wing in the 1950s, given succour and advice to the Roman Catholic, anti-communist groupers and movement, nurtured right-wing dissent, and had even been responsible for gaoling a trade union official. Kerr had a strong sense of duty and a commitment to intensely held personal views on democracy and the shortcomings of the Labor leadership as it had been demonstrated throughout Australia's history. In 1960 he showed his flag in an article written in *Quadrant*, a journal under the patronage of Australia's literary gurus Manning Clark and Leonie Kramer. It was essential, thought Kerr, to combat the absurd theory of democracy that asserted that the great unions of today, often thousands and thousands strong, should be governed not by the principles of representative democracy (i.e. by an elected 'parliament' and 'cabinet') but by those who regularly attended branch meetings. Kerr wore his heart on his sleeve when the huge issues of power and the constitution were concerned.

After the election the Liberals reformed to meet the Labor Party. In March 1975 the daily press canvassed the possibility that Malcolm Fraser would replace Snedden as leader of the conservative opposition. Fraser at first deplored the 'continued and wrong' speculation that he would challenge Snedden as leader and said that Snedden had his full support. Within two weeks he challenged Snedden at a party meeting and took over the party leadership.

As soon as he became leader, Fraser was asked whether he would follow Snedden's example and use the coalition's numbers in the Upper House to defeat the supply legislation and force a general election. Fraser at first hedged, and said that while a government held a majority in the Lower House, it had a right to expect that it would govern. Only in the most exceptional circumstances would he refuse supply – that is, refuse to pass legislation providing funds to allow government of the commonwealth to continue – and he was not prepared to speculate on what the circumstances might be.

The issue that Fraser chose was the legality of the Australian government's loan-raising activities. Here Whitlam was on very shaky ground. The mismanagement of overseas fund-raising was symptomatic of the ALP's inability to deal with economic problems, at least up to Treasurer Bill Hayden's budget, introduced in August 1975.

Labor's economic policies seemed to the middle class to be characterised by incompetence and nepotism to an alarming degree. The middle class had elected Labor to give the under-privileged a new deal and to carry out needed reforms in the country's cities. The first Treasurer, Frank Crean, had presided over record inflation, unemployment, industrial stoppages and grabbed more tax than any of his predecessors. Jim Cairns succeeded Crean when Crean was sacked in December 1974, and Cairns was himself dismissed by Whitlam for misleading parliament over his involvement in overseas loan negotiations.

Cairns's dismissal was the last of a series of scandals involving him. As the idol of the liberal middle-class for his courage and vision in the Vietnam war days, Cairns was irreplaceable. When he went, supporters were irretrievably disillusioned. Cairns was dismissed from the Treasury following a campaign by the Shadow Treasurer, Phillip Lynch. Gradually Lynch was able to pin down a story that had been published in the *Age* that Cairns had offered a commission to a Melbourne businessman if he could successfully broker a huge loan from the Arabs. Cairns repeated in the House of Representatives that he had never offered any businessman commission, but a copy of a letter was produced which proved Lynch correct. Whitlam asked for Cairns's resignation, but Cairns refused, saying that he had at all times acted in good faith, and that he had no recollection of signing the letter. Since Cairns would not leave his portfolio voluntarily, Whitlam went to Kerr and advised him to sack the treasurer. Cairns did not go quietly. He abused Whitlam for having double standards and taunted him for being autocratic, arbitrary and unfair. Cairns had considerable grass-roots support within the party, and Whitlam had to put his own job on the line when he asked caucus to support his moves.

Cairns further damaged the Labor Party by agreeing to interviews in which he discussed his relationship with his secretary, Juni Morosi, in terms that were bound to offend the middle-class supporters of Labor. This group was strongly concerned with social issues and revered the forms of family life. They might be abused for being hypocritical but when Cairns talked of 'being in love' with his secretary to cement their working relationship, middle-class voters frowned all the way to the ballot box. No one expected the Labor ministers to be puritans, but moderation and less obvious enjoyment of the fruits of office were required.

After Cairns's dismissal Whitlam temporarily gained some respite. A special sitting of parliament was held during which the overseas loans matter was debated at length. Using the conservative majority in the Senate, the Liberals called twelve senior public servants, the commonwealth solicitor general, and a group of itinerant international moneybrokers to the bar of the chamber. But the senators were unable to uncover any further evidence of corruption and unconstitutional behaviour. All the public servants claimed crown privilege, and refused to answer any questions. The solicitor-general deflected his Senate interrogators with all the surety that befitted a holder of his high office. The foreign gentlemen came and went and their collection of documents proved nothing. One of the shadow government's front-benchers, Bob Ellicott, even went so far as to say that the evidence brought before him proved that Whitlam was completely blameless. But by then the retreat from Moscow (as Wentworth dubbed it) had become a rout. On 12 November 1974 the Labor government were forced to go back on their idealistic conceptions of economic management. Whitlam himself announced the new measures that were designed to stimulate the economy and reduce unemployment. Taxes were lowered for individuals and companies, and the prices justification tribunal was asked in the future to take into account the need for an adequate return on industrial investment when making recommendations about prices. Tariff increases of 10 per cent could not save the motor manufacturer Leyland. General Motors threatened to lay off 5,000 men in the new year. The textile industry was in ruins. Whitlam's speech at a time when 211,600 Australians – then a huge number – were unemployed was described by Snedden as a 'deathbed confession'. When Whitlam left Australia in December 1974 on a grand European tour intended to show the diplomatic flag, he was bidden farewell at the airport by a crowd shouting, 'Don't come back'. Menzies, the prime minister Whitlam most admired, had never departed like that.

On 9 December 1974 Queensland state election results shocked the federal Labor Party. The Queensland premier, Joh Bjelke-Petersen, had not the slightest doubt that a federal election would follow. The election wiped out two-thirds of the Labor members of the Queensland parliament. Whitlam spoke of the 'dark currents of intolerance and extremism at work in Queensland', but in reality the Queensland election was a personal debacle for Whitlam, who had campaigned extensively. The low spot of the campaign was Whitlam's off-the-cuff aside to an Estonian demonstrator who was protesting against the Australian government's recognition of the incorporation of the Baltic states into the Soviet Union. Whitlam called the woman a 'bloody Nazi bitch'. It was a slip of the tongue that revealed the prime minister's fears. Middle-class Australia had a Janus aspect. A family with a Red Setter often lived cheek by jowl to a family with an Alsatian, and in the Fascist tendencies of middle-class Australia lay one danger for the future. 'Must the democracies concede,' asked Whitlam, 'that only authoritarian regimes can cope with inflation and unemployment?'

Events in 1975 confirmed the trend away from Labor. The Labor Party lost the seat of Bass in a federal by-election; in South Australia the State Labor government held office only after the premier dissociated himself from Whitlam's policies. In federal parliament the Speaker of the House, James Cope, resigned when Whitlam refused to support him in a clash with the front bench. The front bench itself was severely depleted by the loss of Cairns, Cameron, Crean and Connor—all sacked or demoted by Whitlam for their failings.

The remarkable year reached a climax on 11 November 1975, when Sir John Kerr dismissed Prime Minister Whitlam and appointed Malcolm Fraser Acting Prime Minister. Fraser was charged with the task of getting supply through parliament and with forming an interim caretaker government while elections were held for both houses. The governor-general's action led to controversy on a scale hitherto unknown. Analogies were made between Whitlam and Allende, Chile and Australia, Hitler and Fraser. Terms like *coup d'etat* and *putsch* were shouted in the air and in the correspondence columns of the papers as the allies of the protagonists put their point of view. How could it be called a *coup d'etat* when elections followed? How could Fraser become prime minister when he did not command the support of the House of Representatives? Why did the governor-general not invite Whitlam to head the caretaker government?

Opinion polls showed that while the middle class was sorry for Whitlam, and thought that he had been hard done by, they were not prepared to vote for him. In the 1975 election Whitlam saw his party strength reduced from 65 seats to just over 30, and power firmly in the hands of the conservatives in both houses. As the first results were posted in the tally room it was clear that Labor had lost the support of the outer suburb-dwellers on the fringes of Sydney and Melbourne – the voters who brought Labor to power in 1972 and 1974. But it soon became clear that Labor was losing all across the board and that Fraser had won a landslide victory. Whitlam explained his defeat by saying that his party had suffered the fate of a reforming government in time of recession, but his explanation was an anti-climax.

The moments following Whitlam's dismissal were the ones of high drama. There was talk of a general strike and blood in the gutters, but all that happened during the month-long election campaign was that Fraser was hit by a beer can. While 'the burglars were in', and the filing cabinets of the first Labor administration for twenty-three years were being man-handled out of parliament, Whitlam made a fiery speech. Whitlam told the crowd who had assembled to see the governor-general's secretary read the proclamation dissolving parliament: 'Ladies and gentlemen, well may we say God save the Queen, because nothing will save the governor-general!' Fraser, predicted Whitlam, would go down in Australian history from Remembrance Day 1975 as 'Kerr's cur'. The dog metaphor was apt. It was in the parliamentary tradition of invective that specialised in hyenas, packs of dingoes, lying hounds and dirty mongrels. But it showed also that Whitlam had been too long cocooned by his own success. He was a populist leader in touch with the journalists on the VIP BAC 111, but he had lost the power to communicate to the idealistic middle class who put his party into power, and who thought, by December 1975, as their window stickers put it: 'He has had his chance and he has stuffed it'.

CHAPTER 9

The Easy Life

It was to be almost a decade before the Australian Labor Party was to get another chance. A shell-shocked community instinctively turned to the conservative strongman Malcolm Fraser in 1975. Despite bouts of recurrent lung infections and more days off sick than any other prime minister, Fraser's slogan 'Life was not meant to be easy' and his dour Scottish pessimism exactly fitted the mood of the majority of Australians. Fraser's single-mindedness could be mocked, but like many of history's great conservatives he oversaw the completion of monuments of brick that were destined to outlive his political regime. Two of these architectural tombstones, memorials to the Fraser era, stand side by side in the national capital – the Art Gallery and the High Court. The High Court is the Ayers Rock of Canberra. Nothing exists like it in nature, and there is little like it built by man. But, as with many of the memorials of the Fraser administration it was not long before the High Court and the National Gallery were popularly judged as successes. Tourists slipped easily from the National Gallery across to the High Court, ate at the bistro overlooking the lake, and on Sundays watched string quartets play Borodin from the staircases of the multi-tiered courts, while outside security guards quoted odds on the latest State appeal, and the likeliest verdict in sensational murder case appeals. When Fraser left office in 1983, an even greater totem was being constructed around a huge hole in the ground as a new national parliament house site was excavated. By then Fraser was only slightly more popular than was Hitler with wartime Londoners. Many of the country's potential electors were so alienated that they refused to register to vote, and among those who did vote many deliberately spoiled their ballot papers and voted informal.

Fraser took power in a country later described by Billy Snedden (who, as Speaker in the House of Representatives, ought to have known) as on the brink of civil war. As Snedden put it, 'I saw incipient tendencies for insurrection' in the immense anger which built up in the minds of Labor people and politicians. Snedden believed Fraser's brinkmanship and over-throw of constitutional precedent was so dangerous that it ought not to have been attempted.

Events proved Fraser right and Snedden wrong – the gamble turned out to be worth it. The Australian electorate entrusted government to Fraser on 13 December 1975, a bare nine months after he had replaced Snedden as Leader of the Opposition. Fraser's majority in the Houses of Representatives was 55: the Coalition held 91 seats against the ALP's 36, and more important the Liberal-Country Party had a majority in the Senate. The dismissal or resignation of Whitlam's senior ministers Jim Cairns, Clyde Cameron, Frank Crean and R. F. X. Connor, and the clash between the Labor prime minister and the Speaker of the House of Representatives, James Cope, were not swept under the carpet. The Whitlam years became the stuff of apologia, unreliable memoirs and soap opera television series. Bob Hawke, President of the Labor Party on 13 December 1975, spoke like Menzies after the Chifley victory, although in less poetic imagery, saying that the party had had its guts ripped out. Within a decade Hawke, like Menzies, was able to settle the score and lead his party to parliamentary victory.

Hawke knew whom he blamed: Whitlam and David Combe.

Combe, as federal party secretary, had irresponsibly urged Whitlam to raise overseas loans from disreputable and unreliable sources. Hawke was bitterly critical of Combe and Whitlam, and argued that even if the loans had been negotiated, the result would have been that Australia would have been 'in hock, sold down the drain, mortgaged to overseas interests'. The president of the party was on this occasion outmanoeuvred and beaten; within a decade he was able to even the score. The Iraqi loans affair coincided with a period of heavy drinking by Hawke. To make matters worse, as Blanche d'Alpuget, Hawke's official biographer, put it, Hawke was 'objectionable when drunk', a characteristic that had hitherto not been publicised. D'Alpuget attributed this to the fact that the journalists who knew Hawke best were often drunk themselves and, moreover, Hawke was a man who was quick with a libel writ. Since Hawke was becoming a public figure with a portentous political career beginning to develop, by 1975 his heavy drinking had become a matter of legitimate public interest. Mike Schildberger on national television had offered Hawke a list of the questions he was going to ask him, but Hawke, with typical self-confidence, said that he did not want to see them. But then, without too much pressure, Hawke admitted drink was his weakness. Whitlam joked that to hold his position he would have to undertake a rigorous programme of social drinking, and Hawke countered by saying that if he were to become leader of the Australian Labor Party he would give up drinking.

There was plenty to drive them both to drink. Whitlam lost the 1975 election, but decided to stay on as leader and to try to reorganise a party deeply in debt from the unsuccessful election campaign. Whitlam and Combe had planned to pay for the election with money from Iraq. As Hawke put it, however, despite the party's financial plight, 'the dough had not arrived, and the party was therefore in deep financial trouble'. Hawke told Combe to get off his Russian cruise ship, and come back to explain 'the fairy story' of the Iraqi money scandal. Combe was spared at that time the indignity of sacking, remarking, 'Bob's a helluva loyal bloke. He'd stood by me in the past. I didn't have much hope about this one, but he was very strong in saying that, while I'd been a stupid bastard, I'd been trying to do my best by the party in a crisis.' Hawke even wanted to see Whitlam expelled, an idea dropped only because of the damage it would do in the electorate to the idea of Labor solidarity.

After Fraser's victory the Labor Party went into exile and licked its wounds. Fraser began a lengthy struggle to reduce Australia's inflation: all other areas of policy and public administration were subordinated to the one economic idea, in the misplaced hope that once inflation was beaten Australia could begin to enjoy the easy life. It was as well Fraser's aims were limited, as much of his attention was taken by the peccadillos, real and alleged, of his ministers. Whereas the British conservative party specialised in sexual unconventionality, the Australians were often in trouble for minor financial breaches. In February 1976, R. V. Garland, Fraser's Minister for Posts and Telecommunications, resigned while he fought (and won) a case in the courts alleging bribery. The following year Fraser's Treasurer, Phillip Lynch, was forced to resign while allegations of impropriety over land deals were investigated. He too was found innocent. In March 1977, Queen Elizabeth visited Australia in her silver jubilee year, and the Queen's visit overshadowed the growing economic problems of the commonwealth. Curiously, although unemployment had continued to grow, there were few signs of a swing back to Labor. The Australian political pendulum is a very heavy instrument. Repeated political failures and economic mismanagement were not in themselves sufficient to cause Australian voters to change the occupants of the Treasury benches.

On 10 December 1977, Australians again voted in a general

election, Fraser having called an early poll. It was to be Whitlam's Waterloo. Australian voters felt confident with Fraser. Why should they not? Fraser was tough, capable, resourceful and determined. He had gained control of his party with an admirable directness and scorn for niceties – both qualities that appealed to the Australian electorate. Fraser believed in small government, lower taxes and, urged on by the permanent head of the Treasury, John Stone, fighting inflation first. At that time Stone was the most able of a formidable group of intellectual bureaucrats, who included John Menadue, Alan Renouf and Stephen FitzGerald. Unlike his public service peers, however, Stone took the huge jump from private to public life, resigning in due course (after being a headache to Labor and Liberal treasurers alike) to enter the Senate in his own right, as a member of the National Party. In May 1976 Fraser introduced a successful mini-budget, involving modest expenditure cuts and personal income tax indexation. In November, against Treasury advice, Fraser devalued the Australian dollar by 17.5 per cent and again proved successful. Inflation did not stem the profits that flowed from Australia's conservatism, and Fraser was able to offer the electorate 'a fistful of dollars' if they voted for him in the 1977 election. Fraser kept Australian industry behind a high protective tariff barrier, and intervened to keep home-finance interest rates below free market levels.

During the first two years Fraser had the satisfaction of keeping inflation reduced, and although unemployment was still difficult, the electorate, still remembering Whitlam's inability to manage the Australian economy, was not disposed to give Labor another chance. Labor was routed, and the party chose Bill Hayden as its new leader. Hayden would have seemed an odd choice, had the Australian Labor Party ever made anything else. His earliest childhood memories were of his father crashing down drunk on the verandah of his home, which may have influenced his choice of the police force as an early career and his night school reading of Kafka. At the time of his election, Hayden was almost the only man left in the federal Labor top ranks who had not muffed his opportunities, and his successful stewardship of the treasury portfolio was well appreciated by an electorate becoming increasingly demoralised, confused and cynical about the economic policies pursued by Fraser. Fraser was secure in the knowledge that many of the most able social democrats in the Australian Labor Party were in state politics, and that such practical politicians as Neville Wran and John Bannon were taken up, and ultimately overwhelmed, by the difficulties of running successful state administrations.

Fraser nevertheless struggled to cope with the second eleven of Labor leaders, and fought hard against the trade unions. The unions, threatened most by the new technology that led to job shedding, began campaigns to protect their members. Telecom was among the first to feel the backlash as members of the Australian Telecommunications Employees Association placed a series of bans on the telephone, teleprinter and satellite links they operated. The executive of the ATEA was selective in its industrial action, and aimed primarily to affect business customers whose high revenue enterprises were crucial to budget strategy. Fraser's response to these tactics was to pass a new law allowing the redeployment and compulsory retirement of public servants.

Fraser attacked not only his public servant enemies within, but also his old adversaries outside, Australia. When the Soviet Union invaded Afghanistan, Fraser, in a burst of manic hyperbole, described the new strategic situation as being the most serious threat to world peace since World War II. The United States foreign policy was adopted completely and without equivocation, Australian primary producers being forbidden to pick up grain, wheat and wool contracts with the Soviet Union in the wake of the United States trade embargo. In a series of measures designed to cut links with the Soviet Union, scientific interchange was stopped, Russian cruise ships banned, and negotiations with Aeroflot over a direct air link between the two nations was dropped. Things were not as bad as they seemed, however. Australia, while signing no new contracts, pegged trade at the record level of 1979.

In a crucial turning point for the opposition, the Australian Labor Party formed a triumvirate to attempt to combat Fraser. It was a dangerous time for the Leader of the Opposition, Bill Hayden, and marked the moment when his personal defeat became inevitable. The triumvirate consisted of Hayden, leader of the parliamentary party, Neville Wran, the premier of New South Wales, and Bob Hawke, president of the ACTU. Anyone who knew anything of Hawke's style ought to have been reluctant to be part of a triumvirate with him. One does not go on a tiger hunt with a tiger in the party. From his exalted position, Hawke was able to consolidate his national image, and move smoothly from the top of industrial to the top of the federal political arena, a move made easy by the early retirement from party politics of Neville Wran.

At the time, Fraser was distracted by the family problems of Ian Sinclair, a senior minister, whose father had died leaving the family funeral business in a position where the firm's accounting measures were the subject of a police inquiry. Ian Sinclair was charged and later acquitted of fraud, forgery, intending to defraud and making false statements in connection with the annual taxation returns of three funeral companies of which he was a director. He explained that he did not carry the coffins out to the hearses, and took no direct interest in the business, but his embarrassment added to the list of Fraser's concerns, even though embarrassing oversights were to become more common and were not restricted to the Liberal and Country parties.

Fraser's main problems in the 1980s were not concerned with the funeral industry or even foreign policy, they were economic.

Every month seemed to bring worse and worse unemployment figures, and inflation showed little sign of dropping to levels comparable with Australia's major OECD trading partners.

By June 1980, 427,000 Australians were registered as unemployed out of a population of 14,500,000. Fraser justified a high level of unemployment as a necessary component in the fight against inflation. The Australian Labor Party, on the other hand, suggested the establishment of a system of job-creating innovations. The idea that employment should be expanded rather than contracted as a way forward was most forcefully expounded by Labor's shadow Minister for Employment, Mick Young. Young croaked from his West Lakes home in the reclaimed swamp hinterlands of Port Adelaide a continual and imaginative stream of abuse and invective at Fraser's supporters, much of it directed at the hapless governor-general, Sir John Kerr who, for his decision to sack the Whitlam government, Young gave a place in Labor demonology next to Satan and Judas.

When the governor-general arrived to open a Fraser session of parliament, demonstrators threw bricks and yellow paint at his Rolls Royce. Ministers from the Whitlam cabinet stormed and sulked, refusing to join in the schoolboy spirit of celebration attendant on parliamentary session openings and closings. Kerr, who, in his own terms, had only been doing his job when he sacked Whitlam, and who saw his verdict corroborated by Australian voters, was disorientated by the boycott. His ostracism by old friends turned him into a more and more solitary individual, and his spectacular and widely televised public drunkenness at such a great national festival as the Melbourne Cup did little to restore the prestige of the governor-general's office. The Labor Party's republican wing was temporarily enhanced by a glittering star when Nobel Laureate Patrick White added his wit and venom, which he was later to turn back on the Labor Party, to the call for an end to the links with the monarchy.

The opening of the Fraser years saw the tall poppy syndrome triumphant: all the leaders of the community were the subject of national odium. Fraser was so unpopular that it was unsafe for him to travel in the capital cities without the fear of provoking a demonstration. Whitlam was so blamed for mismanaging Labor's national affairs that no state premier wished to be associated with him. And the Head of State, Sir John Kerr, was usually described as a rorty, belching, farting old Falstaff; none painted the negative picture as well as Patrick White.

Fraser approached the task of leading the new Liberals with the energy of a man possessed. He attacked the foundations of the Whitlam era with a bulldozer, not a new broom. Sir John Kerr was only one of tens of thousands of Australians on the public payroll to lose his job. Kerr was both replaced and given a new job in Paris as ambassador to UNESCO. Kerr, respecting the strength of public opinion against him, eventually declined to take up the posting and moved to London where he lived the life of a prosperous expatriate.

Fraser drove himself and his ministers as hard as he drove the country. Described by his friends as a huge brute of a man, Fraser had no conversation apart from cars and the farm, no public hobbies and (at that time) no public vices. He threw himself into office and, once he got there, threw himself about it. Ministers buckled under the huge new workload demanded by 'the head prefect'. The cabinet ceased to be a sheltered workshop, and the wives of ministers begged their husbands to leave politics before Fraser drove them into early deaths from overwork. Fraser's mark of patrician unfriendliness hid a resourceful leader, who was desperately upset by the inability of his ministers to match his executive grasp of action and decision. Fraser's years in office were as productive as Menzies's and, although crammed into a short time, the decisions Fraser made were long lasting and, given the context of the 1970s, beneficial to most Australians when he made them. Fraser never claimed to govern for all. Consensus was an idea foreign to his upbringing and political experience. He would have loved more and better advice and help from his ministers and from the party machine with decision-making if he had been able to find it. But the Liberal and Country Parties were lacking the reserves of administrative skill that later so well served Hawke's government with its meritocratic backbone.

Fraser did not lack a sense of symbolism, and rubbed salt in Labor wounds with the experienced detachment of a primary producer crutching sheep. To wails of outrage, a central figure in the Queensland branch of the Australian Labor Party, Jack Egerton, was knighted, and Fraser threatened to lobby for Prince Charles as governor-general if members of the ALP did not hush their campaign for a republican Australia.

Ties with the mother country were further threatened and traditional institutional links between Australia and the United Kingdom were loosened and changed forever when a new type of cricket was inaugurated by Kerry Packer. Packer, heir to a media fortune and a multi-millionaire entrepreneur with businesses ranging from the *Women's Weekly* to the Perisher Ski resort in the New South Wales alps, was the Malcolm Fraser of the cricket world. He broke all the rules but, persuaded by performance, the Australian cricket spectators followed the new game. Kerry Packer's novel idea involved the establishment of an organisation called World Series Cricket International. This company offered players under contract to it the chance to make large fortunes. Packer changed the way the game was conducted, played cricket at night under lights and before huge international and local television audiences, using the latest in broadcasting technology to pick up the grunts and oaths of the players, and the sounds of ball on jaw. Packer's cricket was show business, with brilliantly coloured uniforms and, when the nation's great sporting heroes defected to World Series Cricket, the role of the game was changed for ever. Players kicked each other, removed their trousers, swore at umpires, sought loopholes in the regulations and were frequently interrupted by nude exhibitionists called 'streakers' rushing onto the field of play. When an Australian bowled an underarm ball in an international match, it seemed to many Australian Labor Party supporters and many others that cricket had fallen as low as politics on 11 November 1975, although it is worth noting in this context that the Australian captain who ordered the underarm ball had ambitions for a political career on the right rather than on the left of the parliamentary spectrum.

As Geoffrey Blainey, one of Australia's most wise, eminent and controversial historians put it, change in Australia moves from small, almost imperceptible beginnings into much larger phenomena: the creeks become rivers slowly. Two important changes in Australia during the Fraser years were the beginnings of a new wave of Asian immigration, and the reliance by the Australian working class on the strike weapon to gain wage concessions in an era of burgeoning unemployment. The first load of boat people contained only 47 Vietnamese refugees. When their craft sailed into Darwin harbour, the boat people were subjected to a typical Australian reaction: a mixture of pity and condescension. As the arrival of refugees from Indo-China increased relative to the decline in traditional migration during the economic downturn of the Fraser years, pity and patronising paternalism soon changed to fear, and Asian profiles soon began to appear in working-class suburbs where the unemployed had most to lose from new competitors in the job market. By April 1978 almost 500,000 Australians were unemployed, and job vacancies stood at one for every twenty-one applicants. Again, there was to be a similar fear of Asians during the Hawke years, although in the late 1980s it was the Japanese rather than the Vietnamese who were cited as the popular cause of economic discontent. While the Vietnamese migrated and lifted themselves up by their bootstraps through hard work and entrepreneurship, the Japanese came to Australia as tourists, but bought large tracts of the country.

Not only unemployed members of the Australian working class ruminated on Fraser's words 'Life was not meant to be easy'. The wheel of fortune turned during the years 1975 to 1983, with an inexorable comprehensiveness which turned many of Australia's winners into losers. Andrew Peacock's accident-prone wife, Susan, who had put him in hot water when she advertised Sheridan sheets in the *Women's Weekly* during 1970, finally ended her marriage with the Liberal Party's brightest rising star, and continued on her daisy chain of marriages. Peacock, like Hawke, had a burning political ambition to rise to the top of his party and govern the nation, but, like Hawke, his career was forced to mark time for almost a decade, and most publicity surrounding 'the colt from Kooyong', as he was affectionately dubbed, centred on his friendships with a series of famous women, ranging from Princess Margaret to Shirley MacLaine.

Perhaps the most symbolic victim, when luck began to run out in the lucky country, was Harry M. Miller. His place at the top of Australian society was marked in various ways: Prince Charles visited him at home, he was a special adviser for the Bicentennial celebrations, chairman of the Queen's Silver Jubilee Commemorative Organisation, a director of the Australian meat and livestock corporation, and on the board of QANTAS. His fortune had been made as a theatrical entrepreneur, and he brought almost all the most lavish theatrical productions that were staged in the capitals. Miller's computerised ticket selling company, Computicket, collapsed, however, and Miller was sentenced to three years jail for fraudulently misappropriating $700,000. Even behind bars (where his VIP status was marked by visits from Doug Anthony),

Miller was newsworthy, especially when it was found that posters advising the sale of prize bulls from his stud estate had been printed in the Long Bay gaol workshops, one of Australia's most interesting commercial coups, and one that earned its author three days in solitary confinement.

The Fraser years were bad for crime, both organised and disorganised. Typical of the new wave of unrest amongst Australia's crime figures was the death of Jack 'Putty Nose' Nicholls, found shot dead on the day he was due to give evidence. Putty Nose Nicholls was a member of the Painters and Dockers' Union, a group which held the highest place in the public's estimate so far as organised union crime was concerned. It was soon to become apparent, however, that crime was spreading into all levels of government and public administration in Australia, even, if the rumours were correct, as far as the High Court.

One of Fraser's most portentous decisions was to support the mining of uranium. And here, curiously, Fraser and Hawke were at one. For while Hayden was opposed to using nuclear power in Australia because of the potential hazards and danger to humankind, Hawke was prepared as he later said, to rip the stuff out of the ground with his own bare hands. In supporting uranium mining, Fraser was working on the basis of a report commissioned by his ALP predecessor. In 1975 the Whitlam government had commissioned Justice R. W. Fox to conduct an enquiry into uranium and the environment. Fox reported twice, in October 1976 and May 1977. Fox pointed out that uranium was a very special metal, insofar as it contained fissile atoms which were potentially dangerous to mankind. The question of how to exploit Australian uranium deposits safely was important to Australians. There were substantial deposits of uranium in the Northern Territory. In 1977, 59 per cent of Australians favoured the development and export of uranium for peaceful purposes.

Fraser's government supported Fox's findings that there should be full and effective safeguards for Australia's uranium exports. By April 1977 an air of urgency entered the debate when US President Jimmy Carter urged that the spread of nuclear weapons should be restrained but the nuclear power industry not. On 24 May Fraser noted that Carter's words were important, because although Australia's known reserves were not the world's largest, the cost of extracting ore was so relatively low that Australia possessed between 15 and 20 per cent of the world's economically accessible reserves. Three months later, on 25 August 1977, Fraser made the historic announcement: 'Uranium mining may now proceed, but only in a way that will not destroy or spoil the national heritage.' Fraser added that when the Australian government decided to allow the export of uranium it would be selective about the countries to which uranium could be sold. It would not be prepared to export uranium to countries where the International Atomic Energy Agency could not inspect safeguards applied under the nuclear non-proliferation treaty. *Pravda* commented in Moscow that Fraser was a hypocrite who was solely moved by greed in his determination to export uranium. The Soviet Union was not to be much happier with Hawke as Fraser's eventual successor as prime minister. Although a member of the ALP, Hawke went further than Fraser and argued that Australia's export of uranium was actually in the interests of world peace, insofar as Australia was responsible about insisting on safeguards under international treaties being given by those to whom Australia supplied yellowcake.

Fraser's election victory was substantial. It was the fourth time in five years that Australians had gone to the polls. The Liberal-Country Party won two-thirds of the seats in the House of Representatives but were faced in the Senate by a new party that was to show strong growth over the next decade. The leader of the new force in Australian politics was Don Chipp, a former

Minister for Customs in the Liberal government, who had become disenchanted with the excessive conservatism of the Liberal party and the Marxist background of many ALP members. Chipp's aim was, as he colourfully put it, 'to keep the bastards honest' by holding the balance of power in the Senate. Chipp was eventually successful in his aim, and his party gained Senate representation in several Australian states, being supported by those voters who were disillusioned by both left and right in Australian politics. The new party was called the Australian Democrats, and was ostentatiously fair and even-minded in its selection of parliamentary candidates, promulgation of rational policy and attachment to popular issues, especially those concerned with the environment, uranium mining and the freedom of the individual in an increasingly conformist and threatening society. Under Chipp, the Democrats occupied the ground taken by the green parties in other societies.

Fraser ignored the Greens, and concentrated on mustering his ministers. He insisted that all his ministers be like Caesar's wife, above suspicion. In August 1978, a Royal Commissioner, Justice D. G. P. McGregor, found that Senator Reg Withers, leader of the government in the Senate, had been guilty of misconduct by using his position to further a political purpose by an approach to the electoral distribution commissioners. This was a small matter to most Australian voters, involving mainly the change of name in a proposed political divison, but Fraser took it seriously and banished Withers to the back bench, where he became a supporter of those like Andrew Peacock seeking to undermine Fraser's popularity and supplant him as prime minister.

Fraser's sensitivity to purity in office was well recognised and many played upon it. Seeking to discredit Liberal-Country Party politicians became an art form, as the Posts and Telecommunications Minister resigned, Treasurer Phillip Lynch was pilloried and retired prematurely, and, in 1982, in the worst breach of all, the Health Minister, Michael MacKellar, and Business and Consumer Affairs Minister, John Moore, were forced to resign by Fraser after they were found to have smuggled a colour television set into Australia, failed to pay the appropriate duty, and tried to cover up the peccadillo. The loudest critic on the Labor benches, Mick Young, was himself to fall victim of a subsequent Fraser directive to Australian Customs – that no minister was to be above the law as far as customs declarations and the import of goods were concerned, and that, far from receiving VIP treatment, all ministers arriving in Australia were to be subject to extra careful scrutiny of their baggage and personal effects.

On 15 May 1978 Sir Robert Menzies died in Melbourne. Menzies's funeral ended a chapter in Australian history. The slow growth and steady economic and political development that had characterised the 1950s and the 1960s were entirely dissipated. Menzies's heirs had to deal with a series of unexpected problems. A popular but useless way to improve Australian job prospects was to cut back on migrant targets, and in June 1978 the Minister for Immigration, Michael MacKellar, announced that a new quota system would change the rules for selecting migrants. The new selection process, introduced in January 1979, was called NUMAS, the numerical multifactor assessment system. This boiled down to a points system, under which prospective migrants scored points for such factors as family ties with Australia, occupation skills in demand in Australia, literacy in their mother tongue, knowledge of English, and prospects for successful settlement. The Vietnamese, of course, did not generally fit well with the NUMAS system, so many of them jumped the queue. By July 1978, 1,600 Vietnamese had arrived in Australia, many of them, according to Labor spokesman on refugees, Bill Hayden, avoiding the necessary guidelines and selection procedures. Hayden spoke of a lucrative racket growing around the importation of Vietnamese refugees, observing that it was widely accepted in Bangkok that the refugees with resources could readily buy a passage to Australia on a boat destined to make a voyage to Darwin. In response, Australian immigration officers were sent to refugee camps in South-East Asia, and told to try to persuade the prospective boat people that they should wait to fly to Australia after an orderly selection procedure that was being greatly accelerated.

In the end, however, it was not Vietnamese migration or failure of his ministers that brought to an end Fraser's seven hectic years of government. Fraser was defeated by the ALP federal caucus which dumped, on election eve, one leader for another, switching Hawke for Hayden. On 3 February 1983, Bill Hayden announced his resignation as Labor Party leader, saying, 'I believe that a drover's dog could lead the Labor Party to victory the way this country is and the way the opinion polls are showing up.'

Reporters asked Fraser (in an unfortunate choice of words) whether the Hawke/Hayden switch had caught him with his pants down. Fraser replied that it made no difference who the leader was. The policy of the Australian Labor Party remained the same, and was not changed by altering the shop front window. 'It will be the first election,' he predicted, 'in which two Labor leaders have been knocked off in one go.'

Fraser hoped that the Australian Labor Party would fight in public and that he could steal the election from them. But the change to Hawke as leader boosted Labor morale. Hawke stole the mantle of national leader during the campaign. His Opera House opening was successful theatre. He stood alone on the stage, invoked John Curtin (whom, as a reformed alcoholic, he resembled), and finished by embracing his eighty-four-year-old father, Clem. Hawke had tears in his eyes.

Fate then took a hand. Bushfires ravaged southern Australia, and for four days Fraser was forced to postpone his attack while he travelled to destroyed areas. The turning-point in the campaign, and the beginning of a decade of Liberal political irrelevance, was on 22 February when Fraser told a Melbourne lunchtime rally that people should not assume their savings were safe in the bank. Fraser said that, under Labor, 'It would be safer under your bed than it would be in the banks. They would be robbing the savings of the people to pay for their mad and extravagant promises.' To this Hawke replied, 'They can't put them under the bed because that's where the commies are.'

The election turned into a landslide. When television station experts predicted a conservative loss, Fraser went into hiding in the manager's suite of the Southern Cross Hotel, Melbourne. With tears in his eyes, Fraser eventually took personal responsibility for the timing and conduct of the election and the defeat of his government. Tamie, his wife, then grabbed him by the arm and led him away from the television cameras and the vultures.

CHAPTER 10

The Banana Republic

Hawke, interviewed shortly after breakfast on the morning after the 1983 election, appeared like a beauty queen in his hotel suite at the Lakeside Motel, Canberra, and unconvincingly told the press that he did not get any joy out of Fraser's tremendous personal human trauma.

Hawke's two senior trusted supporters Paul Keating and Gareth Evans were present. All wore conservative business suits and explicitly eschewed hysteria and wild emotion. Hawke and his colleagues headed for the political centre adopting conservative policies where they considered them appropriate, and forcing the conservative opposition so far to the right that they became marginalised.

Hawke's move from the left began with a decision to call together an economic summit of government, business and labour leaders. Days before the election, the ACTU agreed to co-operate with the Australian Labor Party on a prices and incomes policy, styled 'The Accord'. In the House of Representatives in Canberra, in April 1983, the class war and divisive state interests were put aside, as Australia's business figures, all state premiers (except Queensland's Joh Bjelke-Petersen), and leading trade unionists agreed to help his ALP government attack unemployment and inflation. In the style of Scandinavian social democrats of the 1930s, the unions promised wage restraint, the employers undertook to recommend lower dividends, and the government promised to hold the ring. With such an accord, it was hoped that capitalism would provide and the state distribute. Hawke's summit conference was ridiculed at the time. Wits asked whether 'accord' was a noun, a verb, or the name of a Japanese car. But it marked the signal achievement of seizing the middle ground, and the ALP's moderation was thereafter clear for all to see.

Hawke himself gave up alcohol, took up a conspicuously healthy diet and way of life and made it clear that, from 1983, the Australian Labor Party was operating under new management. First to feel the sting was David Combe, who, in an horrific miscalculation, became entangled with a Russian spy, Valery Ivanov. With text-book indiscretion, Combe and Ivanov held a pre-election dinner party during which Combe mimicked Whitlam. ASIO recorded Combe's impersonation of Whitlam in this way: 'You know, comrade, we've tried winning with policies and no leader, and we failed, but now we're trying to win with a leader and no policies.' Ivanov tried to recruit Combe as an agent of influence who could assist the Soviet Union in the event of a Hawke victory. Combe told Ivanov: 'When they're getting toward the end of their term then I'll say, "Right, I'm entitled to something. I want my job for the boys. Ambassadorship. Moscow will suit me very much."' Since Ivanov had not heard the phrase 'jobs for the boys' before, Combe explained its meaning: 'As former party secretary, I'm one of the boys. I'm entitled to a job, and that will be accepted.'

But there were no jobs for the boys in the new model Australian Labor Party. Combe was ostracised and lost his lobbying livelihood. Ivanov was expelled from Australia, and there was a Royal Commission headed by Justice Robert Hope, which opened a Pandora's Box.

The Hawke government had proved its *bona fides*. There would be no cover-ups, no exceptions made: Hawke was determined to govern in the public interest and not that of party members. The change of direction was marked by intolerance of dissent. The party line became the only line. When John Brown, the Minister for Tourism, unwisely attacked the koala, a symbol unique to Australia, saying it was smelly, had fleas and piddled on its petters, Hawke reprimanded him as publicly as if he had been a hapless koala cuddler. The same treatment was given to Geoffrey Blainey, who, in March 1984, addressing the Warrnambool Rotary Club, canvassed his idea that too many Vietnamese were coming to Australia and too few Europeans. Political correctness became the order of the day.

Having set out the guidelines, Hawke did not waver. No attempt was made to protect Judge Lionel Murphy, who had been ALP Attorney-General in the Whitlam era. Murphy had been responsible for liberal law reform, and sued the French government in the International Court of Justice for its nuclear testing in the Pacific. He became the first High Court Justice to face a criminal charge, and was found guilty of attempting to pervert the course of justice. Sentenced to eighteen months' imprisonment, he was given bail pending an appeal. In April 1986, Murphy was found not guilty by the Appeal Court, and shortly after died of cancer.

A more difficult and intractable problem for Hawke was his friendship with Mick Young. Young was always in and out of hot water, but he had been at Hawke's elbow and guided the party to electoral success on repeated occasions. During the Ivanov crisis, Young had leaked cabinet information and was forced to resign. After reinstatement, he was detected by over-zealous customs officers avoiding duty on a toy bear which had been bought in London. 'The Paddington Bear Affair' lasted for weeks. Young's final resignation and retirement came after misdirection of campaign donations of $A10,000 to the Australian Labor Party.

A vital element in Hawke's success was his 'charisma'.

An almost magical aura was visible in Hawke's early years. He had the capacity to tune into the national mood and capitalise on his personification of 'Australian-ness'. Never was this better illustrated than the occasion of Australia's stunning victory in the world yachting championship 'America's Cup'.

The trophy had not been taken from the United States since it was first won on 22 August 1851. In the year of Hawke's election, 1983, however, *Australia II* defeated the American boat *Liberty* in a never to be repeated illustration of the felicitous collaboration between Australian technology and Australian capitalism. Hawke bathed in champagne, flanked by two of the richest individuals from the richest corporations in Australia, Alan Bond and Laurie Connell. Hawke then incited Australian workers to take the day off, quipping that any boss who objected was a bum. This strategy worked so well that Hawke made 'charisma-appearances' at a football grand final, a tennis championship, and he demonstrated that his government was committed to expenditure on the arts as well as sport, by attending, somewhat less convincingly, a televised performance by the Australian Ballet of *Swan Lake*.

As with the ballet, so with politics: there were internecine squabbles between the company and the principals. Although admitting he had been 'crippled by his mates', the former party leader Bill Hayden took up the Foreign Affairs portfolio and handled it well. The ministry also received deserved kudos for handing back Ayers Rock – Uluru – to its Aboriginal owners in a show of solidarity. But Attorney-General Gareth Evans and Defence Minister Gordon Scholes were soon on the carpet for making unauthorised military flights over hydro-electric dam works in Tasmania. Neal Blewett, on the other hand, added to the Hawke government's stocks by successfully introducing a universal, compulsory medical benefits system, called Medicare, financed out of a levy on income tax.

Hawke's chief lieutenant and his most marketable asset was

his Treasurer, Paul Keating. Keating was described by Paul Kelly, one of Australia's most respected political reporters, as bringing to caucus and machine politics the disciplined infallibility of his Catholicism. 'Dressed with the smart severity of a Jesuit,' said Kelly, 'he slid along the parliamentary lobbies carrying ambition as an altar boy cradles his missal.' Keating cradled missiles as well as missals. At a 1985 tax summit in Parliament House, Keating tried to introduce a consumption tax of 12.5 per cent in return for income tax concessions. The summit turned out to be a political disaster, as Hawke retreated before the hostility of public opinion and dropped the idea of a consumption tax, leaving Keating, who had staked his reputation on the acceptance of his tax plans, to sum up the end of the conference as being 'like "Ben Hur". We crossed the line with one wheel off the chariot'.

The ALP chariot could run for years on one wheel. Keating was quick with an image and followed his Ben Hur idea with the announcement in 1986 that Australia was in danger of becoming a banana republic. The idea of Australia as a banana republic captured the public's imagination. It was so apt. The one megalomanic party system, which Australia was developing, was the chief characteristic of banana republics, but the questions of financial irresponsibility and incompetence were not far behind. In the period of deregulation that followed the election of the Hawke government in 1983, vast fortunes had been made by a relatively large group of entrepreneurs. They all thanked the Australian Labor Party for allowing them – and the state governments – to borrow off-shore, without concern for the disastrous effect on the balance of payments and terms of trade that servicing the interest on such borrowing would have.

The treasurer made feeble attempts to explain away the massive deterioration in international confidence in the Australian economy. Scapegoats were found in many areas:

the fall of commodity prices, the downturn in world demand for Australia's traditional agricultural and mining exports and the new wave of international protectionism. Japan and the United States were particularly attacked for the insensitivity of their policies, Japan for biting the hand that warmed and fed it, and the US for attempting to sell subsidised grain to the Soviet Union. At home, capital and labour were found equally guilty. Keating blasted the leaders of industry for their unwillingness to pay their share of tax, and said that the workers were greedy by demanding excessive wage rises at a time of national crisis.

In a farcical episode, Prime Minister Hawke thanked the pensioners of Australia for forgoing their anticipated and due pension rise (the delay in payment being a matter of government policy in which the pensioners had no choice) and attacked the ALP's rich detractors for not being equally self-sacrificing. The chairman of Elders IXL, John Elliott, was abused for saying that Australia was an inappropriate country for speculators to invest in, an opinion evidently shared by Australia's largest life insurance and superannuation funds, most of whom invested large amounts overseas.

Attacks on and from the industrialists were easy to anticipate and not so politically damaging as attacks from Hawke's own backbench. Senator Graham Richardson pointed out the defects in ALP's public relations during its mid-term slump. Richardson admitted that the Labor government had lost touch with its power base. Richardson warned that Labor would lose the next election unless it stuck to the party platform. Richardson said that the ALP had alienated almost every interest group in the country as well as its own rank and file. The members in the party branches complained that the ALP was too close to the business community and had abandoned traditional ALP philosophy. 'I think we forgot for too long that we were in essence politicians,' said Richardson, 'we became economists with the rhetoric of economists.'

Hawke still remained optimistic. The pensioners (one of whom he described as a 'silly old bugger'), were too disorganised to be a political force, and in any event had even more to fear from the Liberal-National Party. Some of the leaders of industry were critical of his policies, but not all. Even the life assurance offices who invested offshore were only using an aspect of the new deregulated banking system to make the most of their profits, and in time Hawke and Keating expected that dividends flowing from the offshore investments would boost Australia's economy. Moreover, the Hawke government had made considerable progress in its negotiations with trade unions. Under the Hawke wages accord, wage and salary earners bore the brunt of government cost-cutting. The wage and salary earners were persuaded to accept less than full wage indexation, deferred wage increases and a general diminution in their standard of living on the promise of tax cuts in the future. They, like the pensioners, reasoned Hawke, would have to conclude that if things were bad under Labor, they would be even worse under the Liberal-National Party.

Hawke did not have much to fear from the opposition either. Premier Bjelke-Petersen, who was subsequently tried and acquitted for political corruption, celebrated his return to power in the 1986 Queensland state elections with an attack on the federal Liberal Party. His less fortunate Minister for Racing and Main Roads, Russ Hinze, who was tried and convicted, charmed his electors and astonished the critics with an impressive entry in the Gold Coast beer-gut competition. He was less than useful to the party, however, when he vilified the opposition leader, John Howard, as colourless and out of touch and suggested a Peacock take-over would be more acceptable to the voters of Australia. The Liberal Party was further damaged when the former prime minister, Malcolm Fraser, received a set-back to his career as a senior Commonwealth statesman. Fraser was leader of the Commonwealth's eminent persons group charged with finding a solution to the apartheid system in South Africa. In an inexplicable incident far from the Dark Continent, he was found, wearing only a shirt and wrapped in a towel, at the Benbow Inn, Memphis, Tennessee. He had checked in under the name John Jones of Victoria, Australia, lost his diplomatic passport as well as his trousers, and only the dropping of a security curtain stopped further damaging revelations about his conduct. Hawke wept crocodile tears on Fraser's behalf, but declined to pursue the matter, leaving it to Barry Humphries's character, Sir Les Patterson, to proffer sympathy on the grounds that he too had often found himself in similar circumstances.

In 1987 the Hawke government neared the end of its second term with bleak prospects. They were saved by a change of fortune that Hawke was quick to pounce upon. From Queensland came the first signs of a split in the Liberal-National Party Coalition, which widened as the year proceeded. Bjelke-Petersen, misjudging the extent of his own popularity, decided to promote himself as the next prime minister of Australia. Bjelke-Petersen tried to ride the wave of new right sentiment of economic rationalism, and expected that his tough line with trade unions, when combined with a flat tax proposal, would prove irresistible. Bjelke-Petersen grossly misjudged the mood of the electorate.

The conservatives were led by the Nationals' Ian Sinclair and the Liberals' John Howard. Sinclair made only one contribution to the campaign, describing Hawke as the Charles Manson of Australian politics. Howard tried to conduct his strategy without advice from junior ministers, and ran a campaign over-estimating the electors' cynicism and venality. The omens for the Liberals could not have been worse when a former leader of the opposition, Billy Snedden, died *in flagrante* in a Sydney motel, much to the delight of the editor of the *Truth* newspaper who, like the policeman who investigated the death, described the circumstances in too much detail. Hawke would have won in 1987 with no policies and no party, and the Australian Labor Party recognised this by dropping all mention of the party, and simply calling for a vote for Hawke.

While the British *Sunday Times* attacked Hawke as over-emotional, shallow and opportunistic, claiming that he had no deep, unalterable convictions, but on the contrary possessed a ruthless eye for unpopular and disposable policies, most Australian voters preferred him as prime minister. Within five years, however, Hawke became so ineffectual, lachrymose, maudlin and sentimental that a handful of disgruntled caucus conspirators, following the Hayden precedent, dumped the party leader. Hawke's replacement as prime minister of Australia was to be the architect of the banana republic, Paul Keating.

The ALP was destabilised but not mortally weakened by the long running battle for supremacy between the two different party leaders. Hawke, from his Melbourne base, had a clerical-academic background including years at Oxford. Keating was from the Sydney working class and left school with minimal formal education. Both men sized each other up, knowing that it was inevitable that the older would in time yield to the younger. The question was when. In an agreement known as 'the Kirribilli pledge' after the location of its making – the prime minister's Sydney home – Hawke agreed to hand over power to Keating in time for Keating to put his own stamp on the ALP before the next general election. Hawke, however, saw his election victories as so much of an endorsement of his own personal leadership qualities that he was invincible to critics within the ALP, and accordingly he reneged. Keating was forced to dislodge Hawke in a head on clash. The clash of the leader and would-be leader deflected public attention from economic problems and an out of control private sector.

One of the first signs of this was the collapse of L. J. Hooker. Australia's largest and hitherto most respectable property manager, it failed as shopping complexes failed to turn a profit, and house mortgage rates reached 17 per cent, driving home buyers from the market. The economy was further damaged by strikes, lockouts and sackings in the domestic airline industry. John Stone characterised the country as 'a smoking ruin' and he was correct. Even so, Hawke was able to win another remarkable election victory on 24 March 1990, when the conservatives switched their leadership team on the eve of the poll, dumping John Howard and Ian Sinclair, and replacing them with Andrew Peacock and Charles Blunt. Keating summed up popular response to this fatal political miscalculation. He asked Peacock whether a souffle could rise twice. Hawke made political history as Australia's most successful ever ALP prime minister.

But the 1990 election saw bad news for all parties. Charles Blunt, who replaced Ian Sinclair as leader of the National Party, lost his seat. The conservatives made substantial gains in Victoria, where the local ALP government's economic mismanagement was too obvious to ignore. The National Party chose Tim Fischer to lead them, but the Liberals made a more daring choice, selecting John Hewson as their chief. Hewson, at 43 years of age, was relatively new to the parliamentary game, having been elected in 1987. His background was similar to that of Keating, with whom he shared much in common. Hewson's working class home was escaped by climbing the meritocracy ladder, via a doctorate at a minor North American university, a stint at the International Monetary Fund in Washington, and an economics chair at an Australian university. Hewson's entry to the leadership was relatively successful. Initially he provided an alternative to the usual pattern by eschewing personal abuse and vilification. Within months he reduced Hawke's lead in the public opinion popularity polls.

After the 1990 election, the Hawke administration counter-attacked Hewson by moving more and more to the centre, giving the electorate little to choose between. Chifley would have turned in his grave when the ALP cabinet decided to sell part of the Commonwealth Bank, and to embrace privatisation. The Liberals were placed in a difficult position, with the emperor stealing their clothes. Howard quoted with malicious accuracy from Hawke's 'Light on the Hill' speech in 1985, during which Hawke had asked rhetorically, 'What in the name of reason is the justification for breaking up and selling the great efficient national assets, like the Commonwealth Bank, Telecom, Australian Airlines, QANTAS? The fact is that this recipe for disaster represents the heights of economic rationalism, based on a blind and mindless commitment to a narrow, dogmatic and discredited ideology.' During an earlier anti-privatisation campaign Hawke had pointed out that anyone who thought about privatisation knew it meant higher prices, higher costs and higher fares.

Hawke, knowing that he was slipping, seized the opportunity of the seventy-fifth anniversary of ANZAC Day as a way to project his charismatic, heroic-leader image. While the importance of ANZAC Day and the political influence of Australia's old soldiers had been overshadowed by claims for compensation over damage done to Vietnam veterans, Hawke was able to triumph by a tour of the Gallipoli peninsula. Although Hewson travelled with Hawke, all eyes were on the prime minister. He did not disappoint them. Hawke travelled with many of the last survivors of the first world war. Some diggers were nearly a hundred years old and all considered their second trip to Gallipoli more dangerous than the first. A large number of nurses and doctors went with them on a special QANTAS flight bearing the slogan for the occasion 'Spirit of ANZAC'. Hawke made the most of his photo opportunities at the Dawn Service, the most solemn, Jungian moment in the Australian psychic annual calendar. During his speech, telecast live, Hawke wiped aside a tear and prayed, 'Let us hope that the nations of the world are emerging from their self-destructive practices of enmity, and will build, in sunlight, a world of peace.'

There was plenty of sunlight, no peace: Iraq's invasion of Iran turned Hawke the dove into Hawke the hawk. Hawke despatched two warships and a supply ship to the Gulf. Many of the sailors followed their leader by crying on television, protesting that they had joined the navy to travel, and go shopping in South East Asia, not to be shot. In the event, their fear was unfounded. Saddam's military capacity was greatly exaggerated to magnify the victory of the technocrats, and the United States bases in Australia with their handful of defence scientists proved more useful to the war effort than the presence of a small Australian war fleet. Hawke was not able, however, to follow in the footsteps of Margaret Thatcher, and repeat the political triumph of the Falklands campaign. Once the last ship sailed home, Hawke and his ministers were forced to look again at the emerging scenario of financial failure, most alarming in Victoria, where the State Bank of Victoria incurred such huge losses through its merchant banking arm, Tricontinental, that the Commonwealth Bank had to take it over. The collapse of Estate Mortgage Trust hit many small investors and was followed by huge losses in the State Bank of South Australia.

Hawke lost the prime ministership because his ministers were unable to cope with the twin stresses of attack from the Keating camp within the party, and attack by the conservatives on the opposition parliamentary benches over the state of the economy. Keating first challenged Hawke in mid-winter 1991, lost the challenge, and resigned as Treasurer to sit on the back bench, awaiting the moment for a new attack. Keating's departure left Hawke protected by a tired rump not capable of functioning under stress. Australia needed a competent treasurer. Keating may not have been 'the world's greatest treasurer', but he was confident, direct, forceful and decisive. His two replacements at the Treasury, John Kerin and Ralph Willis, were anything but. Hewson made the running with a bold strategy of holding up the prospect of a goods and services tax as the centrepiece of a new economic policy. Kerin was unable to counter-attack, frequently fumbled his opportunities, and was inclined to make thoughtless off the cuff remarks that were damaging to his party and contrary to the Hawke line that Australia was not suffering from a depression, merely a down-turn in economic activity. Kerin had worked as axeman, bricklayer, agricultural economist and served as Minister for Primary Industries before becoming Treasurer. He admitted to journalists (while on a trip to Bangkok) that the record unemployment levels were burning the government, and said bluntly that Australia was in the worst recession it had faced for sixty years. Kerin had once owned a world champion racing lizard. *Perfect Weather* by *Every Day* out of *South West Queensland* won for Kerin the world lizard race championship of 1989. Hawke was forced to send him back to lizard racing, replacing him with Ralph Willis, who was in the treasurer's office for such a short period that his press occasionally confused him with the American film actor, Bruce Willis.

Hawke's desperate switch of treasurers was a response to Keating not to Hewson. The prime minister was rattled by a renewed push, stemming from Senator Graham Richardson's office, to put Keating in The Lodge. Hawke's supporters returned to traditional canine invective, and described Richardson as a slimy mongrel. All the facade of Labor unity was gone. When Keating made the first challenge he lost by a narrow margin, 66 caucus votes to 44. But Keating's disingenuous claim that he had only one shot in the locker did not hold for long. He further destabilised the party by comparing the Australian to the UK scene. He pursued the point that political parties and their leaders needed to evolve, saying that evolution could not be stopped, nor could party leaders be kept until they were 'as old as Methuselah'. Keating concluded, 'The people are quite smart about these things. They've tuned into the healthy process of selection within political parties and democracies,' and he noted with approval how 'the British public' were 'obviously understanding' about what happened to Thatcher, Heseltine and Major.

Australia's Methuselah was only in his early sixties and declined to endorse Keating's Biblical-Darwinian suggestions. Nevertheless, Hawke's most loyal lieutenants explained patiently to him that for the good of the party and to protect his historical reputation, he should retire with dignity, let Keating take over, honour the Kirribilli pledge, and permit the new leader to start afresh in time to beat Hewson at the ballot boxes. Privately, most caucus members thought that Keating would be merely a transition leader, that the ALP was doomed to lose the next election, but that the damage would be lessened if Hawke could be persuaded to go quickly. Hawke, however, refused to respond to the tap on the shoulder. He was desperate to keep the prime ministership, and used every argument to deflect his attackers. He wished to play golf with President Bush, who was about to visit Australia; he wished to have Christmas in The Lodge; he did not want to upset his wife Hazel, who was about to enter hospital for surgery. Hawke listened to his closest friends (who were accurately described as 'the magnificent seven with beer guts'), but ignored their advice. If Keating wished to take his job, Hawke said, he would have to do so by a caucus ballot. Hawke then called a special caucus meeting, at which he resigned, and offered himself for re-election, hoping, he said, that the issue would be resolved quickly in the least disruptive manner. No Labor party prime minister had ever been rejected by his party in a caucus ballot, but on this occasion Hawke lost by five votes.

On 20 December 1991, after eight years of power, there were tears but not beers all round. The opposition leader, remembering Julius Caesar, shook Hawke's hand across the dispatch box and commented that Hawke was a far better man than Keating, who would lead Labor to defeat at the next election. Australians, said Hewson, would never forgive the man whose deliberate high interest rates put home ownership out of their reach, and who cold-bloodedly stalked and then assassinated his own leader. The anti-Keating ALP backbencher John Scott quipped, 'Even a drover's dog could lead us to defeat at the next election.' Hawke's own priority was how to service his debts, and he started 'to rake it in' – as his new agent, Harry M. Miller, expressed it.

Labor lost the by-election for Hawke's seat to an independent. Keating set about to turn around public opinion and set out as his centrepiece a blueprint for prosperity called the One Nation Policy. Keating's 'One Nation' cry was expected to cut the ground from beneath Hewson's equivalent 'Fightback'. However, neither leader could make much impact on the major problem, unemployment. The ALP subtitled the One Nation speech in February 1992 'kickstart', and promised that it would create 800,000 jobs, including 200,000 in tourism. Most of the policy changes were projected so far into the future as to have little immediate impact.

In an initiative of doomed optimism, Keating turned on the British government, and in a series of escalations gradually moved the question of the creation of an Australian republic to central stage. He chose the occasion of a royal visit by Queen Elizabeth to launch his republican campaign. In an exact reversal of the Menzies era, when the Queen was used to boost conservative electoral hopes, Keating fanned the fires of republicanism in a successful attempt to win back Labor supporters who were being crushed by unemployment and deserting the party. Keating began slowly, observing at a Parliament House reception held to welcome the Queen in February 1992, that as Britain sought to make its future secure in the EEC, Australia vigorously sought partnerships in its own region. To underline the point, Keating's wife Annita declined to curtsey to the Queen, and Keating himself offended protocol by putting his arm around her. The Queen herself made no reply, but conservative leaders lambasted Keating as the most petty, mean-minded and ungracious of prime ministers. The conservative front bencher Alexander Downer observed that Annita Keating may have persuaded her husband to give up wearing cream shoes, but had yet to teach him public dignity.

When public opinion proved to be in favour of Keating's republicanism, the prime minister broadened his attack to include not just the Queen but her country. Keating was told that he learned at school 'about self-respect and self-regard for Australia, not about some cultural cringe to a country which decided not to defend the Malaysian peninsula, not to worry about Singapore and not to give us our troops back to keep ourselves free from Japanese domination'. Keating's remarks were attacked by historians and newspaper editors alike. Professor Geoffrey Blainey, Australia's most famous post-war interpreter of contemporary history, disagreed with Keating, saying that Britain abandoned neither Singapore nor Malaysia. Britain, he explained, was so heavily over-extended in the war against Hitler in Africa that Britain gave higher priority to that war against Hitler than it did to the war against Japan. In the UK itself the press ran a gamut between *The Times* recording that Keating had run 'into accusations of *lese-majeste* in so rudely bringing up the issue of republicanism to the Queen's face' to the *Mirror*, which said 'Aussies don't give a XXXX about manhandling the Queen'. The burst of London winter royalism (which sadly did not last long enough to cover the royal marriage problems of the spring) headlined Keating as 'the loudmouthed Lizard of Oz', and said he had insulted 27,000 heroes and forgotten British war dead. The Duke of Edinburgh, in hot water for refusing the opportunity to cuddle a koala, declined to protect his wife by answering reporters' questions about the republican issue. Keating was delighted by the popular response, which, for an instant, put him ahead of Hewson in the see-sawing public opinion polls. He then had another burst of historical revisionism. Whereas Hawke focused on Gallipoli as his chance to influence the swinging voters, Keating decided to shift the emphasis to Kokoda. Keating kissed the battleground where, he said, many teenage Australians died protecting their northern coastline in the battle for Papua New Guinea. This slightly backfired, however, as the Archbishop of Adelaide accused Keating of being offensive to the Pope (who had earned the photo-opportunity monopoly on soil-kissing by his genuine humility). It was, said the *Australian*, an obvious attempt to deflect public attention from the economic conditions of Australia.

By 1993, the banana republic predicted by Keating was much closer. Retribution for economic mismanagement in the 1980s fell on the public, the politicians and the entrepreneurs who made transient fortunes in the deregulated era. Losses were in billions not millions, and a procession of financiers were called to account by shareholders and, in some cases, the criminal courts. Alan Bond was jailed for dishonesty, and Laurie Connell charged over the collapse of a merchant bank. Some escaped Australian jurisdiction (Abe Goldberg fled to Poland, Christopher Skase to Spain), and some, like John Elliott and John Spalvins, stayed to face the music. The Australian Labor Party was badly scorched by the falls from grace of parliamentary leaders in Victoria, South Australia and Western Australia. Royal commissions and government enquiries tried to explore the dividing range between dishonesty and incompetence.

Australia, in the 1990s, had experienced *The Change*; its economy had become as menopausal as Germaine Greer, whose cult book bore the *zeitgeist* title. In the heady days of feminism which were marked by *The Female Eunuch*, social democracy was in the ascendancy. By 1993, the party system was as moribund as the ageing feminist's follicles. Although she would not have recognised it, her attack on HRT – hormone replacement therapy – was in tune with public opinion on the political equivalents, Fightback and One Nation. Voters recognised that political slogans were no more likely to kickstart the Australian economy than mares' urine was likely to bring back youth to middle age.

Keating and Hewson went into the 1993 election campaign trying to project the confident image of respectable gynaecologists, each armed with their own brand of conjugated oestrogens. Keating took the initiative and prescribed his own version of Premarin: a five-week election campaign during which he was gradually able to gain the upper hand. Hewson preferred to rely on the stirrups. Both leaders were trying to do the impossible. Keating was attempting to lead the Australian Labor Party to a record number of victories, five straight; Hewson was trying to win an election with a programme with, however much he tried to disclaim it, the imposition of a new tax as its centrepiece.

The 1993 election was to be a turning point for Australia's conservatives. During the five-week campaign, Keating turned every question into an opportunity to ridicule the GST, and Hewson was unable to create any confidence that this new tax would lead to an economic revival, reduce unemployment, or even create incentive for private enterprise. Hewson made the great mistake of avoiding contact with the Fourth Estate. Keating was happy to debate issues with the megalomaniacal journalists of the Australian press, and was able to get across his views that under Hewson Australians would see Medicare dismantled and industrial relations return to anarchy. The experience in Victoria, where Premier Jeff Kennett's heavy-handed attack on established workers' privileges led to mass street demonstrations, would, Keating, argued, spread nationwide. Keating described Hewson as a right-wing radical. In any other society the term 'right-wing radical' is a polite expression for 'fascist'. Hewson complained that the press was against him and that Keating was running a scare campaign, but the leader of the opposition was unable to convince the patients who were frightened by the depth of Hewson's conservatism. The electors saw GST as extrinsic to their culture, and rejected it.

It is difficult to say exactly when victory changed sides. Certainly Hewson looked like a winner when Keating took the bold and imaginative step of calling the election in the wake of a smaller than expected defeat for the state Labor Party in the Western Australian elections. Perhaps the decisive moment was when Annita Keating allowed herself to be glamourised by *Vogue* and appear as a glossy, sophisticated covergirl. Carolyn Hewson was touted as a Hilary Clinton look-alike, and stepped into her husband's shoes when he eventually lost his voice, exhausted from bellowing at crowds at lunch-time public meetings. Both leaders took part in television debates on US presidential lines, a mistake on Hewson's part as Keating had gone into the election competition as underdog. Keating's official campaign opening was held at the Bankstown Town Hall, against a minimalist backdrop conceived by the creator of the popular Australian cult film *Strictly Ballroom*. Keating delivered his campaign speech in a despondent, weary voice, hesitant and muffing his lines, reading his text as if it were the first time he had ever seen it, and bearing an uncanny physical likeness to Dr Goebbels, some of whose old footage was broadcast by the Australian Broadcasting Corporation at about the same time.

The election was not fought on the issues of defence, foreign affairs or trade. Many electors made up their minds at the last moment, leaving both parties bewildered about the likely outcome until well after the counting of votes began. Republicanism, which was to be a big issue after the election, was not high on the election agenda in 1993. There was no chance of the conservatives calling for a royal visit to save them, as Menzies had done in 1954. *Prince Charles at Play* would have conjured up a different set of images forty years later. The heir and successor to Her Majesty Queen Elizabeth II had all but wrecked the credibility of the monarchy by his variation of the frog-prince myth: instead of the frog dreaming of turning himself into a prince, the prince dreamed of turning himself into a tampon. Hewson's GST was seen as a threat to culture, and artists of all kinds rallied to Keating. Writer and activist for republicanism, Thomas Keneally, tried to demolish Hewson's residual enthusiasm for the governor-general and links with the British monarchy by commenting that Prince Charles was an inappropriate person for Australia to swear loyalty to. His place of domicile was uncertain, he said, Prince Charles having expressed a wish to reside permanently in an English horse-woman's underclothes.

By late on the night of the election, Hewson must have wished there was room there for him also. Showing what Senator John Button called 'a ton of political ability and vision', Keating was elected prime minister in his own right. Keating was a cruel victor, crowing, 'This is the sweetest victory of all – this is the sweetest.' Hewson was ungracious in defeat. The conservatives recognised that their party had gone backwards and that they had neglected to pay sufficient attention to the voice of women. Sections of the women's movement deplored the way in which it appeared (correctly or incorrectly) that Hewson's new conservatives believed a woman's place was in the home. Beryl Beaurepaire reminded conservatives that Menzies's Liberal Party stood for equal gender representation on all party committees. Keating was shrewd enough to employ writer and feminist Anne Summers as an adviser, and his foresight was rewarded: in 1993 gender preferences for political parties changed, and most women voted Labor. As writer and commentator Bob Ellis predicted on ABC radio on 2 March 1993, when the leader of the opposition failed to win the arguments, the public went sour and left Hewson 'looking like a dickhead in a wet T-shirt'. Keating, on the other hand, as he promised when he won, exerted his own firm authority over ministry selection. No leader since Menzies had been in a stronger position. Keating selected a new and young team, and charged them with the difficult task of avoiding all the old, mouldy mistakes and inventing another satisfactory series of beautiful new lies to suit Australia in the third millennium.

CHAPTER 11

Core Promises

When Keating just squeaked in he did not forget that many of his ministers and most of his party expected him to lose. The new Keating ministry saw a burst of ageist discrimination, with most of the new cabinet being younger than 50, if not younger than springtime, and seasoned elder statesmen (like Neal Blewett, who had steered through parliament long-lasting and beneficial reforms to the health funding system) banished to diplomatic appointments on early retirement. Initially, Keating had a dream run: the conservatives dumped Hewson and replaced him with Alexander Downer who, at that stage, came across as urbane, intelligent and thoughtful, and accordingly was not to last long in the job. But after the fifth election victory there was no honeymoon period of supportive public opinion for the ALP. Australia won the world-wide competition to bring the 2000 Olympic Games to Sydney, but this good news was almost the last, as scandals of bribery and corruption were uncovered in the Olympic Games selection process. To make matters worse, former prime minister Bob Hawke attacked Paul Keating, highlighting Keating's remark that Australia was 'the arse-end of the world', and predicted that Alexander Downer would be the next prime minister of Australia. Hawke was correct about the short-term future of the Liberal Party, but wrong about its new leader and the future prime minister, who turned out to be John Howard.

In the closing years of the twentieth century, Keating sowed the last of his dragon's teeth, cocooned in his suite of offices – arrogant, vindictive and completely under-estimating Howard's political skills, which turned out to be formidable. It was Keating's dream that an Australian president would declare open the Sydney 2000 Olympic Games. Keating, as a prime minister with all the cocky self assurance of a working-class Catholic lad who barely finished primary school, appointed Sir William Deane to replace Bill Hayden as Australia's forty-second – and, Keating hoped – last governor general. Keating's characteristic misreading of Irish history gave him an atavistic dislike of the English monarchy – displayed earlier when, according to the British press, he goosed Queen Elizabeth II – and re-iterated his insistence that Australia ought to be a republic on what he took to be the Irish model.

The attempt to pursuade a largely Anglo Saxon, conservative and insular community to dump the Queen turned out to have an unexpected outcome in the last days of the century, as did Keating's relentless commercial enthusiasm for Indonesia and Indonesian foreign policy. Keating met President Suharto in Bali in September 1995, and cemented the warmth of a relationship which began in auspicious circumstances when Australia supported Indonesia's struggle for self-determination in the late 1940s. Friendship was reinforced by joint training exercises between the Australian and Indonesian military forces, and Indonesia's willingness to withdraw a candidate for the position of ambassador to Australia on the grounds that Australians believed he was too close to a massacre in East Timor in 1992. At foreign minister level, Australian–Indonesian links were also strong, both Gareth Evans and Ali Alatas being concerned about the connection, and Evans not yet concentrating on the seductive qualities of the leader of the Australian Democrats, Cheryl Kernot. Cheryl Kernot became the Democrats' leader in May 1993, winning the post with an enviable vote of 81 per cent. In 1994 she launched the 'Inspiring Women' calendar for 1995. She was Miss April. The slogan with her photograph was 'strength and courage' which in retrospect was probably better than 'keep the bastards honest'. Kernot's quote from Emmeline Pankhurst, 'Women will only be truly successful when no one is surprised that they are successful', was of no interest to the prime minister, although the attorney general, Gareth Evans, pricked up more than his ears.

By March 1996 Keating faced an election in which the Australian Democrats were an irritation not an obstacle. His pessimism was such that on election eve he spent long hours planning his post-retirement ownership of the largest piggery in the southern hemisphere, a megalomaniacal dream in keeping with his Napoleonic collection of French antique timepieces. The 1996 election campaign had an *Alice in Wonderland* air to it, with both political leaders acting like mad hatters. Keating in his heart suspected he was finally doomed in 1996, and his opponent, John Howard, was so hardened to disappointment that he also planned his defeat speech. The campaign was run by two political leaders who both confidently expected to lose: each adopted the same campaign strategy, going to great lengths to avoid any spontaneous contact with the Australian electorate, and talking exclusively to hand-picked groups of their own supporters, in set pieces of television sound bites.

As it turned out the electorate, weary of Keating, dumped him and chose Howard. Australians wanted a less radical future. Howard's critics said that from the moment he took office John Howard mastered time travel and stepped backwards towards a vision of Australia before Aboriginal land rights, women's liberation, social democracy or even a sense of national identity. His every movement was a backward one. Nineteenth-century political economy was the order of the day, with a Darwinian doomsday scenario under which the weakest went to the wall in a vision of antipodean Thatcherite capitalism red in tooth and claw. Australia had always had the world's most dangerous collection of spiders, sharks and fish. To this was added in the twenty-first century the most retrogressive political perspective in the developed world, with an economic performance so poor that by 2002 the only local currency the Australian dollar consistently outperformed was the Papua New Guinean Kina.

Keating was sent on his way by the former Governor General Bill Hayden who, under privilege, attacked Keating, implying that he was homosexual. While in theory, in a multicultural tolerant society like Australia, this should have caused no more offence than describing him as a vegetarian, the gasps from the press gallery showed that Hayden had successfully succeeded in turning the blowtorch of public opinion away from the conservatives and moving it towards the ALP's bottom. Hayden's efforts to diminish the prestige of the vice-regal office were, however, to be overshadowed by Howard's own personal choice for governor general in the third millennium, Peter Hollingworth, whose bedside reading must at one stage have included *Lolita*.

Australians were confused by the ALP's policy changes over the previous decade, some of which were totally out of sync with appropriate historical ideological perspectives. Keating seemed to be undoing all of the social democratic economic reforms of the Chifley and Whitlam eras. His government started the process of privatising national assets like the Commonwealth Bank, Telstra, and Qantas. The ALP, in its enthusiasm for the 'user-pays' school of political economy, reintroduced university fees, and reduced the numbers allowed into the welfare and health safety net. All these changes were part of an unexpected bonus which meant that John Howard, Keating's successor as prime minister, was truthfully able to say that he was merely carrying out reforms begun in the Hawke–Keating era.

Not that truthfulness was the most appropriate word to describe Howard's stunningly successful succession of electoral campaigns. Howard invented the concept of the 'core promise', the promise that had to be kept, as opposed to 'ordinary promises', which could be broken.

Keating's defeat saw the end of the ALP as it had more or less existed as a coherent entity throughout the twentieth century. The ALP was to face the twenty-first century under new management, and with an approach to political issues quite removed from its earlier attachment to the class war, to such an extent that in 2002 it tried to distance itself from its trade union roots, believing this to be the only way it could regain power.

Keating left the party leadership with the same goal as his predecessor – to earn as much money as possible in the shortest time. Like Hawke, his marriage ended with the collapse of his political fortune. While Hawke married his glamorous biographer, Keating contented himself with the smug observation (which he later regretted) that to lose one's wife was a small price to pay for the *gloire* of being prime minister. This was rather unhelpful to the ALP, as Annita Keating had been often been paraded as an icon of domestic felicity, so different from the unhomely image of the teary and once beery Hawke menage. In addition, Mrs Keating had put runs on the board. Her speeches in favour of Sydney's bid for the 2000 Olympics were credited with having a special influence in Australia's narrow two-vote win over China. While Paul Keating's mind turned to thoughts of pork, his wife was left like Hazel Hawke to rue the passing of her salad days, when her face beamed out from the cover of the *Australian Woman's Weekly* in months during which Royal scandals were thin on the ground.

Keating was replaced by Kim Beazley, a former minister of defence whose hobbies included the study of military history. Beazley's after-hours reading on battles and gun fire ill-equipped him to cope with the grim tragedy in Port Arthur, where, in April 1996, an unhinged English migrant shot dead 35 people in a random act of senseless killing. The Port Arthur massacre was

Howard's finest hour. It was the only time in his period as prime minister when his critics were unable to describe him as mealy-mouthed and weasel-wording. Howard decided that automatic and semi-automatic rifles and pump-action shotguns had to be banned, and by May 1996 he had banned them. Mountains of guns were turned into scrap. Their barrels were cut off, their firing mechanisms fused, and the metal muck was incinerated under high-security supervision. It was an act of phallic destruction worthy of Alicibides. Australia's shooting rednecks protested, but riding a wave of popular enthusiasm Howard brushed aside their moans and grizzles, paid them compensation, and was for a short time overwhelmingly popular for his statesman-like approach to healing a traumatised country. Criminologists later calculated that Howard had saved hundreds of future lives, and millions of dollars in costs associated with murder and copycat killings, which, after 1996, all but disappeared in Australia. The grim appropriateness of the massacre taking place in Port Arthur, site of the worst atrocities in Australia's penal history, underlined Howard's determination to rid Australia of both the convict stain and, as far as possible, of the means of mass murder by deranged weapon collectors and gun club members.

Keating saw Howard's policy on gun ownership as irrelevant, nursed his contempt of the new prime minister and described the coalition as the most vicious and partisan government since the war. Howard's greatest legacy, said Keating, would be to seriously interrupt the drumbeat of Australia's engagement with Asia. The characteristic illiteracy of Keating's split infinitive, like his incorrect but pretentious sprinkling of such French phrases as *fait accompli*, was derived not only from Catholic ill-education but also from paranoia. 'The media crucified me,' declared Keating, leaving no doubt who it was he identified with. But Keating was wrong in fact as well as pronunciation. Whether or not it was the example of the operation of chance in history, Howard made lasting changes to the fabric of Australian society, and forestalled the march of historical inevitability. In his first term of office, Howard introduced legislation to modify the High Court's voting on Aboriginal land rights, began a massive alteration to the Australian taxation system and, in a Machiavellian masterpiece which was a great political achievement, set out to destroy the campaign for an Australian republic begun by his predecessor. His peculiar midget myopia was precisely the correct response to the right-wing radicals emerging in Queensland, led by Pauline Hanson. By the beginning of the twenty-first century Howard had saved the Queen, destroyed Pauline Hanson and turned Australia into a nation of fugitives from Goods and Services Taxes.

Howard realised early that Pauline Hanson was a potential threat to his power greater than that posed by the Aborigines, the republicans, the ALP, or even his treasurer, Peter Costello, engaged as he was in a bitter battle with his sibling, the Reverend Tim Costello, who, from his eminence as a power broker in the non-conformist church, tore into the Howard government whenever the opportunity presented itself.

Hanson was a baby-boomer and a battler. She joined Howard's Liberal Party as a rising business woman owning a fish and chip shop and was perfectly suited to the small-scale vision of her first leader. Although Hanson probably would not have known it, her views were echoed throughout contemporary Europe from Norway to Sicily, where public opinion was generally focused on the harm being done to stable communities by immigrants who were most likely unemployed and illegal. As in Austria, Italy, France, Germany, Norway and Finland, the racial difference between the existing inhabitants of Australia and the new economic refugees was high on the popular list of anxieties. Howard made the correct decision to chuck her out of the Liberal Party on the very eve of the 1996 elections. By then liberals like Alexander Downer were warning of the damage

Hanson was doing to Australia's overseas image, particularly in South East Asia. Against the odds, like Jean-Marie Le Pen in France, Hanson won a seat in parliament. Her maiden speech contained observations which Australia's gutter journalists found irresistible, even though they were a gross over-simplification of Hanson's complex and sincere views. In September 1996 Hanson told the Australian parliament that she thought that Australia's unemployment was caused by Asian immigrants and Aborigines.

Howard had delivered into his hand a demon he could disown. Pauline Hanson's speeches were to the right of his own views, and he made some headway by denigrating racist populism, which was said to attract at its core a following of disgruntled English migrants. He agreed with Hanson on only one issue. Like Hanson, Howard refused to apologise to Indigenous people for past injustices, explaining that in the Howard household as a child he had been taught that he did not have to apologise for something he had not done.

Hanson, as an independent cut free from the Liberal Party, repeated in parliament that Australia was in danger of being overrun by Asians, who took the jobs needed by Australian citizens, and made no effort to assimilate. She called for Asian immigration to be halted, foreign aid to be stopped, and returned to her theme of the excess generosity of the Australian Treasury in distributing money to undeserving Aborigines. Hanson said she was fed up with being told by Aboriginal Australians: 'This is our land'; she asked rhetorically: 'Where the hell do I go?' I was born here, she declaimed, and so were my parents and children.

Early in the twenty-first century, Howard's popularity continued to fall, and Hanson's to rise. Both drew support from the insomniac listeners to late-night talkback radio, where listeners could telephone the 'the shock-jocks' with such representative comments as the view that Australia's growing heroin problem could be laid at the door of the Vietnamese and Chinese boat people. Errol Simper in the *Weekend Australian* identified the kings of Australian talkback radio as 'the foot soldiers' in rallying public opinion behind John Howard's refugee policies, and certainly talkback radio announcers were crucial in beating up xenophobia, never far from the surface in Australia.

Few can doubt that in an objective sense Howard turned out to be a political genius, with a Napoleonic grasp of strategy so conspicuously lacking in Keating, despite his penchant for fondling French clocks. Howard's mastery of the enemy in the republic debate changed the direction of Australian politics for a generation. He began the process of decimating his republican opponents by carefully selecting the group of delegates to attend a key convention, set for February 1998, during which it would be decided how to deal with the monarchy versus republic debate. Howard appointed 76 delegates, 40 of whom were members of parliament, 20 from the Commonwealth and 20 from the states. Popular voting decided the other delegates who were to carry out the convention mandate of deciding whether the constitution should be amended, which model of a republic would be best, and what the timetable for changes would be.

Although Bob Hawke pointed out that a minimalist republic was unworkable, the ALP followed Keating's minimalist republic concept, an idea which was rooted in Keating's Irish conservatism. The Irish were the most conservative revolutionaries in history. They admitted it. All they wanted to do after the Easter Rising and the Anglo–Irish Treaty was paint the letter boxes green. Keating took the Catholic conservative Irish approach to the republican issue in Australia and, like the twentieth-century Irish nationalist governments, never had the courage to go the whole hog. Consequently, just as Irish have left the Ulster question unresolved, so Australians in the first republican referendum lost a great chance for sweeping and comprehensive reform.

Howard amended his game plan to take advantage of what appeared to be reverses and literally forced victory to change sides. Initially, the republicans were buoyed to find that the key convention voted to support Australia becoming a republic. Howard responded by calling a referendum to be held in 1999 so that Australians could decide if they approved a change to the constitution designed to replace the queen with a president chosen by two-thirds of a joint session of both houses of the federal parliament.

The republicans fell for Howard's trap hook, line and sinker. They were divided, and divided they fell. The stumbling block to success in the republican referendum was the question of direct election. Republicans could not agree on whether they wanted a popular vote – as in the United States, the Finnish, and most normal presidential elections or whether they wanted a president chosen by politicians from the federal parliament. The politicians themselves argued that politicians could not be trusted to elect a president. Who could disagree with that? The matter stopped there. Fifty-five per cent of Australians who voted on 6 November 1999 were persuaded that the election of an Australian president could not be entrusted to the untrustworthy. The Australian result was greeted with disbelief around the world. Even the British royal family agreed with the old ALP slogan 'It's Time'. The optimists among the republicans, including expatriates, and the editor of the *Sunday Times*, described the election as a pyrrhic victory for John Howard, advised the royal family to go before they were pushed, and believed that a republican Australia was inevitable. Howard joined in the celebrations of the monarchists, and warned his republican colleagues in the Liberal Party that henceforth the matter was closed.

Nevertheless, election victory seemed, despite the success of the anti-Republic campaign, a forlorn hope for Howard in the third millennium. Although Beazley as leader of the opposition had done virtually nothing of note besides accept Cheryl Kernot's defection from the Democrats and appoint her to the

Labor shadow front bench, Australians were tired of Howard as they had become tired of Keating. Prime Minister Howard went into the 2001 election holding only a tiny majority. But, after trailing the ALP in the public opinion polls for most of the election campaign, a dramatic and complete turnabout put Beazley out of the race and Howard found himself with the unexpected prize of matching Malcolm Frazer's three election victories, and naming his own retirement date.

Howard's 2001 re-election took place as Australia celebrated 100 years of federation. The gala celebration of federation in Melbourne was a closed-shop event almost exclusively attended by politicians from Australia's over-stocked houses of parliament. While Howard pessimistically watched over the proceedings, retirement plans were on his mind. Public opinion polls since his previous victory had shown a steady erosion of his popularity and that of Australian conservatives generally. Successive election losses left Australia in 2001 with only one conservative state premier, in South Australia, and Howard's party was demoralised and fearing the worst in the run up to the campaign. When Mike Rann subsequently became ALP premier of South Australia, there were no conservative state governments left on the continent. Even in the Northern Territory, where the conservative Country Liberal Party had governed for 26 years, Labor's Clare Martin defeated Denis Burke, and put the ALP into office for the first time. Shane Stone, the president of the Liberal Party, leaked a memo in May 2001 in which he pointed the finger at Peter Costello, saying that the Howard government was 'too tricky, mean, out of touch and arrogant' and much of the blame was the Treasurer's.

Australia had been through a cultural revolution in the Keating era. The banner of Keating's revisionist red guards had been adopted by Howard's conservatives, who re-badged themselves as centre right. For a time the 'greed is good' policies of Howard and Costello carried on the blueprints of Keating and

Dawkins reforms. The guard dogs and balaclava-wearing thugs added by minister Peter Reith to speed up the process of industrial workplace reform merely accelerated what was already afoot in a disturbing period of social change. But as they approached the 2001 election after long stints at the helm, Australia's conservatives were acting and looking tired. Howard, for a time, trailed Beazley in the public opinion polls, and on the eve of the election the ABC published figures putting the ALP in front, and predicting that the ALP would win 18 conservative-held marginal seats. The pollsters were wrong. A year earlier Keating had published a book in which he also prematurely wrote Howard's political obituary. Keating underestimated Howard in 1996 as did Beazley in 2001. Howard's luck held when out of the blue a Norwegian oil tanker, the *Tampa*, picked up almost 500 Afghan refugees, and sailed with them for Australian territory at Christmas Island.

The *Tampa* was international news. Not since a crocodile had been thrown into a swimming pool to ginger up Australian Olympic swimmers had the world's press taken such an interest in the Antipodes. When Howard sent the SAS to board the *Tampa* in rubber inflatables and despatched commandos armed to the teeth and looking like pirates to force the Norwegian ship to stand offshore, the *Sunday Times* likened Howard's refusal to let the Afghans set foot on Australian soil to the 'Voyage of the Damned', during which a boatload of Jews fled Hitler and were refused entry to a string of countries. The *Sunday Times*, like the rest of Howard's critics, was soon forced to eat crow as the *Tampa* case was followed in quick succession by a re-run of Pearl Harbor, when in September 2002 international terrorists from Al Quaeda destroyed the twin tower blocks in New York and put the Pentagon itself out of action for a time. The first Australian minister to catch a whiff of the public opinion change which began with the *Tampa* and was accelerated by September 11, was Philip Ruddock, who alerted the prime minister. Within hours of the government's decision to stop the illegal immigrants landing in Australia the Howard government had changed the public opinion polls around. Overwhelming popular support came almost instantly in talkback radio programs, and almost all callers demanded that the refugees, who were illegal immigrants, be sent back to where they came from.

In a prescient editorial on 2 September, nine days before S11, the *Sunday Times* observed that Australia, like Britain, was a prime target for refugees from poor countries. The *Sunday Times* added that those responsible for the *Tampa* crisis were not in Canberra but in Kabul. There, said the *Sunday Times*, the cynical Taliban, who harboured the terrorist leader Osama Bin Laden, demanded that Australia admit Afghan nationals and allow them the right to lead a normal life. This was the first time a major link had been stressed between the Taliban and the *Tampa*, the elements which, after September 11, Howard used as artful smoke and mirrors to anchor his election victory. When the kamikaze attacks destroyed the twin towers in New York, and Bin Laden was given the credit for the chaos and destruction, Howard could hardly believe his luck. Like Britain's Tony Blaire he quickly took the opportunity to offer troops, fell in with the war against terrorism, and saluted the stars and stripes, giving himself the opportunity to be in command of a nation at war. He was incorrectly lampooned as a little man, although he was taller than Bob Hawke, his Labor mentor in the niceties of Gulf Warfare. President Bush did not spot him in New York in 2002, and initially did not think it was worth meeting his most bellicose outrider.

Howard, however, managed the Australian media skilfully. In the immediate aftermath of S11 Australians were on the whole in favour of the Bush crusade. Even in multicultural Australia Howard's strong stand against Afghan refugees was so popular that it was itself a type of political anthrax, which wiped out Pauline Hanson's hitherto high-profile xenophobic pre-eminence.

Howard became prime minister for a third time, and as his head hit the pillow at night he reflected that he was indeed, as he had always thought, the heir of R.G. Menzies not Billy MacMahon.

Howard's self assessment was not universally popular. Critical views (which were bipartisan) were best summed up by ALP federal politician Anthony Albanese, who earlier quoted Sir Paul Hasluck's description of Prime Minister Billy McMahon as describing John Howard equally well. Hasluck believed that Australia had to go back to McMahon to find a prime minister who approached Howard for petulance, pettiness and sheer grinding inadequacy. As a conservative governor general describing a conservative prime minister, Hasluck was speaking of a colleague, not an enemy. I confess (said Hasluck) to a dislike of McMahon: 'The longer one is associated with him the deeper the contempt for him grows, and I find it hard to allow him any merit. Disloyal, devious, dishonest, untrustworthy, petty, cowardly – all these adjectives have been weighed by me and I could not in truth modify them or reduce any one of them in its application to him.'

'Howard,' said Albanese, was 'Billy McMahon in short pants.' But most of 12.5 million voters who went to the polls in 2001 wanted Howard as prime minister and on 10 November 2001 they got their wish. In Howard's honeymoon period as thrice-elected conservative prime minister he had little to fear from the ALP. The defeated leader of the opposition went off to the doghouse to lick his wounds, ruefully noting that there was nothing to compensate him for not being leader of the opposition. The new Howard ministry were not re-assembled until February 2002, when they were asked to swear allegiance on the Bible to 'Her Majesty Queen Elizabeth the Second, her heirs and excesses', due to an antipodean slip of the tongue, when 'successors' and 'excesses' were unwittingly transposed. In the case of the royal family, the confusion was understandable.

Howard faced a cat's cradle of crises when he first stood at the dispatch box at the opening session of the new parliament. The prime minister's initial survival depended on his ability to chart a plausible course through the unravelling of the coalition's claims during the election campaign that children had been thrown overboard by refugees. Indeed the centrepiece of Howard's election victory was his revelation that asylum seekers, in an attempt to blackmail HMAS *Adelaide* into picking them up, threw their children overboard. By February 2002 Howard regretted his allegations over asylum seekers, and told the misled voters, 'I can only speak the truth and the truth is I was not told, the original advice was wrong.' In the confused mix-up which followed, Peter Reith, Minister of Defence, said his mobile telephone was malfunctioning when he was being told the initial reports were wrong. Air Marshal Angus Houston, who was acting Chief of Defence, said he told Reith on 7 November 2001 that no children had been thrown overboard. The Chief of the Defence Forces, Admiral Chris Barrie, confused matters and rejected the view that no such incident took place. The opposition made heavy weather of their attempts to get the true story behind the 'children-in-the-water-gate', as the ALP was still split between those who wanted softer treatment of refugees, and those who wanted to maintain a bipartisan approach to border sovereignty and people-smuggling. As the *Australian* put it, 'Out of the blue, a big whopper'.

With politics all at sea, truth gone overboard, and Howard rugging up, a further disaster hit the prime minister when Governor General Peter Hollingworth turned overnight from Father of the Year, Australian of the Year, respected icon of Anglican Conservativism, to the central figure in sexual abuse allegations. Hollingworth joined the church as a supporter of nineteenth-century High Church Anglicanism, committing himself to working with the poor. Between 1984 and 1990 he was one of the leaders of the Brotherhood of St Laurence and, as executive director, fought with Bob Hawke over Hawke's failure to deal with child poverty. During the Australian gay nineties he was Archbishop of Brisbane, reaching his penultimate career apotheosis as chairman of the Council for the Centenary of Federation. There his vice-regal ambition was signalled by the Reverend Tim Costello, who highlighted Hollingworth's withdrawal of support for a republic at the Constitutional convention in 1998. Hollingworth was not the only community leader to be caught in the crescendo of investigations into child sex abuse in Australia. His clerical colleague, the Catholic Archbishop of Sydney, Dr George Pell, was forced to step aside while an inquiry found him not guilty of what appeared to be convincing audition for a small part in *The Devil's Playground*, a film novel by Thomas Keneally, professional Irishman and republican.

Howard's decision to appoint Hollingworth governor general backfired on him in much the same way as Gough Whitlam's appointment of John Kerr. Not only did Hollingworth face claims that he did not adequately deal with allegations of sexual abuse within the Anglican church when he was Archbishop of Brisbane, but he went on national television and made it clear that he thought a fourteen-year-old girl had taken the initiative in a sexual relationship with a priest. At that point the Queensland premier led the charge by state leaders calling for Hollingworth to be sacked. Even veteran shock-jock John Laws told the prime minister that for the first time he was out of step with Australian public opinion, which was overwhelmingly against Hollingworth remaining as governor general. At that point Simon Crean, Beazley's replacement as leader of the opposition, made an uncharacterisically brave political choice, and contacted the governor general asking him to resign. And, when that failed and Hollingworth said he was determined to stay on, Crean skilfully painted Howard into a corner. Howard immediately decided to back the governor general, as he could not be seen to be following the Labor lead by sacking the viceroy.

In the months following the *Tampa* election victory, Howard showed signs of reneging on his promise to retire before the next federal election and hand the job of prime minister to Peter Costello. Things started to go right for Howard. The ALP was embarrassed by the conviction of Andrew Theophanos, one of its federal members, for taking bribes. To make matters worse, Kym Beazley said in June 2002 that had he known of the love affair between Gareth Evans and Cheryl Kernot, Ms Kernot would not have been permitted to defect from the Australian Democrats and join the ALP.

Howard's grip on his party became even firmer when, in a tragic example of international terrorism, almost 100 young Australian holiday-makers to the Indonesian resort island of Bali were blown to bits by a car bomb. The bombers were Muslim fundamentalists, proud of their handiwork. From that moment on, Howard took an uncompromising stand on foreign relations, seized the diplomatic initiative and tied Australia as closely as he could to a military alliance with the United States. Howard and many others saw the Bali bombing as Australia's S11. It was proof of the evil links between international terrorists, and gave the prime minister the moral authority – in his terms, the ethical justification – for a just war against the enemies of the United States who had in Bali manifested their animosity to Australia.

At the opening of the 2003 Australian Football League season, Howard boldly appeared on oval television screens to link the Bali bombing with the danger to Australia and the war on terrorism. It was an attempt to justify his decision to send Australian troops to the Gulf in advance of a United Nations resolution to declare war on Iraq. The prime minister sent letters to all Australian homes containing helpful advice on how to deal with local terrorists. The publication, *Let's Look out for Australia*, subtitled *Protecting our way of life from possible terrorist threat*, contained the number for a twenty-four-hour national security hotline, an email address, and added usefully: 'If you wish to report suspicious activity and do not speak English well, call this translating and interpreting service'. Beneath the emu and kangaroo coat of arms on the A4-size booklet, four pictures showed sun-bronzed Aussies on the beach (the largest picture), a barbecue picnic, a policewoman talking to another woman, and sixteen ten-year-olds, one wearing Muslim headdress. A large but flimsy fridge magnet was included in the pack, so that Australian households could be continually reminded of the danger from terrorists.

From the Bali bombing and the decision to commit Australian troops to George Bush's 2003 crusade in the Gulf, Howard spent hundreds of hours flying between Canberra, London and Washington, storing up kudos for Australia as a reliable ally in the event the going got tough (and making it more and more difficult to disengage pre-deployed Australian troops in the event the US went to war against United Nations authority).

Unlike the French and the German leaders – representatives of what the US dismissed as 'old Europe' – Howard was prepared to put Australia out on a limb and go for broke in the interests of enhancing the Pacific alliance.

By February 2003 the prime minister was not being universally thanked for his efforts. Howard returned from a genial meeting with the President of Indonesia to an Australia in ferment.

During the Iraq crisis, the ALP concentrated on tarring the Howard government with the label 'liars'. Crean tried to make 'Honest John' a ludicrous nickname. Crean's ridicule accelerated in 2003 when, against a background of economic reverses, Howard became even more convinced of the need to protect Australia from terrorism and weapons of mass destruction by becoming an indispensable ally of the United States during President Bush's Iraq adventure. In a variation on 1960s' diplomacy Australia joined a troika with the United States and Britain in leading that charge to defang the United Nations and set up western – one might almost say wild western – values as compulsory role models for international relations. Howard was happy to use such simplified descriptions as 'rogue states' to describe North Korea and Iraq, but much more circumspect than Bush in thinking in 'crusader' terms. Howard went out of his way to brave Indonesian popular wrath, calling in on the president of Indonesia on his return from a sabre-sharpening tour conferring with his powerful friends George Bush and Tony Blair. Australia's relations with Indonesia, dented by Australia's role in helping East Timor's independence struggle, were repaired by the collaborative efforts of Indonesian and Australian police to bring to trial the organisers of the Bali bombing. Howard wanted to keep sweet with Indonesia – which had the world's largest Muslim population – and went out of his way to try to explain that the proposed war on Iraq was not anti-Muslim, but anti-Saddam Hussein. Howard's boldness as a foreign policy innovator elevated Australia to an international status it had never had before. As one of the three western nations determined to lead 'the coalition of the willing' and use force against Iraq, Australia became a prime target – not *the* prime target, of course, Washington and London had that distinction – for the enemies of western capitalism.

Certainly the Australian middle class was not so neurotic in 2003 as it was in 1949, when Menzies was able to exploit the fear of communists in the trade unions. The Bali terrorist attack was horrific, but there was no enemy at the gate in 2003 as there had been in 1940. Bali was bombed, not Darwin.

Australians asked, Is the war against Iraq the result of genuine concern about terrorism, evidenced by S11 and the Bali bombing, or is it a cynical grab for Arab oil? Are Australian troops and politicians liable to be tried for war crimes if Australia joins the US and the UK and the coalition of the willing to invade Iraq without United Nations approval or direction?

In February 2003, 500,000 Australians marched in protest against the looming war in Iraq, their pacifism and non-belligerent demonstrations distinguishing them from the angry protestors of the Vietnam era. They were not just worried about war in the Gulf, but what war in the Gulf would do to their already declining standard of living. Australian material prosperity had slumped in the new millennium. Billions were wiped off superannuation accounts. Targeted welfare meant fewer qualified for state support. The health services were in ruins. Education was in a parlous state. Major companies collapsed, or were in the process of doing so. What had not collapsed was becoming absorbed by globalisation, or ruined by managerial incompetence. You name it, it was dead, gone, or going: HIH, Ansett, BHP, Southcorp, BRL Hardy, Orlando-Wyndam, Telstra. Howard described the crowds who marched in Australian streets as a 'mob'.

The marchers were overwhelmingly representative of the Australian bourgeoisie. They wanted a saviour and they did not see him or her coming from the ALP. In 2003 every state in the Commonwealth had an ALP premier, but Howard was overwhelmingly preferred as prime minister. Crean's background as a trade union aparatchik and the son of an ALP minister ill-fitted him to keep in touch with ALP rank and file. Like Beazley, also the son of an ALP minister, the mindset of middle Australia was outside his ken. Since Crean could not lift his personal popularity in the dark hour of Australia becoming involved in the most unpopular war its troops were ever to fight, there seemed no hope for him or his party.

When Howard described the protest groupies as traitors to Australia who brought comfort to Saddam and Bin Laden, Crean repeated his droning mantra that Howard was a serial liar. Calling Howard a liar was not enough. And if Howard was a liar, the ALP were masters of odious prevarication. Only the Greens spoke with a complete lack of ambiguity. Crean's popularity was not helped by his nemesis Mark Latham. From the Labor benches, Latham described Howard as an 'arse-licker' and his parliament's conservative MPs as 'a conga line of suckholes'.

What truly sank Crean's prime minsterial hopes were the divisions in the third millennium Federal ALP. Carmen Lawrence's disaffection, caused by her reaction to the ALP's gutless attitude to refugees' imprisonment, was one brick removed from the wall. Laurie Brereton's courageous early attack on Bush's destruction of the norms of international relations and respect for sovereignty was another. In the event of actual war as compared to proposed war, the ALP would divide into those who supported war in the event of UN approval, and those who opposed war on any terms as 'US imperialism'.

To make things easier for Howard, the ALP had continued its acts of self-indulgent vandalism when Kim Beazley challenged Simon Crean for the party leadership, lost, and left the Liberals with a number of frank assessments of the ALP's weaknesses, as seen from the shadow cabinet. Even at that moment of presumed invincibility, Howard, like his cautious forebears, took nothing for granted. Although he decided that for the good of the nation he would sit Peter Costello on the potty, and not relinquish the prime ministership during his sixty-fifth year, Howard warned his followers that the future for conservatives would not be easy, and that glowing, favourable opinion polls and routed enemies did not necessarily lead on to easy victory.

The key to understanding Howard's strength and appeal was on the public record as early as 2001, when the *Irish Echo* asked him on election eve 'Are you of Irish heritage?' Howard answered 'Yes, in part'. Unfortunately the *Irish Echo* did not establish which part of him was Irish, but since Howard admitted to having only visited Ireland once, as Minister for Special Trade Negotiations, warm and fuzzy feelings towards ancestral roots in Erin can be ruled out. Bearing in mind that Howard was baptised Winston and not Patrick, described himself once as a Christian with a Methodist heritage, the Ulster connection is pretty clear. Howard's motto is No Surrender. If there is one thing dear to an Ulsterman's heart, it is the Monarchy. For love of the monarchy Ulstermen like Ian Paisley or Edward Carson were prepared to overthrow the constitution in the name of the constitution. Nor did they see this as mendacious. Edward Carson, who was the idealogue responsible for the success of the Ulster partition, started off his career like Howard as a Protestant lawyer. There is not much chance of Ian Paisley retiring. Being in a minority has never worried Ulstermen, and it doesn't worry Howard. As Dennis Shanahan put it, Howard's social attitudes were grounded in his 1950s and 1960s suburban monocultural Liberal upbringing which left him with immature fears of republicanism. Shanahan argued that Howard had always resisted a republic, although he actually believed an Australian republic was inevitable, yet powerful personal experience when Howard was growing up instilled a fear of sectarianism, which came to be embodied in a Paul Keating-led Catholic republican movement.

During the premature victory celebrations at the beginning of the war on terror in Iraq, Howard, in an almost Roman triumphal victory tour, called in at London on his way home from the US, where he had discussed Australia's role in the post-Saddam future with George Bush, grateful and effusive as ever. As protocol demanded, Howard called not only on his wartime ally Tony Blair, but on his sovereign, Queen Elizabeth. In Buckingham Palace, quicker than a Corgi's piddle, the Queen left Howard in no doubt that she wanted Bishop Hollingworth out as governor general. By that time Hollingworth had been forced to defend himself not only from a sexual abuse report from the Anglican church (which was helpfully tabled in the Queensland parliament), but also from an affidavit in the Victorian Supreme Court claiming that the Governor General had raped a woman at an Anglican church youth camp at Bendigo in the 1960s. The queen was unconcerned about foolish claims of rape, but as Head of the Church of England and as such directly responsible to God, she could not stomach the thought that her governor general had been, traduced or not, accused of covering up clerical pedophile networks. The queen made it clear Howard needed to rid them both of a troublesome ex-priest. Howard's face was black with rage, not jetlag, when he left the palace, whose masters of spin thoughtfully briefed the London press on the dialogue between the queen and the Australian prime minister. By June 2003 the removalists had crated away Hollingworth's effects from the viceregal residences, and Howard had chosen Major General Michael Jeffery as Australia's 24th governor general.

Major General Jeffery was the unknown soldier. Google could not find him. As an infantry company commander in Vietnam with the 8th battalion, Royal Australian Regiment, he was awarded the Military Cross. A courageous and outspoken fighting soldier, he was embarrassed when asked what he did on operational service, and how it felt to command the SAS. Howard's push to keep security and the war against terror in the public mind found a perfect foil in the new Governor General, and consistent with the prime minister's medieval view of how politics should be run in a twenty-first century parliamentary democracy: by queens, bishops, generals and prime ministers. Jeffery was a human fridge magnet with out-of-step views on homosexuality, single parents, Aboriginals and juvenile crime. His appointment was full of contradictions and incongruities. Certainly he will look more convincing at Gallipoli on Anzac Days than the former archbishop. But Howard's description of him as a man of the people was simply incredible.

With audacious insight Howard decided to fight the 2004 election on the issues of belief, trust and responsibility. During the long campaign he convinced the electorate that trust mattered in one area only: economic management. The ALP, despite the warnings, installed a revolving door to the leader of the opposition's parliamentary suite in Canberra, so Howard's task was made easier by the L-plate leader Mark Latham. Latham lost argument after argument with Howard as the tide of public opinion ebbed and flowed. By not going in hard on the treatment of refugees, or the lack of weapons of mass destruction in Iraq, Latham alienated a large group of potential supporters. His equivocation over Australian troop withdrawal dates could not match Howard's determination to stay and finish the job. He was unable to bribe key electorates over the most sensitive environmental and employment relationships. Howard's finesse of the Tasmanian timber workers' electorate knocked the ALP out of the ring.

In choosing Latham to lead them the ALP caucus were hoping to avoid an election train wreck under the sincere but soporific Simon Crean, or the weaving and dodging Kim Beazley. On the eve of the 2004 election Latham was notorious only for describing George W. Bush as 'the most incompetent and dangerous President in living memory' and for breaking a taxi driver's arm in a dispute over a cab fare. It was not just cab drivers who refused to take Latham seriously as a potential world statesman. The ALP also decided it would be prudent to replace him. Latham left parliament within months of the election loss, retiring on health grounds. The ALP avoided a train wreck, but they got a derailment, putting Kim Beazley into the office with a revolving door. In 2005 Howard took control of both houses of parliament, sent extra Australian troops to Iraq, saw interest rates rise and the balance of payments deficit blow out to a disastrous number. Nor was public opinion impressed when a German-speaking ex-Qantas flight attendant, Cornelia Rau, was imprisoned for months in the outback Baxter detention centre with Muslim asylum seekers, on suspicion of being a possible unlawful non citizen. Howard's conservatives were secure in their future, with Kim Beazley having every prospect of spending his last years not as prime minister, but as a dunny cleaner on the *Titanic*.

Select Bibliography

Advertiser, Adelaide

Age, Melbourne

Alexander, F., *Australia since Federation* (Nelson, Melbourne), 1976

Alomes, S., *When London Calls: The Expatriation of Australian Creative Artists to Britain* (Cambridge University Press, Cambridge), 1999

Argus, Melbourne

Australian, Canberra

Ball, D., and Horner, D., *Breaking the Codes: Australia's KGB Network* (Allen and Unwin, Sydney), 1998

Barrett, J., *We were there: Australian soldiers of World War II tell their stories* (Viking, Melbourne), 1987

Bennett, B., and Strauss, J., *The Oxford Literary History of Australia* (Oxford University Press, Melbourne), 1998

Blainey, G., *A Shorter History of Australia* (Heinemann, Melbourne), 1994

Blewett, N., *A Cabinet Diary* (Wakefield Press, Adelaide), 1999

Bolton, G., *The Oxford History of Australia, Volume 5 1942–1988; The middle way* (Oxford University Press, Melbourne), 1993

Booth, D., and Tatz, C., *One-Eyed: A View of Australian Sport* (Allen and Unwin, Sydney), 2000

Britain, I., *Once an Australia: Journeys with Barry Humphries, Clive James, Germaine Greer and Robert Hughes* (Oxford University Press, Melbourne), 1997

Broome, R., *Aboriginal Australians* (Allen and Unwin, Sydney), 1982

Browning, J., and Critchley, L., *Dynasties* (ABC Books, Sydney), 2002

Brune, P., *Those ragged bloody heroes: From the Kokoda Trail to Gona Beach 1942* (Allen and Unwin, Sydney), 1991

Bulletin, Sydney

Caine, B., (ed.), *Australian Feminism: A Companion* (Oxford University Press, Melbourne), 1998

Canberra Times, Canberra

Carr, B., *What Australia means to me* (Penguin, Melbourne), 2003

Cashman, R., *Paradise of Sport: The Rise of Organised Sport in Australia* (Melbourne University Press, Melbourne), 1995

Catley, R. and McFarlane, B., *From Tweedledum to Tweedledee. The new Labor government in Australia* (ANZ Books, Sydney), 1974

Clark, M., *The Ideal of Alexis de Tocqueville* (Melbourne University Press, Melbourne), 2000

Clark, M., *The quest for grace* (Viking, Melbourne), 1990

Commonwealth Parliamentary Debates

Communist Review, Sydney

Connors, L., Finch, L., Saunders, K. and Taylor, H., *Australia's frontline: Remembering the 1939–45 war* (University of Queensland Press, St Lucia), 1992

Courier Mail, Brisbane

Coward, D.H., *Out of Sight: Sydney's environmental history 1851–1981* (Australian National University, Canberra), 1988

Crisp, L.F., *Ben Chifley: a biography* (Longman, Melbourne), 1961

Crowley, F.K., *Modern Australia in documents, 1939–1970* (Wren, Melbourne), 1973

Damousi, J., *Living with the Aftermath: Trauma, Nostalgia and Grief in Post-War Australia* (Cambridge University Press, Cambridge), 2001

Darian Smith, K., *Challenging Histories, Reflections on Australian History* (Australian Historical Studies, Special Issue, Melbourne), 2002

Davidson, A., *From Subject to Citizen: Australian Citizenship in the Twentieth Century* (Cambridge University Press, Cambridge), 1997

Davidson, J. and Spearitt, P., *Holiday Business: tourism in Australia since 1870* (Melbourne University Press, Melbourne), 2000

Davison, G., *The Use and Abuse of Australian History* (Allen and Unwin, Sydney), 2000

Day, D., *Curtin* (HarperCollins, Sydney), 1999

de Bono, E., *Why I want to be king of Australia* (Penguin, Melbourne), 1999

Dixson, M., *The Imaginary Australian: Anglo-Celts and Identity, 1788 to the Present* (University of New South Wales Press, Sydney), 1999

Dovers, S., *Environmental History and Policy: Still Settling Australia* (Oxford University Press, Melbourne), 2000

Economist, London

Edwards, I., *Keating* (Penguin, Melbourne), 1996

Edwards, P.A., *A Nation at War: Australian Politics, Society and Diplomacy during the Vietnam War, 1965–75* (Allen and Unwin, Sydney), 1997

Ellis, B., *Goodbye Babylon* (Penguin, Melbourne), 2002

Evans, G., and Grant, B., *Australia's Foreign Relations: In the World of the 1990s* (Melbourne University Press, Melbourne), 1995

Far East Economic Review, Sydney

Ferrier, C., and Pelan, R., *The Point of Change: Marxism/Australia/History/Theory* (University of Queensland Press, Brisbane), 1998

Fraser, M., *Common Ground* (Penguin, Melbourne), 2002

Frost, F., *Australia's war in Vietnam* (Allen and Unwin, Sydney), 1987

Funnell, W., *Government by fiat* (University of New South Wales Press, Sydney), 2001

George, K., *A Place of their own: the men and women of war service land settlement at Loxton after the Second World War* (Wakefield Press, Adelaide) 1999

Goldberg, S.L. and Smith, F.B. (eds), *Australian Cultural History* (Cambridge University Press, Cambridge), 1988

Golding, Peter, *Black Jack McEwen* (Melbourne University Press, Melbourne), 1996

Gollan, R., *Revolutionaries and reformists. Communism and the Australian Labor Movement 1920–55* (Australian National University Press, Canberra), 1975

Graetz, B., and McAllister, I., *Dimensions of Australian Society* (Macmillan, Melbourne), 1994

Grattan, M., *Australian Prime Ministers* (New Holland, Sydney), 2000

Grey, T., *A Military History of Australia* (Cambridge University Press, Cambridge), 1999

Griffen-Foley, B., *Sir Frank Packer: the Young Master* (HarperCollins, Sydney), 2000

Griffen-Foley, B., *The House of Packer: The Making of a Media Empire* (Allen and Unwin, Sydney), 1999

Griffiths, A.R.G., 'Australia', *Encyclopaedia Britannica Year Book* (Encyclopaedia Britannica, Chicago), 1966–2003

Guy, B., *A Life on the Left: A Biography of Clyde Cameron*, (Wakefield Press, Adelaide), 1999

Hamnett, S., and Freestone, R., *The Australian Metropolis: A Planning History* (Allen and Unwin, Sydney), 1999

Hancock, I., *John Gorton, he did it his way* (Hodder, Sydney), 2002

Hancock, I., *National and Permanent? The Federal Organisation of the Liberal Party of Australia, 1944–1965* (Melbourne University Press, Melbourne), 2000

Hasluck, P., *Light That Time Has Made* (National Library of Australia, Canberra), 1993

Hasluck, P., *Mucking About: An Autobiography* (University of Western Australia, Perth), 1994

Hasluck, P.M.C., *The government and the people, 1942–45* (Griffin Press, Adelaide), 1970

Haynes, R.D., *Seeking the Centre: the Australian Desert in Literature, Art and Film* (Cambridge University Press, Cambridge), 1998

Head, B. and Walter, J., *Intellectual movements and Australian society* (Oxford University Press, Melbourne), 1988

Henderson, G., *Australian Answers* (Random House, Sydney), 1990

Herald, Melbourne

Hollingworth, P., 'People of the Past?', *Australian Historical Studies*, 117, 2001, 387–8

Horne, D., *Ideas for a Nation* (Pan, Sydney), 1989

Horne, D., *Looking for leadership* (Penguin, Melbourne), 2001

Horner, D., *Inside the War Cabinet: Directing Australia's War Effort, 1939–45* (Allen and Unwin, Sydney), 1996

Hudson, W., and Bolton G., *Creating Australia: Changing Australian History* (Allen and Unwin, Sydney), 1997

Hudson, W.J., *Casey* (Oxford University Press, Melbourne), 1988

Hughes, C.A. and Western, J.S., *The mass media in Australia* (University of Queensland Press, St Lucia), 1971

Hutton, D. and Connors, L., *A History of the Australian Environment Movement* (Cambridge University Press, Cambridge), 1999

Inglis, K.S., *Observing Australia: 1959 to 1999* (Melbourne University Press, Melbourne), 1999

Inglis, K.S., *Sacred Places: War Memorials in the Australian Landscape* (Melbourne University Press, Melbourne), 1998

Iremonger, H., Merritt, H. and Osborne, C. (eds), *Strikes* (Angus and Robertson, Sydney), 1973

Jensen, P.R., *From the Wireless to the Web: The Evolution of Telecommunications, 1901–2001*, (University of New South Wales, Sydney), 2000

Johnson, M., *Fighting the Enemy: Australian Soldiers and their Adversaries in World War II* (Cambridge University Press, Cambridge), 2000

Jupp, J., *Immigration* (Sydney University Press, Sydney), 1991

Kerr, J.R., 'The struggle against communism in the trade unions: the legal aspect', *Quadrant* (1960)

Kiernan, C., *Calwell* (Nelson, Melbourne), 1978

Kmenta, J., 'Economic mobility of immigrants in Australia', *Economic Record* (1961)

Knightley, P., *Australia: Biography of a Nation* (Brough, London), 2002

Lake, M., *Getting Equal: the History of Australian Feminism*, (Allen and Unwin, Sydney), 1999

Leach, M., *The rise and fall of one nation* (University of Queensland Press, Brisbane), 2000

Lee, C. and Henschel, R., *Douglas MacArthur* (Holt, New York), 1952

Long, G., *MacArthur as military commander* (Angus and Robertson, Sydney), 1969

Lowe, D., *Menzies and the 'Great World Struggle': Australia's Cold War, 1948–1954*, (University of New South Wales Press, Sydney), 1999

MacArthur, D., *Reminiscences: General of the Army – Douglas MacArthur* (McGraw-Hill, New York), 1964

Macintyre, S., *A Concise History of Australia* (Cambridge University Press, Melbourne), 1999

Macintyre, S., *A History for a Nation* (Melbourne University Press, Melbourne), 1994

Macintyre, S., *The Oxford History of Australia, Volume 4 1901–1942: The succeeding age* (Oxford University Press, Melbourne), 1993

Macintyre, S., *The Reds: The Communist Party of Australia from origins to illegality*, (Allen and Unwin, Sydney), 1998

Mackay, H., *Generations, baby boomers, their parents and their children* (Macmillan, Sydney) 1997

Maddock, K. and Wright, B. (eds), *War: Australia and Vietnam* (Harper and Row, Sydney), 1987

Maddox, G., *Australian democracy in theory and practice* (Penguin, Melbourne), 1985

Maddox, G., *The Hawke Government and Labour Tradition* (Penguin, Melbourne), 1989

Manne, R., *The Australian century* (Text Publishing, Melbourne), 1999

Manne, R., *The Barren years* (Text Publishing, Melbourne) 2001

Manne, R., *The Petrov Affair: Politics and espionage* (Pergamon, Sydney), 1987

Mansergh, N., *The Commonwealth experience* (Weidenfeld and Nicolson, London), 1969

Marr, D., *Patrick White: A life* (Random House, Sydney), 1991

Martin, A.W., *Robert Menzies: A Life, Vol 2, 1944–1978* (Melbourne University Press, Melbourne), 1999

Martin. A.W., *Robert Menzies* (Melbourne University Press, Melbourne), 1993

May, A.L., *The Battle for the Banks* (Sydney University Press, Sydney), 1968

Mayer, H. (ed.), *Catholics and the free society: an Australian symposium* (Cheshire, Melbourne), 1961

Mayer, H. (ed.), *Labor to power* (Angus and Robertson, Sydney), 1973

McLachlan, N., *Waiting for the revolution. A history of Australian nationalism* (Penguin, Melbourne), 1989

McLaren, J., *Writing in Hope and Fear: Literature as Politics in Post war Australia* (Cambridge University Press, Cambridge), 1996

McMaster, D., *Asylum seekers* (Melbourne University Press, Melbourne) 2002

McQueen, H., *A new Britannia: an argument concerning the social origins of Australian radicalism and nationalism* (Penguin, Melbourne), 1970

Menzies, R.G., *The measure of the years* (Cassell, Melbourne), 1970

Mercury, Hobart

Molony, J., *The Penguin History of Australia* (Penguin, Melbourne), 1988

Murphy, J., and Smart, J., *The Forgotten Fifties* (Melbourne University Press, Melbourne), 1997

Murphy, J., *Imagining the Fifties: Private Sentiment and Political Culture in Menzies' Australia* (University of New South Wales, Sydney), 2000

Murray, R., *The Split: Australian Labor in the fifties* (Cheshire, Melbourne), 1970

National Times, Sydney

Nelson, Hank, *Papua New Guinea: black unity or black chaos?* (Penguin, Melbourne), 1972

Noone, V., *Disturbing the War: Melbourne Catholics and Vietnam* (Spectrum, Melbourne), 1993

Parkinson, T., *Jeff, the rise and fall of a political phenomenon* (Penguin, Melbourne), 2000

Pemberton, G., *All the way: Australia's road to Vietnam* (Allen and Unwin, Sydney), 1987

Pierce, P., *The Country of Lost Children: An Australian Anxiety* (Cambridge University Press, Cambridge), 1999

Pike, D., *Australia: the quiet continent* (Cambridge University Press, Cambridge), 1962

Playford, J. and Kirsner, D. (eds), *Australian capitalism: Towards a socialist critique* (Penguin, Melbourne), 1972

Polizzotto, C., *The factory floor: A visual and oral record 1900–1960* (Fremantle Arts Centre Press, Fremantle), 1988

Read, P., *Charles Perkins: A biography* (Penguin, Melbourne), 1990

Rees, P., and Fischer, T., *Tim Finder's outback heroes* (Allen and Unwin, Sydney), 2002

Reid, A., *The Gorton Experiment* (Shakespeare Head Press, Sydney), 1971

Reid, A., *The Power struggle* (Shakespeare Head Press, Sydney), 1969

Renouf, A., *Let Justice Be Done* (University of Queensland Press, Brisbane), 1983

Reynolds, H., *Frontier* (Allen and Unwin, Sydney), 1989

Reynolds, H., *The Other Side of the Frontier* (Penguin, Melbourne), 1982

Richie, J., *The Wentworths: Father and Son* (Melbourne University Press, Melbourne), 1997

Rickard, J., *Australia: A cultural history* (Longman Cheshire, Melbourne), 1988

Rinton, S. (ed.), *Ashes of Vietnam: Australian voices* (William Heinemann and the Australian Broadcasting Commission, Melbourne), 1987

Rowse, T., *Australian liberalism and national character* (Kibble Books, Melbourne), 1978

Rowse, T., *Obliged to be Difficult: Nugget Coombs' legacy in Indigenous Affairs* (Cambridge University Press, Cambridge), 2000

Scott, E., *A short history of Australia* (Oxford University Press, Melbourne), 1947

Serle, G., *Robin Boyd: A Life* (Melbourne University Press, Melbourne), 1995

Shaw, A.G.L., *The story of Australia* (Faber, London), 1960

Sherington, G., *Australia's immigrants 1788–1988* (Allen and Unwin, Sydney), 2nd edition, 1990

Stokes, G., *The Politics of Identity in Australia,* (Cambridge University Press, Cambridge), 1997

Stubbs, J., *Hayden* (William Heinemann, Melbourne), 1989

Summers, A., *Damned whores and god's police: the colonisation of women in Australia* (Penguin, Melbourne), 1975

Sunday Mail, Adelaide

Sydney Morning Herald, Sydney

Terrill, G., *Secrecy and Openness: The Federal Government from Menzies to Whitlam and Beyond*, (Melbourne University Press, Melbourne), 2000

The Times, London

Thomson, R.C., *Religion in Australia: A History* (Oxford University Press, Melbourne), 1994

Torney-Parlicki, *Somewhere in Asia: War, Journalism, and Australia's Neighbours 1941–75* (University of New South Wales Press, Sydney), 2000

Truman, T., *Catholic action and politics* (Georgian House, Melbourne), 1959

Walker, D., *Anxious Australia: Australia and the Rise of Asia* (University of Queensland Press, Brisbane), 1999

Walter, J., (ed.), *Australian studies: A survey* (Oxford University Press, Melbourne), 1989

Warhurst, J., and Parkin, A., *The machine* (Allen and Unwin, Sydney), 2000

Wark, M., *The virtual republic* (Allen and Unwin, Sydney), 1997

White, R., and Russell, P., *Memories and Dreams* (Allen and Unwin, Sydney), 1997

Williams, J.F., *Anzacs, the Media and the Great War* (University of New South Wales, Sydney), 1999

Yarwood, A.T. (ed.), *Attitudes to non-European immigration* (Cassell, London), 1968

Index

Scandinavia

at war with trolls

A history from the Napoleonic era to the third millennium

TONY GRIFFITHS

Since the Napoleonic era the two great Scandinavian kingdoms of Denmark and Sweden have been transformed into model parliamentary democracies. The Finns are now no longer seen only as quarrelsome and unintelligible knifefighters, the Swedes as swaggering, boastful introspective materialists, the Norwegians as a scattered group of bovine alcoholics and the Danes as bicycling pornography enthusiasts.

Tony Griffiths has blended together in a fascinating way their culture, history and politics over two hundred years, and describes how, even in the third millennium, the Nordic nations continue their metaphorical struggle with malevolent trolls.

'There is an astonishing amount of information in Scandinavia's pages, yet the lively style makes page after page read like a good story.' – Marjatta Forward, *Australian Book Review*

ISBN 1 86254 591 X

For more information visit www.wakefieldpress.com.au

Wakefield Press is an independent publishing and
distribution company based in Adelaide, South Australia.
We love good stories and publish beautiful books.
To see our full range of titles, please visit our website at
www.wakefieldpress.com.au.

Wakefield Press thanks Fox Creek Wines
and Arts South Australia for their support.